REMARKABLE
→ WASHINGTON ←
WOMEN

REMARKABLE
⇥ WASHINGTON ⇤
WOMEN

THIRD EDITION

L. E. BRAGG AND
CHRISTY KARRAS

TWODOT®

ESSEX, CONNECTICUT
HELENA, MONTANA

A · TWODOT® · BOOK

An imprint of Globe Pequot, the trade division of
The Rowman & Littlefield Publishing Group, Inc.
4501 Forbes Blvd., Ste. 200
Lanham, MD 20706
www.rowman.com

Distributed by NATIONAL BOOK NETWORK

British Library Cataloguing in Publication Information available

Library of Congress Cataloging-in-Publication Data available

ISBN 978-1-4930-6875-3 (paperback : alk. paper)
ISBN 978-1-4930-6876-0 (ebook)

∞™ The paper used in this publication meets the minimum requirements of American National Standard for Information Sciences—Permanence of Paper for Printed Library Materials, ANSI/NISO Z39.48-1992.

I accomplished what I have always dreamed of and feared impossible, and from my experience nothing could be taken.

—FAY FULLER, AFTER REACHING THE SUMMIT OF
MOUNT RAINIER ON AUGUST 10, 1890

WASHINGTON

CONTENTS

PREFACE

The stories of the women found within these pages illustrate the unique history that made the state of Washington what it is today. Although the credit for building this great state usually is given to its male citizens, women played equally important roles. These eighteen women, all of whom were either born in or migrated to Washington in the nineteenth or early twentieth centuries, epitomize the spirit of the Northwest.

It was my goal to tell the stories of an ethnically and geographically diverse group of women from a great variety of vocations, and I ended up including a doctor, a lawyer, and the daughter of an Indian chief. Their lives of courage, dedication, and achievement laid the foundation for the Washington of today. Professor Edmond S. Meany's famous statement about Seattle could well be said for all of Washington: "The foundation of Seattle was laid in a mother's tears." Some died tragically, some fell from grace, some are still revered and remembered, while others are forgotten. This book is intended to honor the memories of these remarkable Northwest women.

—L. E. Bragg

It was a great pleasure to delve into the lives of the three women whose stories I added to this book for the third edition. As with the others in this book, their lives epitomize the times in which they lived and women's ever-ongoing struggle for equality, opportunity, and recognition. Emma Smith DeVoe fought tirelessly for Washington women's suffrage and built on work by her predecessors and colleagues to finally gain the vote after decades of setbacks. Susie Revels Cayton wielded her considerable network and persuasive talents to educate Seattle citizens of all backgrounds about the Black community and the potential for progress.

Along with thousands of other Japanese Americans living in Washington, Kara Matsushita Kondo was forcibly incarcerated during World War II. She used her experiences as a springboard for community action and positive change. I have tried, in some small way, to do these women justice. I hope this introduction to their lives spurs curiosity and encourages readers to find out more about them, their communities, and the times in which they lived. I am grateful for their work.

—Christy Karras

ACKNOWLEDGMENTS

Special thanks to Joy Werlink of the Washington State Historical Society; Lisa Love of the *News Tribune;* Nancy Gale Compau of the Spokane Public Library's Northwest Room; Karen De Seve of the Cheney Cowles Museum; and Carolyn J. Marr, librarian at the Museum of History and Industry. A large number of individuals also provided assistance for individual chapters; their names can be found in the bibliography under each chapter listing.

For their expertise and attention to detail, I would like to thank and acknowledge the editors of both volumes of this book: Megan Hiller, Julie Marsh, and Meredith Rufino.

This book is dedicated to my nineteenth-century, Washingtonian great-grandmothers: Jessie Penola (Gordon) Bragg of Colfax, Washington; Hannah Mary "Marie" ("Von" Sapp) Eckles of Sunnyside, Washington; and Elizabeth (Paddock) Lee of Seattle, Washington. Not to be forgotten is Mary Ann (Johnston) Nixon of Ballymena, County Antrim, Northern Ireland. Thanks also to my Oregonian-Washingtonian mother, Mary Pauline "Polly" (Nixon) Bragg, for reading and editing every word I have ever written.

—L. E. Bragg

Our online age has made researching history more exciting than ever, although it has also increased the chances of falling down digital rabbit holes. I am grateful for every library worker, historian, volunteer, and work-study student who has toiled creating digital copies of everything from diaries to magazines for researchers like me. Gratitude is also due to the folks who act as institutional memory for their communities—people like John Baule, director emeritus and archivist at the Yakima

Valley Museum, who is a generous one-person repository of knowledge about the area's history. The Washington State Historical Society's very accessible Women's History Consortium and Suffrage Centennial collections were especially helpful aids for researching this book. The Denshō project is recording precious personal histories and ensuring that the lives of Japanese Americans, particularly those incarcerated during World War II, are remembered.

—Christy Karras

Narcissa Prentiss Whitman

1808–1847

TRAGEDY AT WAIILATPU

The deadly blade of the tomahawk, previously cloaked beneath the attacker's blanket, dealt two sharp blows to the back of the doctor's head, knocking him senseless to the floor of the tiny mission kitchen. Seventeen-year-old John Sager drew his pistol upon the intruders. The men swarmed into the kitchen, and one of them grabbed the gun barrel before John could shoot and stabbed him in the head. Telaukaikt (who had been studying to become a member of the church) later entered the room and began to beat and cut the doctor about the head and face, leaving him with his throat cut—life pouring out of him. Mortally wounded, both Dr. Marcus Whitman and John Sager lived only until nightfall.

Gunshots began to ricochet about the mission yard. Upon hearing the shots, Narcissa Whitman ran to the kitchen and came upon her fallen husband. Narcissa bent over her bloodied mate, attempting to comfort him. Tears of fear and grief flowed together with her spouse's blood. She and another woman moved Dr. Whitman from the kitchen floor to a couch in the parlor.

Mr. Rogers, a young missionary, escaped from his attackers in the yard with a broken arm and bloody head wound. He rushed into the house, shutting the door in a feeble attempt to keep out the hostile invaders. Mr. Kimball, his arm broken as well, joined Mr. Rogers in barricading themselves in an upstairs bedroom.

Still anguishing over her dying husband, Mrs. Whitman attempted to quiet the terrified screams of the mission's children. Crying children flew around the house in panic. As Narcissa passed by a window in order to reach the children, she was shot through the right breast by a Canadian of mixed blood named Joe Lewis. Her body crumpled to the

Narcissa Prentiss Whitman National Park Service, Whitman Mission National Historic Site

floor. She sat up and dragged herself to the settee where her husband lay. Here, Sister Whitman commenced to pray for the lives of all at the Whitman Mission, especially the children.

∽

Narcissa Prentiss was born in Prattsburg, New York, on March 14, 1808, the eldest daughter and third of nine children born to Judge Stephen Prentiss and Clarissa Prentiss. She grew up and attended school in Prattsburg and was a member of the first class of girls to attend Franklin Academy, a seminary school for women in Troy, New York. Following her graduation, Narcissa taught school.

In 1832, four Flathead Indian leaders visited St. Louis to encourage teachers to come live among them and teach them of "The Book of Truths." Their speeches were published in the *Christian Advocate* in March of 1833 and stirred great excitement in the East. At age twenty-six, Narcissa attended a meeting where the Reverend Samuel Parker, a missionary explorer for the American Board of Commissions for Foreign Missions, made an appeal for missionaries and money to support his goal of establishing missions among western Indian tribes. Narcissa felt her true calling. She approached the Reverend Parker and asked if there was a place for an unmarried female among his western missionaries. Both the Reverend Parker and Narcissa Prentiss made a request of the board to allow her to travel west as a missionary. The board denied the requests, thinking the West an unsuitable match for a single woman.

A young medical doctor, Marcus Whitman, was slated to travel with Parker on his expedition. When the two met to plan the journey, Parker mentioned Narcissa Prentiss and her great desire to perform missionary work among western tribes. Further, Parker suggested that if Whitman was serious about becoming a missionary and wanted a wife, he should contact this woman and propose marriage. A month later Narcissa and

Marcus were engaged to be married. Narcissa reapplied to the mission-ary board, not as a single female, but as a missionary wife.

Meanwhile, Dr. Marcus Whitman and the Reverend Samuel Parker set out on their expedition to explore the possibility of building missions in the Oregon Territory (which at that time encompassed the present-day states of Oregon, Washington, and Idaho). This territory was not part of the United States, but was held jointly with England and virtually ruled by the English Hudson's Bay Company.

Marcus and Samuel traveled as far west as Rendezvous, on the Green River in Wyoming. Here, the two decided that Samuel would go west to select sites for missions, while Marcus would return to New York for additional recruits. Marcus left Rendezvous on August 27, 1835, with two Nez Perce Indian boys, Richard and John, as guides. He had six months to recruit a party to join the American Fur Company's caravan, a safe party with whom to travel to Rendezvous in 1836.

When Marcus returned to New York, he and Narcissa were married on February 18, 1836. Richard and John attended the wedding, where they sat mesmerized by the ceremony. Narcissa, who sang soprano in her church choir, filled the church with her golden voice as she sang the last stanza of her final wedding song.

The next day they left on their honeymoon—a three-thousand-mile trip to the Oregon Territory. With them were Reverend Henry H. Spald-ing; his wife, Eliza; William H. Gray; two teamsters; and, the two Nez Perce boys. Narcissa grew to love John and Richard, who proved to be excellent guides and took good care of the stock. The two hired men proved much less useful.

At first, the Whitman party traveled in the relative comfort of boats. From Pennsylvania, they cruised on the Ohio, Mississippi, and Missouri Rivers. The plan was to meet the American Fur Company caravan at Council Bluffs and travel in the company of several hundred men and six hundred animals to the Oregon Territory. The men of the American

Fur Company heard that women were in the party that was to join them. Not wanting to travel with females, the group moved out earlier than planned, leaving without the Whitman party.

Discouraged, but undaunted, Dr. Whitman and his group decided to go alone and try to catch the American Fur Company expedition. After a month of traveling, the small party caught up with the caravan.

Although they encountered many dangers and treacherous terrain while crossing the plains, the journey agreed with Narcissa Whitman. In a letter to her family, she wrote, "Our manner of living is far preferable to any in the States. I never was so contented and happy before. Neither have I enjoyed such health for years."

When in buffalo country, members of the American Fur Company caravan were designated hunters and were assigned to supply the meat— a diet of buffalo, antelope, deer, bear, and birds. Buffalo jerky and tea were sometimes the main meal. Eliza Spalding became sick on the diet; in contrast, Narcissa developed quite a taste for buffalo meat.

They began their ascent of the Rocky Mountains at South Pass, a natural road discovered by early trappers. Crossing the pass meant driving over dangerous, narrow, steep passages. For this reason, the party decided to leave the larger wagon behind. The women, who had alternated between riding in the wagon and on horseback, would now spend more time astride a mount. Narcissa preferred to ride horseback and so spent the rest of the journey in the saddle. In this manner, Narcissa and Eliza became the first white women to cross the Continental Divide.

The first tribe the missionaries saw was the Pawnee. Like other tribes they later encountered, the Pawnee were fascinated with the white women—the first they had ever seen. Narcissa wrote that when they arrived at Rendezvous, Wyoming, she was greeted warmly with kisses from the Indian women. A mountain man, Isaac P. Rose, described such a scene in his autobiography, *Four Years in the Rockies:*

Mrs. Whitman was a large, stately, fair skinned woman, with blue eyes and light, auburn, almost golden hair. Her manners were at once dignified and gracious. She was by both nature and education, a lady, and had a lady's appreciation of all that was courageous and refined, yet not without an element of romance and heroism in her disposition strong enough to have impelled her to undertake a missionary's life in the wilderness. Mrs. Spalding, the other lady, was more delicate than her companion, yet equally earnest and zealous in the cause they had undertaken. The Indians would turn their gaze from the dark haired, dark eyed Mrs. Spalding to what was to them the more interesting golden hair and blue eyes of Mrs. Whitman. . . .

The American Fur Company traveled only as far as Rendezvous. A group of Nez Perce Indians offered to guide the party to Fort Walla Walla along a steep mountainous northern route. Wagons and stock would have to be left behind, and the Whitmans feared they would not be at Fort Walla Walla before winter. Soon, a party from the Hudson's Bay Company's Fort Vancouver base arrived at Rendezvous and offered the Whitman party a shorter route through desert terrain. Members of the Flathead, Nez Perce, and Snake tribes guided the Whitman party, now including members of the Hudson's Bay Company, to Fort Hall (Idaho). There, the Indians went north to their preferred route, while the missionaries and members of the Hudson's Bay Company traveled west.

After leaving Rendezvous, the travelers were far less likely to encounter parties traveling east, by whom they sent letters home to their families; so, Narcissa began to keep a journal chronicling her life on the trail. In it, she wrote that she found travel with the Indians more difficult than it had been with the fur company. The fur traders made two stops per day, while the Indians were accustomed to making camp only once a day.

Again, the party traveled on mountain trails, some described as so narrow a horse's hoof would barely fit on the trail. Some of the wagons slipped off the trail sending their contents tumbling down steep slopes. At some spots the wagons were eased over the mountainsides using long ropes. Much to everyone's dismay, Dr. Whitman insisted on bringing his wagon. When the trails became too narrow, his wife secretly hoped he would discard the contraption. Instead, the inventive doctor removed the front wheels, making the wagon into a cart. Later it was decided they should dispose of some of their belongings to lighten the wagon's load. Marcus convinced his bride that she must leave a treasured trunk, a gift from her sister.

After another month's journey through mountains, rivers, and deserts, the party arrived at Fort Walla Walla on September 1, 1836. When the pioneers arrived at their destination, Narcissa Whitman was nearly three months pregnant. In a letter to Samuel Parker dated October 24, 1836, she wrote of her feelings about the journey:

> . . . [Y]ou ask whether I regret coming by land? I answer No! by no means. If I were at home now, I could choose to come this way in preference to a seven month voyage. Nothing can equal the purity of the mountain air; and its exhilarating effect on the system; together with the healthful exercise of a horseback ride. Never have I slept more sweetly, than after a day thus spent. How unlike the close atmosphere of stages, boats, and disturbed rest of a crowded cabin, together with such an appetite as one has in this traveling. I found so much pleasure, mixed with the little suffering and fatigue endured; that the fatigue is entirely forgotten. I once could not believe such a journey could be made with so little inconvenience, to a lady, as I have experienced. I believe I was prepared for the worst, but happily have been disappointed. True! I have had some hindrances, and been hungry at times,

because we had nothing but buffalo meat dried in the sun by the Indians to eat. . . .

Once in the new territory, the first order of business was to meet with the ruling authorities, the Hudson's Bay Company, headquartered at Fort Vancouver. This trip was made by boat, traveling west on the waters of the Columbia River. Dr. McLoughlin, the chief factor of the Hudson's Bay Company, was very impressed by the rugged trip the doctor and his fair bride had made. He suggested that the Whitmans make their mission near Walla Walla, and the Spaldings 125 miles to the east, at Lapwai (Idaho). Narcissa and Eliza remained at Fort Vancouver while their husbands returned east of the Cascade Mountains to start construction of the missions. While at Fort Vancouver, Narcissa instructed Dr. McLoughlin's daughter in her school studies and music.

Mr. Spalding returned for the women a month and a half later, telling them homes had been finished enough to provide them shelter. The women arrived at the mission site to find little but a lean-to enclosing a fireplace and chimney. The structure had a floor of rough hewn boards, but not a door, window, or bit of furniture, not even a bed! The site for their home was a peninsula between the branches of the Walla Walla River and Touchet Creek. The local Cayuse Tribe called this place Wai-i-lat-pu (rye grass place). The mission was located twenty-five miles east of Fort Walla Walla. Each year additions were made to the main house and accompanying buildings. Marcus traveled up to 1,500 miles in search of timber. He built a small grist mill to provide corn, rye, and wheat meal. By 1839, the Whitmans had fenced 250 acres and cultivated 200 acres with grain. Forty to fifty Indian children ages seven through eighteen attended the mission school with Narcissa as their teacher. The Cayuse were attending Sunday church services quite regularly, with Narcissa leading the services when Marcus was away.

Marcus's efforts to instill Christian values in the Indians included trying to interest them in helping him build the mission. In Cayuse society it was traditional for the men to hunt, fish, and fight, while the women built and tended the homes. Although the local Native men were intrigued with the mission church and school, they saw the construction of the buildings as women's work, and chose not to participate. Marcus attempted to induce the locals to build permanent homes, plow, plant, sow, and raise cattle or sheep even though this also was not their way. The Cayuse were a proud people, wealthy with horses, who traveled to different encampments each season following their food sources. At the camps they hunted, fished, and traded for salmon, deer, elk, and buffalo.

Although Narcissa showed great love for individual Indians, she regarded the majority of them as heathen, both because they had not been "saved" and because of conflicts between the two societies—Mrs. Whitman often found herself at odds with Native custom. The mission was situated on Cayuse land and the Cayuse, therefore, recognized no boundaries, including doors. She became accustomed to them entering the kitchen unannounced but objected to their tendency to roam the house, bedrooms included. This clash of cultures caused some of the Native people to regard Narcissa Whitman as haughty.

The custom of polygamy also disturbed the pious Mrs. Whitman. She believed that Indian wives were mistreated, and regretted that early in the mission years she had little contact with Cayuse women, as only the men ventured to Waiilatpu. One Cayuse man questioned Dr. Whitman's practice of taking his wife with him everywhere he went. Dr. Whitman tried to explain that his wife was his partner, but this explanation did not sit well. The Cayuse were displeased with the equal treatment Narcissa received.

On March 14, 1837 (the evening of Narcissa's own birthday), Alice Clarissa was born to Narcissa and Marcus Whitman. Alice Clarissa was born on Cayuse land, thus the Cayuse considered this first child born to American parents in the Oregon Territory their child. The baby had many visitors from chiefs and important tribal members on a daily basis. As Narcissa described in a letter to her parents on March 30, 1837,

Fee-low-ki-ke, a kind, friendly Indian, called to see her the next day after she was born. [He] said she was a Cayuse ten-ni (Cayuse girl), because she was born on Cayuse wai-tis (Cayuse land). He told us her arrival was expected by all the people of the country— the Nez Perces, Cayuses and Walla Wallapoos Indians, and, now she has arrived, it would soon be heard of by them all; and we must write to our land and tell our parents and friends of it. The whole tribe are highly pleased because we allow her to be called a Cayuse girl.

Alice Clarissa grew to be a very bright and talkative toddler. To the great delight of the Cayuse, Alice began to sing hymns and converse in the Indian languages surrounding her. Narcissa wrote in a letter home:

Alice has become so familiar with [the Nez Perce hymns] that she is repeating some part of them most of the time. Situated as I am, I know not how I shall succeed in training her as I ought. So many Indians and children are constantly in and about our house, and recently I discover her much inclined to imitate and talk with them, or they with her. It makes them very much pleased to think she is going to speak their language so readily. They appear to love her much. The old chief Cut Lip says "he does not expect to live long, and he has given all his land to her."

Dr. and Mrs. Whitman made every effort to learn the local language, although he did better at it than she. To do this, they needed to spend time with the tribal members, who traveled a great deal. It was not unusual for the Whitman family to leave their home and camp with the tribes. Narcissa described one such occasion when her family traveled sixty-five miles and spent three cold, winter weeks camping with the Nez Perce. She wrote to her family of how much she enjoyed these encampments and felt the riding and camping outdoors agreed with Alice's health. They also thought that such close associations with the Indians afforded them more opportunity for converting them to Christianity, as well as learning their language and customs.

Unfortunately, Narcissa seemed to have been influenced by other missionaries to remove her child from such frequent contact with the Indians. They scolded her, telling her of the "evils of allowing her to learn the native language." Confused, Narcissa prayed about the matter and had decided to remove herself and her daughter from such daily contact when tragedy struck.

One evening in June of 1839, two-year-old Alice Clarissa disappeared while the evening meal was being prepared. A search ensued, and when two tin cups were found floating in the river, hope faded. The rescuers waded the river in a last hope of finding the baby alive before an old Indian man dove under water, found Alice, and brought her lifeless little body to the surface. Narcissa grieved incessantly, and her health began to fail, even though she believed the child to be in a better place.

When a boundary dispute between the United States and the British threatened the Oregon Territory, Marcus went to Washington, D.C., and met with President Tyler and Congress to convince them that the Oregon Territory was worth having. The Hudson's Bay Company had been successful in keeping the secrets of the Oregon Territory to themselves. It was in their best interest if the population of the East believed the land worthless. Unlike the missionaries, the company had no desire to change the way the Indians lived as long as they were kept in constant supply of rich fur pelts.

In Congress the view was expressed that the "Oregon Territory was a barren worthless country fit only for wild beasts and wild men. . . . it is shut off by impassable mountains and a great desert which made a wagon road impossible." Whitman informed the legislators that it would be a mistake of enormous magnitude to listen to the enemies of American interests in Oregon. "Six years ago I was told there was no wagon road to Oregon, and it was impossible to take a wagon there, and yet in spite of pleading threats, I took a wagon over the road and have it now." Dr. Whitman's pleas were successful in reviving American interest in the vast territories comprising the present-day states of Oregon, Washington, and Idaho.

When Marcus returned in the spring, he had with him a large group of emigrants bound for Oregon—one thousand men, women, and children—and one thousand head of stock—cattle, horses, and sheep. The emigration that ensued, following Marcus Whitman's speech, brought the population of Americans up three-to-one over the British and Canadians in the territory.

Whitman foresaw the wealth and importance of the country and knew that his mission must serve as a supply station to the annual emigrations. As hundreds and thousands of emigrants came to the mission, worn, hungry, sick, and destitute, the Whitmans cared for them all. They provided them with food, clothing, and medicine, often without pay. Frequently, the doctor would give away his entire food supply and have to send to the Spaldings for grain to get them through the winter.

Meanwhile, Narcissa was called upon more and more to minister to wagon loads of emigrants now traveling to the Oregon Territory. Both Indian and white children were left as boarders at Waiilatpu, where Narcissa was the only teacher until she was assisted in later years by others. Narcissa also kept busy with a family of seven children who were placed in the Whitman's care after their parents had died on the trail west. The Whitmans legally adopted all seven of the Sager children though Dr.

Whitman feared the emaciated baby would be too much of a burden on the frail Narcissa.

The Indians became increasingly dismayed by the huge influx of emigrants. They did not mind so much as long as the wagon trains were just passing through, but they did not want more settlers on their lands. Both the Hudson's Bay Company and the local tribes blamed Whitman for opening up the territory after his arrival with such a large caravan of emigrants. These feelings became even more pronounced when England lost the Oregon Territory through a treaty signed in 1846, ending the Hudson's Bay Company's domination of the territory.

In addition to the unrest among the tribes, there was a growing animosity between the Protestant missionaries and the Catholic priests moving into the territory. Each group claimed theirs was the only true religion, thereby causing confusion and mistrust among the Indians.

Though they were spending more of their time on the needs of the settlers, the Whitmans were not unsympathetic to the plight of the Indians. Narcissa wrote, "We feel that we cannot do our work too fast to save the Indian—the hunted, despised and unprotected Indian—from entire extinction."

With the settlers came the white man's diseases. In 1847, a measles epidemic caused a great deal of sickness among both settlers and Indians. The Indians, who had little resistance to the disease, died in much greater numbers than the whites. The Cayuse were led to believe that Dr. Whitman was poisoning them.

One night, under the cover of darkness, Dr. Whitman's friend, Istikus, came to him. Risking his own life, Istikus told the doctor of threats against his life, advising him to leave the mission, "until my people have better hearts." Mrs. Whitman was devastated by the news. She locked herself in her room and cried all night. Though he refused to leave, Marcus realized the gravity of the situation and advised others at the mission to remove their families to safer places. It was the first time Marcus

Whitman had been so alarmed or thought that his Indian friends could be capable of attempting such acts.

The next day, November 29, 1847, was like many others. Dr. Whitman had returned from ministering to Cayuse Indians who were sick with the measles, and he was now at rest, reading in the mission's small kitchen. Like most afternoons, the kitchen was filled to capacity with members of the Cayuse Tribe. It was under the guise of asking for medicine that the attackers entered the house, approached Dr. Whitman, and administered the blow that began the incident that came to be known as the "Whitman Massacre."

With Dr. Whitman's life ebbing away from the slash to his throat, the others convinced the wounded Narcissa to leave her husband's side and hide herself upstairs in a bedroom with Messrs. Rogers and Kimball and the women and children of the mission. They remained huddled in fear until well after dark. The sounds of breaking glass and shattering wood emanated throughout the house, as the attackers plundered through the Whitmans' belongings. Several times the intruders climbed the stairs toward the terrified captives. Mr. Rogers found a broken gun barrel and thrust it through a crack in the door. The trick worked and he was able to fool them into thinking he was armed. With their original tactics not working, the men then attempted to coerce Mr. Rogers and Mrs. Whitman downstairs by alternately threatening to burn the house down and ensuring their safety if they did come down. The adults, fearing for the lives of the orphans, eventually agreed to descend the stairs. Narcissa, weak from loss of blood, fainted. Her limp figure was carried to a couch by Mr. Rogers and Miss Bewley. The rifles of the captors who crowded into the room remained trained on the missionaries. As the settee containing the wounded Mrs. Whitman was carried outdoors, a volley of gunfire erupted both outside and within the house. Mr. Rogers and Mrs. Whitman were riddled with bullets. She groaned and fell to the ground, but still lingered on until mutilated by one of the raiders.

Thus ended the life of a dedicated missionary wife and one of the first two non-Indian women to cross the Continental Divide.

The leader of the assault was the half-Indian Canadian Joe Lewis. It may have been his falsehoods that brought the conspiracy to the boiling point. Dr. Whitman had fed and clothed Lewis for months. Soon, the doctor discovered Joe's dishonesty and lack of character and tried to get rid of him. Joe Lewis returned and set about breeding distrust among the Cayuse. Several who took part in the killings had been frequent guests at the mission and had expressed interest in joining the church.

Thirteen people in all were killed, nine the first day—including Marcus and Narcissa (the only woman to die)—and four more over the next eight days. The last two men killed were dragged from their sick beds at the mission, beaten and stabbed before the eyes of the women and children who were now hostages at the mission. The mangled bodies were left by the door. For two days, the captives had to step over the dead to get food and water.

Forty women and children became hostages, later joined by two families to make the sum forty-seven. Several of the women were molested, and three were forced to become wives to their captors. Eliza Spalding, age ten, daughter of the Spaldings who had traveled west with the Whitmans, later described the constant horror and fear the hostages endured. She was forced to translate for her kidnappers, since she was fluent in their language.

When the chief factor of the Hudson's Bay Company, Peter Skene Ogden, heard of the carnage and the captives taken, he traveled to Fort Walla Walla, arriving on December 12. Ogden succeeded in ransoming all of the hostages with a supply of blankets, shirts, guns, ammunition, and tobacco. The total value of these goods was placed at approximately $500.

No arrests were made until two years after the attack. Five Indian men were hung in Oregon City for participating in the "Whitman Massacre," including one who evidently was not present there at all. Joe

Lewis and another mixed-blood accomplice named Finley escaped to Montana, where it is said Lewis was killed some years later during a stagecoach robbery. The numbers of the Cayuse Tribe were greatly diminished by the epidemics, influx of settlers, and repercussions from their participation in the raid. The Cayuse Tribe is now one of the Confederated Tribes of the Umatilla Reservation, located near Pendleton, Oregon.

The Whitmans, who died for their cause of converting the Indians to Christianity, are remembered by some as martyrs. Samuel Campbell, who lived at the mission for two winters, never tired of telling

of the grandly Christian character of Mrs. Whitman, of her kindness and patience to all, whites and Indians alike. Every evening she delighted all with her singing. Her voice, after all her hard life, had lost none of its sweetness, nor had her environments in any sense soured her toward any of the little pleasantries of everyday life.

KICK-IS-OM-LO

1811–1896

PRINCESS ANGELINE—
SEATTLE'S LAST ROYALTY

Coins collected by Seattle schoolchildren paid for this princess's headstone. When she died on May 31, 1896, her friends carved her a casket in the shape of a canoe. The funeral service was held at Our Lady of Good Help Cathedral, which was packed to capacity with an audience of Seattle citizens. A black hearse, drawn by matching dark horses, carried the unique coffin. The noblewoman was buried in the canoe-shaped coffin with a paddle laid across the stern. During the burial, a sprig of cedar was dropped into the grave, and local children tossed flowers atop the mound. Seattle's prominent pioneer families buried the princess in their cemetery, Lakeview Cemetery, on Capital Hill. Her grave is marked with a simple granite boulder bearing the inscription, "Princess Angeline."

Few cities in the late nineteenth century could claim an Indian princess among its citizens. A frequent sight on the streets of Seattle, this princess's crown was a red bandanna tied over wiry gray locks; the staff she carried, a bent, fire-charred, walking stick; her robe, a tattered shawl; her gowns, well-worn, calico skirts topping mismatched water-soaked shoes, if she wore any at all. The royal palace in which she lived and died was a tiny, ramshackle, wood hut on Seattle's waterfront.

Princess Angeline, or "Kick-Is-Om-Lo" in the language of her tribe, is believed to have been born in 1811. She was the daughter of Chief Seattle,* chief of the Suquamish, Duwamish, and six allied tribes, and

---

* According to Chief Seattle's friends William DeShaw and Doc Maynard, the pronunciation of the chief's name was closest to "Seattle." "Sealth" is a later interpretation.

Kick-Is-Om-Lo Museum of History and Industry

namesake of the city of Seattle. The daughter of Chief Seattle's first wife, Princess Angeline told a newspaper reporter in 1891 that her father was twenty-five when she was born. She outlived three brothers and two sisters born to the chief and his second wife.

The name Angeline was bestowed upon her by her friend, Catherine Maynard, the wife of one of Seattle's more colorful pioneers, David "Doc" Maynard. When the princess was introduced to Mrs. Maynard by her married name, Kick-Is-Om-Lo Dokub Cud, Catherine Maynard replied, "Why you are much too good looking a woman to carry around such a name. I now christen you, Angeline." In her later years, she was commonly referred to as "Old Angeline," or "Princess Angeline," by the people of Seattle.

The Suquamish were one of several coastal tribes living on Puget Sound. Angeline's father, Chief Seattle, was the hereditary chief of the Suquamish Tribe who was later made chief of six allied coastal tribes for his acts of wartime bravery and skill. The people of the tribe, including young Kick-Is-Om-Lo, lived in rectangular houses made from poles, bark, and boards of cedar, with woven mats covering the doorways. The cedar roofs were each constructed with a hole to allow smoke to escape from the fires within the homes. They made clothing from deer and other animal skins that they sometimes adorned with shells and feathers. Capes and hats woven of cedar and reeds repelled the moisture from the area's frequent rainstorms.

The Northwest rains nurtured a great variety of plants, wildlife, and sea creatures, giving Chief Seattle's people a wealth of choice in food. The Suquamish and Duwamish found deer, bear, cougar, and small game plentiful in the woods, an abundance of waterfowl and fish in the many freshwater lakes, and salmon and shellfish in and around Puget Sound's salty shores. Women dug for clams from the beaches and roots in the meadows and picked several types of berries. The men of these coastal tribes were known for their skill in carving cedar canoes, and the women for their weaving skills in creating baskets and clothing.

Kick-Is-Om-Lo witnessed the coming of the first white settlers to the area, beginning with the Hudson's Bay Company and settlers at Fort Nisqually near Tacoma. She and her father befriended and aided the first settlers to land on Elliott Bay. By some accounts, it was Chief Seattle who recommended to the Denny party, the first white settlers to the area, that they would have better shelter if they resided at the site of the present-day Seattle, rather than on Alki Point where they first landed. Both Chief Seattle and Princess Angeline were converted to Christianity by the early settlers.

The princess and her people showed the pioneers the bounties of the environment. On such an occasion, Angeline and her daughters took several pioneer women with them in their canoe to find the succulent blackberries growing at the water's edge. The party left the canoe tied to a rock on the shore during a low tide and ventured inland in search of berries. The women, engrossed in their harvesting of blackberries, did not notice that the tide was coming in rapidly. When they tried to return to their boat, they found it to be high tide, and their canoe was now quite a distance from the shoreline. Not only was the canoe beyond their reach, but the rock tied to the canoe was now an anchor under several feet of water.

Without saying a word, one of Angeline's daughters dashed onto the beach, removed her clothing and moccasins, and dove into the frigid waters of Puget Sound. She swam to the canoe, dove down, and retrieved the line anchoring the craft. Once the line was above water, Princess Angeline's daughter climbed into the canoe and paddled to shore to retrieve her mother and the other women.

According to legend, Princess Angeline had heard from other Indians that an attack was planned on the early pioneers' village, but she did not know exactly when this was to occur. When she heard the warriors in the woods surrounding the town signal to each other using "hooting" type sounds, Angeline knew the attackers were near and hastened to tell her settler friends. Other accounts say she paddled her canoe across Puget Sound in a raging storm to warn her friend Henry Yesler and the other settlers that the Northwest's inland and coastal tribes would soon attack. The 1856 Battle of Seattle followed.

The warship *Decatur* sailed into Elliott Bay to protect the city. Its captain, having been informed of the plan for attack, fired *Decatur*'s guns into the forest at the edge of Seattle. The shot was answered by yells and gunfire from the warriors. Settlers who heard the guns rushed to the blockade at the foot of Cherry Street. The fighting ensued. Two settlers were killed, yet the number of Indian casualties was never known. According to the legend, Angeline regretted warning the settlers of the attack after her Indian lover was killed during the shelling. Two houses within the city were burned, one after looting by the warriors, the other ignited when fired upon by the ship's guns. When the fighting slowed, women and children were moved from the blockade to the ship. By morning, the warring party had gone.

Whether or not Angeline paddled her canoe across the sound to warn the settlers is disputed, but the legend contributed to her celebrity status. Yesler later denied that Angeline was responsible for warning of the attack, instead giving credit to a Native man who was nicknamed Salmon Bay Curley. Mrs. Maynard maintained the legend was true.

It is, however, undisputed that in March of 1892, Angeline marched into the Seattle Police headquarters to warn the citizens of Seattle that the world would end in June of that year. Wah-Kee-Wee-Kum, the spirit of a great medicine man, had visited her to impart this knowledge and Angeline, in her typical magnanimous spirit, decided to share this information with her white neighbors. City officials, to whom she reported her prophesy, made light of the warning by asking her if she could predict which city employee their cantankerous mayor would fire next.

As a young woman, Princess Angeline was married to Dokub Cud, a half-Cowichan chief of the Skagit Tribe. By midcentury, Dokub Cud died, leaving Angeline a widow. Angeline gave birth to two daughters, Betsy and Mary, both of whom married white settlers. Mary wed William DeShaw, a respected local merchant. DeShaw accumulated wealth through a variety of enterprises, including smoking salmon for market. No doubt, Mary enjoyed a better life than that of her sister.

Daughter Betsy suffered much abuse from her mean-spirited, alcoholic husband. As a way of escaping this abuse, Betsy hanged herself with a red bandanna tied to a beam in a shed on Commercial Street. Angeline discovered the body of her daughter hanging from the rafters of her cabin, her baby boy wailing in a basket at her feet. Betsy's infant son, Joe Foster, went to live with his grandmother. Angeline raised the child with love, but he took after his father. He was always in trouble, frequently in jail, and he caused her much grief.

It was a common sight to see Angeline sitting on city sidewalks, hawking her wares. Angeline sold clams and baskets on the streets of Seattle and moccasins to people arriving in ships at the waterfront piers. She also did wash for many of Seattle's founding families. These tasks would have afforded her a comfortable living had she not spent most of her earnings posting bail and paying fines for her wayward grandson, Joe Foster.

A favorite subject for visiting journalists and photographers, her fame spread, and Angeline was invited to tour the world with George Francis Train in his quest to promote the Northwest. After a purse of several thousand dollars was raised for her fare, a delegation of local citizens visited her to propose the promotional trip. The delegates were dumbfounded when the princess flatly refused their offer. She explained that her revered father (whom she called "Hy-as Ty-ee," or "Great Father") would be so angry at her for running off with a crazy man that he would turn in his grave.

Carnival operators and dime museum owners also offered Angeline money to travel with them as she became known nationwide. Aiding in the spread of her fame were souvenir spoons and dishes bearing her likeness, which were sold to tourists. Though she would not hear of leaving her home, and she refused to be displayed in such a manner, Angeline did enjoy being shown off as a local celebrity and became the most photographed face in the city, although no photos of her as a young woman exist. Never wishing to leave Seattle, she expressed a desire to be buried with her pioneer friends, or "tillicums."

The farthest Angeline ever traveled from home was on a trip to Olympia with her famous father to protest the naming of the city after the great chief. The law among the Duwamish and Suquamish tribes was that when a person died, his name was not to be spoken aloud for five years. If the deceased was a chief, the silence was observed for ten years. When the name was passed on to a son, this law became moot. Should the tradition not be observed, the dead chief would roll over in his grave every time his name was spoken. Chief Seattle was horrified when the founding fathers proposed naming the city after him. Wishing to avoid a terrible fate, he took his entire family to Olympia to ask the governor to intercede. The governor was eventually able to convince Seattle that his last sleep would be peaceful. Reportedly, the chief was ultimately pleased with the honor.

On May 6, 1891, President Benjamin Harrison arrived for an official visit to Seattle, and the people of Seattle did their best to honor the occasion despite a torrential rainstorm. Angeline was presented to the President as the daughter of Chief Seattle and the head of her nation. Although she understood English, she always spoke in the Chinook jargon (the common language of traders and the various Northwest tribes).

The princess shook President Harrison's hand, curtsied, and greeted him, "Kla-how-ya."

"Hello, how are you?" the usually staid head of state responded politely in turn.

As she aged, Angeline became quick tempered and sensitive to insult. Often teased by the local boys, she carried rocks in her skirt pockets that she tossed with great accuracy to ward off such attacks.

One pioneer woman recounted her experience with the wrath of Angeline. After moving to Seattle in 1880, she and Angeline had become friends. Angeline frequently visited her home, always bringing freshly dug clams with her. On one occasion, the young mother was strolling the city streets with her small daughter and pushing her baby in a buggy. Not seeing Angeline sitting on the sidewalk, she rolled the wheels of the stroller over Angeline's toes. Angeline leapt to her feet and began to curse profusely at the startled woman. No apology would do, and from that day on whenever the woman encountered Angeline on the streets of Seattle, Angeline would point to her foot and proceed to swear at the embarrassed lady. The most hurtful thing for the pioneer woman was that Angeline never again returned to her home for a friendly visit.

The early Seattleites owed their lives to Chief Seattle and his people. Perhaps they looked after Angeline in her later years because they felt responsible for her fate. Although this woman of noble birth lived her later years immersed in the white man's world, she always seemed out of place in the bustling "modern" city.

Angeline's needs were simple; she never took anything she did not need. If she had extras, she "potlatched" the item, or gave it away in the Indian manner. After she could no longer dig clams, gather firewood, or work for a living, the charity of the early settlers kept her going. When she needed shelter, Henry Yesler donated lumber from his mill to build the princess a waterfront cabin.

At the onset of her illness, her well-meaning, pioneer friends placed her in Seattle General Hospital. Angeline railed against being taken from her simple home and placed in what she deemed a jail. After much wailing and thrashing about, she was returned to her cabin, where she died on May 31, 1896. A black crêpe drape was hung across her doorway on the day of her death.

When she died at the estimated age of eighty-five, the population of Seattle was more than 60,000. Angeline had witnessed the growth of her small Indian village into a log-cabin settlement; and, by the end of her life, the land over which her father once reigned had become a thriving metropolis.

MARY ANN BOREN DENNY

1822–1910

MOTHER OF SEATTLE

In preparation for the journey north from Portland to Puget Sound country, the young mother, Mary Ann Denny, laundered her family's clothing and washed and starched her sun bonnet until the brim was properly stiff. She laid a cloth on the grassy ground and ironed her bonnet and dress so that she would appear well groomed for the trip.

Mary Ann, her husband Arthur, two young daughters—Louisa (seven) and Lenora (four)—and her newborn son, Rolland, who had been born in Portland just twelve days after her arduous four months of travel across the country by wagon train, set sail on the schooner *Exact* on November 5, 1851. Bound for Puget Sound with the Dennys were Mary's brother, Carson Boren, and his family; her sister, Louisa Boren; Arthur's brother, David Denny; the Low family, whom they had joined on the Oregon Trail; the Bell family, with whom they had become acquainted in Portland; and Charles and Lee Terry from New York by way of Olympia. With the twelve adults on the excursion were twelve children, all under the age of nine. The *Exact* was taking gold prospectors north to the Queen Charlotte Islands and settlers to Olympia, which was one of the few "settled" towns north of Portland.

As they waited to board the *Exact,* Mary bought salmon from local Indian vendors. There was a small cookstove aboard the ship, so the wives took turns cooking the fish for their family meals. Before they could even finish cooking, the women began to feel ill. One by one, men, women, and children became incapacitated by seasickness. Whole families took to their bunks below deck as the ship was tossed and turned by the rolling sea.

Mary Ann Denny Museum of History and Industry

The wind, which caused so much discomfort to the passengers of the tiny schooner, was a great boon in sailing up the Pacific coastline; just eight days after leaving Portland, the ship sailed into Puget Sound. The captain dropped anchor in the middle of the sound and sent his passengers ashore in rowboats. Mrs. Alexander, a passenger aboard the *Exact* headed for Olympia, described the women of the landing party in a newspaper interview:

> *I can't never forget when the folks landed at Alki Point. I was sorry for Mrs. Denny with her baby and the rest of the women. You see, it was this way. Mr. Alexander and me went on to Olympia, but the rest stopped there. I remember it rained awful hard that last day—and the starch got took out of our bonnets and the wind blew, and every one of 'em, and their sun bonnets with the starch took out of them went flip flap, flip flap, as they rowed off for shore, and the last glimpse I had of them was the women standing under the trees with their wet bonnets all lopping down over their faces and their aprons to their eyes.*

It was 8:00 a.m. on the morning of November 13, 1851, when the Denny party landed at Alki Point amid a typical Puget Sound winter storm. Winds howled and rain poured. The women and children of the party huddled on the rocky beach. Shivering with cold and drenched to the skin, their long calico frocks were plastered to their forms. The ship had already been partly shrouded by a curtain of driving rain, and they found themselves on a rocky shore at the base of a high sandy bank, with an endless expanse of dark, forbidding forests beyond that.

Mary Denny hugged her baby to her chest in a futile attempt to keep him warm and dry. The rain ran in rivulets from her limp bonnet. She and the other women sought shelter for their children as the men secured their household goods from the incoming tide.

Surely Arthur's brother, David, who had gone ahead to explore the Puget Sound region and had stayed there to build cabins for the families would have completed several homes for the group. Mary and the others were dismayed to find just one partially constructed log cabin, sans roof. They watched forlornly as the *Exact* sailed out of Puget Sound and out of sight. Baby in arms and daughters at her side, Mary Denny sat down on a soggy, fallen, old log and began to cry. Arthur Denny described the scene as he found his wife upon returning to Alki Beach:

> *We were landed in the ship's boat when the tide was well out, and while the men of the party were all actively engaged in removing our goods to a point above high tide, the women and children had crawled into the brush, made a fire, and spread a cloth to shelter them from the rain. When the goods were secured I went to look after the women, and found on my approach, that their faces were concealed. On a closer inspection I found that they were in tears, having already discovered the gravity of the situation. . . . My motto in life was never to go backward and in fact if I had wished to retrace my steps it was about as nearly impossible as if I had taken up my bridge behind me. I had brought my family from a good home, surrounded by comforts and luxuries and landed them in a wilderness, and I did not think it at all strange that a woman who had, without complaint, endured all the dangers and hardships of a trip across the great plains, should be found shedding tears when contemplating the hard prospects then so plainly in view.*

Noted University of Washington history professor Edmond S. Meany aptly stated, "The foundation of Seattle was laid in a mother's tears," regarding Mary Denny's welcome to the area.

Members of Chief Seattle's* tribes—the Duwamish and Suquamish—witnessed the landing of the Denny party. They peered curiously from the woods, and some ventured cautiously onto the beach. An Indian mother showed Mary how to extract milk from the clams that were profuse on Alki Beach and how to nurse the baby with clam's milk. Mary Denny had been so sick during the trip from Portland, as well as stricken with fever in Portland, that she could not produce milk to feed her baby. Indian babies were often fed with the nectar of clams, on which they thrived, as it provided excellent nutrients. The baby, Rolland, was fed with clam nectar and broth until the party was able to bring its cattle north early the next year. The cattle had been left to winter in the Willamette Valley with Arthur Denny's father, who settled in Portland while the Dennys traveled north to the Puget Sound region.

The local Duwamish women were fascinated with the baby, Rolland. They stared intently at this tiny white-skinned child, with light curly hair atop his head. Then they would shake their heads at the pale, fragile child and cluck their tongues, "Acha-da! Acha-da! Memaloose—memaloose!" which is translated, "Too bad! Too bad! He die! He die!" In fact, Rolland lived well into old age as the last living member of the Denny party.

That night on Alki Point, twenty-four people and their belongings took cover from the pounding rain within the confines of the roofless cabin. Indian mats provided some shelter from the downpour. The Denny party's introductory night on Puget Sound left them wet, cold, and miserable by morning's light. This scene could not have been imagined by Mary Denny when she agreed to move west.

* Denny's granddaughter, Roberta Frye Watt, reports that Chief Seattle himself was present when the Denny party first arrived at Alki. Other sources, including Arthur Denny's book, *Pioneer Days on Puget Sound,* do not mention Chief Seattle's presence on that day.

Mary Ann Boren was born November 25, 1822, in Nashville, Tennessee. In 1843, at the age of twenty, she married a young civil engineer, Arthur Armstrong Denny, and the couple settled in Illinois. Letters from friends who had ventured into the vast Oregon Territory enticed Arthur Denny to move his family west. Arthur had a good position as the county supervisor for Knox County, Illinois. Still, when the word came east of the Oregon Territory's virgin forests, majestic mountains, mild year-round climate, and fertile soil, Arthur Denny got the bug. However, Arthur would not uproot his wife and two young daughters unless Mary Ann would consent to the move. When he finally summoned up the courage to ask her, Mary agreed to go west.

As Mary and Arthur told family of their plans, the size of their traveling party increased. On April 10, 1851, Mary and Arthur, along with many in their extended families, left their home in Cherry Grove, Illinois. The Denny-Boren party included Arthur and Mary Denny with their two little daughters; Arthur's father, John Denny (a widower who had married Mary's mother, Sarah), wife, Sarah, and their baby daughter, Loretta; Arthur's four unmarried brothers, James, Samuel, Wiley, and David; Mary's unmarried sister, Louisa Boren; and Mary's brother, Carson Boren with his wife and child. The group left Illinois in four wagons pulled by teams of horses and accompanied by a few head of cattle and two dogs. These brave pioneers left behind comfortable homes to venture west into the new Northwest territory.

In an attempt to retain some of the refinement of her home in Illinois while on the trail, Mary set the table properly for supper each evening, made up the beds with linen sheets for her family, and changed into nightclothes before retiring. One ferocious storm changed all of this by drenching their linens, bedding, and clothing thoroughly. From then on, the pioneers were so fatigued at the end of a day's travel that they gratefully fell into their bedrolls wearing whatever they had on at the time.

Conventions were often lost on the Oregon Trail. Mary's shoes soon wore out, and she finished the journey wearing buckskin moccasins. One of her daughters lost her only pair of shoes, so the two little girls were forced to share a single pair. They took turns wearing the shoes— one going barefoot, as the other went shod.

The small wagon train endured many hardships and dangers while crossing the barren plains, climbing winding mountain trails, and traveling through hostile Indian territory. The women bravely bore their travails. Mary Ann Denny was pregnant with her third child throughout the journey and not long after leaving Illinois, her two daughters came down with whooping cough. In addition to her trail-side duties, Mary now had two children to nurse. The young mother worried about the lack of clean water and fresh fruits and vegetables to feed her little girls. Biscuits cooked over campfires and wild game were their staples.

The Denny party encountered additional hazards along the Oregon Trail: scorching deserts, sudden storms, droughts, rattlesnakes, wild animals, quicksand, stampeding of their own livestock, and an attack by a warring tribe. After four months of such grueling overland travel and a treacherous ride down the Columbia River, the party arrived in Portland on August 22, 1851. Once in Portland, members of the party, including Arthur and Mary, became gravely ill with malaria.

While on the trail, Arthur heard tales of the Puget Sound region from another traveler. When they arrived at their original destination in the Willamette Valley around Portland, they found it to be already inhabited by settlers. The members of the Denny-Boren party decided that John Low and David Denny would go north and explore the region. Along the route they were joined by Lee Terry in Olympia and while there, met Captain Robert Fay, who took them by boat to Puget Sound.

When Low, Denny, and Terry arrived on the shores of Elliott Bay on September 25, 1851, they found an encampment of Indians on the beach, fishing for salmon. By some accounts, Chief Seattle was among those camped there that day. David Denny was reported to have been greeted by the chief and resolved then to learn the language of the Native people of the region. Low, Denny, and Terry slept near this camp their second night on Puget Sound. Two of Chief Seattle's men were hired the next day to take the men exploring. After their excursion, the men decided the gently sloping beaches of gravel and sand, surrounded by tall fir timbers on a peninsula the Indians called Smaquamox, was the place to start their settlement. Smaquamox was the southwest point of land, across Elliott Bay from Seattle's present site.

Terry, who was from New York, gave their town the name "New York." The three men envisioned a great city at this site, as great as any on the Atlantic seaboard. Since their vision was still far in the future, the name "Alki" was suggested. This was the Chinook term for "bye-and-bye." The town then was known as "New York Alki." The name Alki remained with the peninsula after the pioneers later moved north along the bay.

Low returned to Portland to bring his family north; he brought with him a letter from David Denny to his brother, Arthur, urging him to come up as well. The two remaining men cleared the land to lay foundations for cabins. Terry and Denny notched the logs, and began to build the walls of the first log home. When Terry went in search of needed tools, David Denny stayed behind to build shelters so the families would be safe from the elements when they arrived.

Local Indians, curious as to the source of the fires, began to paddle by in canoes. Chief Seattle's daughter, Princess Angeline, paddled her canoe to see what the huge fire was all about. They were surprised to see the outline of just one log cabin in the clearing, with such an enormous fire beside it. Princess Angeline and her party were told that the land was being cleared for other settlers, and that a boatload of people was expected, including a baby. Word of the new arrivals quickly spread among the local tribes, and many of them were on shore to greet the boat when it arrived from Portland.

Unfortunately, David Denny, left alone to finish the cabin, cut his leg and became ill before the rest of the Denny party arrived. For this reason, twenty-four wet and miserable men, women, and children found themselves attempting to keep dry in a single, roofless dwelling.

After the rest of the party had arrived, the men's first order of business was to finish construction of their shelter's roof. With a new roof now over their heads, Mrs. Denny and the other women suddenly realized that Christmas was fast approaching. Although they were surrounded by evergreens and could have easily found a perfect Christmas tree, the women decided that they did not have room for a wet tree in the crowded cabin. Improvising, the ladies put a ladder against the wall and draped it with a sheet.

Christmas Eve, while the children slept, Mary and the others scoured their possessions for materials to use in making presents. The women sewed bits of lace, velvet, and ribbon into decorative collars for the little girls. The mittens and scarves the pioneer wives had knit while traveling west were pinned to the sheet so that each child had a present on Christmas morning. The party said prayers and sung hymns in celebration of the Christmas holiday. Christmas dinner consisted of a roasted goose, prepared on Mary's cookstove, and a Native Northwest salmon side dish.

The first business enterprise for the new settlement was initiated by the arrival of the ship *Leonesa,* which dropped anchor off of Alki Point several months after the Denny party had settled there. The ship's captain requested the pioneers supply him with logs for market in San Francisco. In exchange for sorely needed cash and provisions, the settlers and their Indian friends began the task of logging. While the captain waited for the logs to be harvested, he entertained the women and children of the Denny party with stories of his high seas adventures. The Denny women, in turn, told tales of their adventures in crossing the plains to Oregon. When the ship had been loaded with lumber, the captain paid the settlers and Indians in provisions he could spare and the balance in cash. The settlers also placed orders for merchandise and provisions with the captain for his return voyage.

More ships followed in search of timber and exchanged compensation with the settlers and their Indian friends. The women looked forward to the conversation and provisions that the captains of the ships would bring. The ladies wondered about current fashions and complained that the clothes they had brought had become shabby and full of holes. Mary and her friends urged the captains to bring fabric with them from San Francisco on their next trip north.

One captain, upon bringing a bolt of fabric with him to Elliott Bay, bet his crew that before the ship was loaded with logs for return to California, all of the women in the settlement would be dressed alike. The captain won his bet, but as more ships ventured north to trade with the new settlement, a variety of dress material and other provisions became available. The ships became busy markets when they dropped anchor in Puget Sound, as the settlers were eager for provisions and news from the outside world.

When the new citizens of the Northwest weren't trading with docked ships, they prepared to construct a cabin for each family. Before long, many local Indian families were moving tepees onto the lots the pioneers had staked out for themselves. The Indians explained that they wanted to be close to the settlers for protection from enemy tribes. The Denny party was soon surrounded by an encampment of up to one thousand Indians who were extremely curious about their neighbors. Cultural differences caused some misunderstandings, as the Native people felt free to enter the cabins and help themselves to what they found. On one occasion, an Indian man entered Mary Denny's cabin as she was frying up a large fish. As the man reached into Mary's frying pan, she was forced to defend her dinner by striking the man on the hand with a spoon.

Another custom that caused confusion was that of young Indian men placing their tepee poles so that they obstructed the doorways of the cabins. It was their custom that if a woman touched the poles to move them aside, then she must become the pole owner's wife. Several of the Native men had designs on Louisa Boren. Once informed of the plan by a tribal elder who had learned Chinook (the language of trade among early trappers and various Northwest tribes) from the Hudson's Bay men, the settlers quashed the matrimonial plan. Louisa, the Sweetbriar Bride (she brought sweetbriar seeds with her from Illinois), later married David Denny in a ceremony that caused great intrigue among the local Indians.

Confrontations sometimes occurred between Native people and settlers. Mary Denny, while outside the family cabin, was confronted by Nisqually Jim, who, without saying a word, leveled his rifle directly at her. He got no response from the brave pioneer woman, as she stood unflinchingly, returning his stare. He then lowered the gun and retreated. Mary's explanation for the incident was to say that, "I suppose he did it to show that he could shoot me if he wanted to."

Certainly, the new settlers to the area and the Natives were not always at odds. Mary and the women of the settlement formed valuable friendships with Native women who showed them how best to obtain and use the Puget Sound region's bounty of edible goods. Indian women often came to visit bearing gifts of food, such as baskets full of ripe blackberries.

After the first winter in Alki, Chief Seattle reportedly pointed out to the Denny party that the land to the northeast, sheltered within Elliott Bay, would be a more desirable location to build a town. Arthur Denny explored the area, noting the deep water harbor, which he used Mary's clothesline to measure, and nearby trail over the Cascade Mountains. In 1852, the Denny, Boren, and Bell families moved to that site, where downtown Seattle is located today. This new location provided far better shelter from the wind and winter storms.

Within the next year, many more pioneer families moved to the area. In 1853, the territorial legislature selected the name "Duwamps" for the new town, and mail was addressed to "Duwamps via Olympia, Oregon." Later, the town's name was changed to "Seattle," and after a conflict with its namesake was resolved, the name stuck and the town prospered.

In 1855, warring tribes from east of the Cascade Mountains incited violence against the settlers in the Puget Sound region. The year before, Washington territorial governor Issac Stevens had begun organizing treaties with Indian tribes within the territory. In exchange for cash and trinkets, the tribes were moved to reservations and their original lands were opened to settlers. In protest, some eastern Washington Indians from various tribes rebelled against prospectors and pioneers. As the warring tribes moved west, settlers in the Duwamish Valley were killed, along with two young men killed in Seattle during the fighting. Cabins were ransacked, and some burned to the ground. Mary Denny's treasured wedding dress was taken from her cabin, and she often wondered who wore it through the woods after that. The Denny families and Seattle's settlers took refuge in the old blockhouse that stood at the corner of the present-day streets of First Avenue and Cherry Street. The war, known as the Battle of Seattle, was ended rather abruptly by the presence of the warship *Decatur* in Puget Sound. When she saw the ship, Mary Denny's daughter, Louisa Catherine, remembers her mother exclaiming, "Thank God! Our prayers are answered!"

Mary and Arthur Denny became wealthy, well-respected members of Seattle society. In addition to bringing the first non-Indian baby to Seattle from Portland, Mary Ann Denny also gave birth to the second non-Indian baby, and first male child in Seattle. The baby boy, Orion Orvil, was born to them in July of 1853. The Denny's homestead fronted First Avenue and covered several present-day city blocks north to Union Street. Arthur used his civil engineering skills to survey and lay out Seattle's streets. He was instrumental in governing the young city and territory—serving in the first Territorial Legislature* and being elected as a delegate to the United States Congress. Building the city's economic foundation, Arthur helped to bring a road across the Cascades, shipping to Puget Sound, and the railroad to Seattle. Without Mary's support, Arthur would never have made the journey west.

Mary Denny was known for her benevolence—giving anonymous gifts to poor families and generously buying presents for children in need. Mary's memories kept alive the pioneer spirit. She told of making the trip between Seattle and Olympia (the nearest real town) in Indian canoes, sailing vessels, steamships, trains, and automobiles, and it was her ambition to make the journey by "flying machine." She recalled Secretary of the Interior William Seward visiting Seattle in 1869 on his way to inspect his purchase of Alaska. Seattle at that time had approximately one thousand residents, but Seward predicted future greatness for the city, calling Puget Sound the "Mediterranean of the Pacific."

Mary Ann Boren Denny passed away on December 30, 1910, at the age of eighty-eight. On the day of her death, boldface headlines in the *Seattle Daily Times* proclaimed, "Woman Founder of City Passes Away." The article stated:

> [w]ith the demise of Mrs. Denny there passed one of the oldest human landmarks in the history of the city. She was the first white woman to land on the shores of Puget Sound and together with her husband played a prominent part in the upbuilding

---

* The Washington Territory was officially formed from the Oregon Territory in 1853.

of this city. Her death took from Seattle not only one of its most interesting characters, but one of its noblest women.

A group of descendants of the Dennys and Seattle's other founding families was formed in 2004 to thank the Duwamish Tribe for helping the settlers survive their first winter on Alki. The "Descendants Committee" organized the "Coming Full Circle" ceremony at the Museum of History and Industry to acknowledge the tribe's contributions. The committee went on to raise funds to help build the Duwamish Longhouse, a tribal cultural center and the only property owned by the tribe since ceding the land under the city of Seattle to the federal government. The group of first families continued their work to raise awareness of the Duwamish Tribe's fight to gain federal recognition. Ironically, the tribe of Chief Seattle has struggled to be recognized by the U.S. government since signing the treaty that gave away their land.

MOTHER JOSEPH

1823–1902

CHIEF OF THE LADY BLACK ROBES

Clouds of dust erupted as the stagecoach wheels ground to a halt on the narrow mountain road. Four masked gunmen greeted the startled passengers with the cold steel barrels of their revolvers. "Get out of the stage, and throw your bags to the side of the road! Now!" barked the gang leader. Pistols were trained on the terrified travelers as they disembarked. A middle aged nun among the passengers whispered to the others, "Pray, pray!"

Once the luggage had been deposited by the roadside, the people were herded back into the stagecoach as the robbers began to rifle through the baggage. The nun looked up from her praying as if seized by a sudden impulse. She jumped to her feet and called out, "Mister . . . Mister. . . ." Her co-passengers, thinking they might all be killed any minute, urged to her to be quiet.

The sister was undaunted and spoke more authoritatively, addressing the youngest member of the gang with a thick French accent, "Mister . . . my boy." The young thief started, as if no one had ever spoken to him in such a manner. For a moment, he stopped his pilfering.

"My boy, please give me that black bag!"

While the other passengers, cowering in the stage, looked on in horror, the young man asked, "Which?"

"That one—the black one over there."

The boy searched through the pile of luggage, then held one up with a questioning look toward the sister.

"No, no."

He continued to sort through the bags, eventually coming upon a large carpetbag, and held it up for the nun's approval.

"Yes, my man. Give it to me. There is nothing in it you would want."

Mother Joseph Sisters of Providence Archives, Seattle, WA

Stunned by the nun's audacity, the bandit brought her the bag.

"Thank you. God bless you," commended the sister graciously. The boy then returned to looting with his gang, and the nun rejoined her companions in the stage. She winked at the petrified young nun traveling with her and patted her bag. Several hundred dollars the sisters had collected that day from miners had been saved from the bandits.

The two nuns, Sister Mary Augustine and her bold superior, Mother Joseph of the Sacred Heart, continued on this begging tour through the mines of Oregon, Idaho, and Colorado for another sixteen months. The Sisters of Providence sought contributions from generous miners to fund the building of an orphanage in Vancouver, Washington Territory. The stagecoach robbery was but one of many adventures and hardships that Mother Joseph endured while on her begging tours throughout the West to raise money for her charitable endeavors.

∞

She was born Esther Pariseau in French-speaking Saint Elzear, Quebec, on April 16, 1823. Esther was the third of twelve children of Joseph and Francoise Pariseau. During the snowy winter months when he could not farm, Joseph Pariseau worked as a coach maker, a talent he became well known for throughout the region. As a young girl, Esther worked beside her father in his shop, learning to love the tools and wood crafting at which her father was so skilled.

Madame Pariseau, educated by the Sisters of Notre Dame in Montreal, taught her children to read and write. When she was seventeen, Esther entered the Saint Martin de Laval boarding school run by Mademoiselle Elizabeth Bruyere in 1840. Strong and direct, Esther had a dignified presence and a natural capacity for organization and leadership. She loved school and adored her instructor, Mademoiselle Bruyere, but it did not surprise Esther when her teacher announced she was leaving the school to become a nun.

Shortly after her instructor left, Esther felt her own calling. She was inspired to work for the poor and infirm by a visit from Monseigneur Bourget to her family's farm. Father Bourget told of a new order of nuns, the Sisters of Providence, who were serving the poor with wonderful works of charity for the sick and destitute in Montreal. The priest sought money to construct a convent, the Asile of Providence, for the new order of nuns.

Joseph Pariseau brought his young daughter to this newly built convent, the Asile, on December 26, 1843. As Joseph respectfully approached the dignified Mother Superior Gamelin, he stated his purpose and introduced his daughter.

Madame, my daughter, Esther, wishes to dedicate herself to the religious life. She is now twenty years of age, and for some time she has prayed with the family for enlightenment as to the decision she is about to make. . . It is a great sacrifice for me to part with Esther, but if you will accept her into your company, she will be a real acquisition. She has had all the education that her mother and I could give her, besides what the Parish school could offer. My daughter can read, write, figure accurately, sew, cook, spin, and do all manner of housework. She can even do carpentering, handle a hammer and saw as well as her father. She can also plan for others, and succeeds in all she undertakes. I assure you, Madame, she will make a good superior some day.

Esther cried out in embarrassment, "Oh, Father, please! *Pour l'amour de Mon Dieu!* Must you tell all my accomplishments, my talents, and the work my mother taught me?"

"Let your father speak, child," interrupted the mother superior, "What he says interests me very much."

Joseph continued, "Only twenty now, Esther is healthy and strong, has never been ill. She is clever and knows her mind. She is very well determined to give herself to God in the Providence to answer the appeal of Monseigneur Bourget for helpers."

"And you, Monsieur Pariseau, are you willing to make the sacrifice of your daughter?"

"Certainly, Madame, that is why I brought her today. This is her Christmas offering to the Divine Child, the gift of herself."

After arranging Esther's dowry and a hug goodbye, Joseph was gone. Esther now entered into a new life. She took her vows in 1845 and with them the name Sister Joseph in honor of her father.

When, in April of 1852, Father Francis Norbert Blanchet (Archbishop of Oregon City) and his brother, Father Magloire Blanchet (Bishop of Nisqually) visited the Asile, the direction of Sister Joseph's life changed again. Father Magloire Blanchet had spent six years in a remote wilderness called the "Oregon Territory," most recently as the Bishop of the Nisqually Diocese. Father Francis Norbert Blanchet had been in the territory since 1838. All at the Asile were intrigued with tales of the Oregon Territory, including Sister Joseph, who had dreams of going west and working with Native people.

The Fathers Blanchet had been well received by the Hudson's Bay Company, the entity that controlled the Oregon/Washington Territory for Great Britain. The Hudson's Bay enclave Fort Vancouver was the dominant settlement in the Washington Territory at that time. Catholics were welcomed by Dr. McLoughlin, the head of the Hudson's Bay Company, and the trappers who were mostly Catholic. The priests had a huge job in covering all of this territory and were in need of sisters to help them. Upon this return to the Asile in 1852, the Bishop of Nisqually spoke of this need for sisters to serve in the new land. Sister Joseph volunteered, but the council in Montreal refused to let her go, as she was much needed there.

In November of 1856, after a previous expedition of nuns had failed, Sister Joseph was allowed to be part of a new expedition. Frightened and confused by the wild country, winter storms, and floods, the first group of nuns had sailed for home, only to end up settling in Chile. The new party of five mostly French-speaking nuns was led by Father Magloire Blanchet. The priest appointed Sister Joseph as their mother superior, a job she reluctantly accepted. She was given the title, "Sister Joseph of the Sacred Heart."

Due to strong anti-Catholic sentiments of the time, the nuns were advised not to wear their habits when traveling, especially not in New York City, where they were to embark upon their journey. Having borrowed and purchased used clothing for their travels, the women, in their unfashionable attire, attracted far more attention than a few habits would have drawn. While riding cabs through the streets of the city they heard cries such as, "Look at the Quaker ladies!" The waiters at the Catholic-owned hotel where they stayed could hardly contain their laughter when the women first entered their dining room. Following dinner, the maitre d' tipped the sisters that they had nothing to fear were they to wear their habits in the hotel, on the boats, or even in the city itself. The sisters must have breathed a collective sigh of relief. From this time on, Mother Joseph was never without her habit.

On November 6, 1856, the party sailed from New York to Panama, where they crossed the Isthmus of Panama by train. The sisters were lucky to have a train in 1855, as the expedition of nuns in 1852 had crossed Panama on mules. Even so, this train ride of forty-seven miles took them five hours.

Once at the Pacific Ocean, the nuns boarded a ship to San Francisco. Then, after a few days rest, they transferred to a steamer bound for Vancouver. This was to be the hardest part of the trip. Winter storms made for turbulent seas. Ferocious waves tossed the ship like a toy boat, and trunks and baggage were thrown about by the violent lurching of the boat. Everything not tied down flew around the cabins as the vessel creaked and groaned. The main mast was blown over. It was impossible for the passengers to leave their bunks, as they could not stand without being heaved through the air. The nuns were chilled to the bone and seasick—so much so that Mother Joseph thought she might die.

When the seas finally calmed, the Captain announced they were entering a place known as the "Grave Yard," due to its hidden shoals and shifting sands. Many ships had been lost crossing the sandbars at the mouth of the Columbia River. Landing safely at Astoria, Oregon, they traveled on the Columbia to Vancouver.

Along the Columbia, the nuns saw dense forests with trees so tall they disappeared into the fog. They saw little civilization, but for a few log cabins. At Fort Vancouver, the party was greeted by a small crowd of what seemed to be all young soldiers. Fort Vancouver, once run by the British Hudson's Bay Company, was now an American military post where there were only a few women and no Indians.

At the Vancouver Mission, the women found no housing and a priest who opposed their staying at Vancouver. Vicar General Brouillet thought it more appropriate that the sisters reside in Olympia, the new capital of the Washington Territory. The vicar argued with Bishop Blanchet that the women would be better provided for in Olympia. Here they had only a shed to give them for quarters. Mother Joseph, overhearing the conversation, offered to stay in the shed.

The nuns spent their first night in Father Blanchet's dusty attic, which they first had to clean! Their bedding consisted of dirty old quilts used by settlers and Indians who took refuge at the mission during the Indian Wars. The following months were also spent with Father Blanchet, crowded into his simple board house over which the nuns assumed care. Mother Joseph constructed a dormitory-refectory-community room. Using the skills acquired from her father, she built bunk beds, a table hinged to the wall, and cupboards.

The sisters spent the unfamiliar rainy winter planning for a convent and a school. On Ash Wednesday, February 22, 1857, the nuns moved to their own small, wood-frame house. In it Mother Joseph had constructed an attic dormitory and chapel complete with an altar and tabernacle.

Prior to the school's opening, the nuns received their first little pupil. Three-year-old Emily Lake arrived at the convent with a mother eager to leave her behind with the nuns. The child was fatherless, of mixed race, and appeared dirty and neglected. Mother Joseph was delighted to take the girl; she held the tiny, grimy hand tightly and assured the mother they would care for Emily. The mother showed no emotion, just relief, and made a quick exit, never to be seen again. Mother Joseph adored little Emily, and for the first time in her life, Emily was wanted and protected. She could often be seen following Mother Joseph around in the garden and in the chapel.

Before long, a baby boy named William was placed with the sisters. Mother Joseph pitied the little orphans, often placed with guardians who mistreated them and raised them without morals. Such guardians sometimes traveled hundreds of miles to the mission to abandon these poor children.

Next, an eighty-five-year-old man, feeble and poor, asked to be taken in. There was so little room at the tiny convent that the old man's bed was put next to the stove in the kitchen.

On April 15, 1857, the first Catholic school in the Northwest opened its doors to seven little girls. The school was small and plain, but impeccably clean. A language barrier impeded the teaching of these American pupils as only two of the nuns spoke English. Mother Joseph, who spoke very little English, often wrote to her mother superior in Montreal of the need for more English-speaking nuns. She particularly hoped that the mother superior might send a music teacher west.

Mother Joseph found Vancouver to be a town full of sin. She was aghast at the lifestyles of her fellow French Canadians. In her letters to her mother superior, she noted that Vancouver's population was a mixture of people from everywhere, and that both the Catholics and Protestants had been poorly schooled in religion, although the Protestants welcomed religious instruction for their children.

Initially, the sisters' mission was to create schools and orphanages. Mother Joseph had hoped to work and live among Indian people but, to her dismay, she learned that "these poor unfortunates" had been driven to the mountains by an increasing number of white settlers. She longed to establish Indian schools, but the Indian Wars of the mid-1800s made for turbulent times. Bishop Blanchet, on occasion, brought orphaned Indian children to the convent from east of the Cascade Mountains.

From the time they arrived, the sisters had visited Vancouver's sick and infirm. In the spring of 1858, they were called to take in a young man named John Lloyd who was afflicted with tuberculosis. Though they wanted to help the poor, sick, homeless man, they had no place to house him. The vicar proposed building a hospital. The ladies of the town—Catholic, Protestant, and Jewish alike—assembled to assist in the endeavor.

Mother Joseph had built a tiny clapboard cabin, which she intended to be used for a laundry and bakery. The town's ladies offered to complete the interior and furnish the small building if Mother Joseph would allow them to use it as their hospital. Mother Joseph agreed, and Saint Joseph's, the first hospital in the Northwest, opened in April of 1858, with only four beds. Before long, young John, the waiting patient, was admitted to Saint Joseph's and was soon followed by many sick and injured Northwesterners. Thus, the nuns had created the first official school, orphanage, and hospital in the Northwest.

In the spring of 1861, a mentally ill woman was placed in the sisters' care. They then devoted two small buildings to housing the "mentally deranged." By 1866, there were twenty-five patients cared for under a contract with the Washington Territory. The patients later moved to a more spacious house, but when the territorial government revoked their contract to care for the insane over a dispute resulting from Mother Joseph's insistence on being paid in gold coin rather than "greenbacks," the home to Saint John of God Asylum became the new Saint Joseph's Hospital.

At the urging of priests, the sisters founded Saint Vincent's in Portland, Oregon, in 1875 and Providence Hospital in Seattle in 1877. These were the first of twenty-nine institutions Mother Joseph established during her forty-six years in the Pacific Northwest. Although high mortality rates in the logging camps around Seattle were creating an urgent need for hospitals, the sisters often met with less than enthusiastic welcomes from the citizens they came to serve. At the time, Seattle was a rough, muddy, sparsely populated, Protestant or atheist, logging and seaport town. The people were suspicious of the French-speaking nuns and of Catholics in general. However, the sisters persisted, and the people came to depend upon them.

In 1881, after the hospital had outgrown two buildings, Mother Joseph designed a new elaborate Providence Hospital in Seattle. This stately building was like nothing the city had ever seen, with its gas-lighting system and steam-driven elevators. Mother Joseph conducted the final inspection of Providence Hospital in a sawdust-covered habit with her hammer swinging from her tool belt.

Although Mother Joseph's first preference was to work with a hammer and saw, she recognized the need to raise money to build and run these institutions. Asking for financial support from the community flew in the face of tradition, but the industrious sister would do what was necessary to get the job done and then later pray for forgiveness. Mother Joseph and her nuns traveled on begging tours throughout the West, appealing to miners to fund their charitable works. To Westerners they were known as the "Lady Black Robes," with Mother Joseph designated, by the Indians, as their chief.

Mother Joseph's description of one such begging tour can be found in the annals of the Sisters of Providence for July of 1866. Mother Joseph and Sister Catherine had traveled by boat to Wallula, near Walla Walla, and then by stagecoach to Walla Walla and on to Idaho City where they collected $3,000 from the miners. During their six-week begging tour in Idaho, they met with varied reactions from those they appealed to for alms. In Idaho City, the nuns were received cordially even by "infidels and Protestants who marveled at [their] daring, and commended [their] perseverance." Often in the mining camps the sisters encountered cold indifference, and even abuse. In her habit, Mother Joseph made perilous descents into the black mines, hundreds of feet below the earth's surface, in order to contact the many miners who worked underground.

Encouraged by good fortune in Idaho, the two nuns set out for Montana. The miners of Montana were not as enthusiastic as those in Idaho, yet the sisters still collected $2,000. Following a visit with four, lonely sisters at the Saint Ignatius Mission forty miles north of Missoula, the women set off for home on horseback. They would no longer have the luxury of traveling by boat or stagecoach. Only on horseback could they pass through the forests that lay between them and the lower Columbia country. The sisters at Saint Ignatius loaned them saddles and riding habits—the Jesuit Fathers provided the horses.

"In the last days of September our little caravan set out. It was composed of Father Louis Saint-Onge, an Indian named Sapiel from the mission, Father Joseph Giorda, S.J., who went with us as far as Missoula, Sister Catherine and myself." With them were two pack horses with provisions and a tent. They traveled through dark forests and steep, precipitous mountains on narrow Indian trails. Except for some lone miners, the party met no one.

Every evening they looked for a clearing, with water and grass for the animals, in which to make camp. Father Saint-Onge hunted for game, Sapiel cared for the horses and collected firewood, and the sisters took charge of cooking crêpes and fresh meat. They ate, conversed, sang hymns, and prayed before the light of the fire. In preparation for bed, they pitched their tent, wrapped themselves in blankets, and with saddles for pillows, retired for the night.

One day while riding on steep Rocky Mountain trails, a fierce storm broke upon them. Low, dark clouds hung overhead menacingly. When the clouds broke, the gradually increasing rainstorm gave way to a relentless downpour, thunder, and lightning. Traveling in the deep mud was challenging, as was building a fire in the driving rain. By the time camp was set up, all were soaked to the skin. With great difficulty, Sapiel was able to set a small fire inside the tent. They lay down that night in the mud, as near to the fire as possible. Several nights later, an enormous tree fell just three feet from the tent in which the two nuns were sleeping.

Traveling through dense forests over an animal trail, they would often lose sight of each other on the winding paths. On the ninth day of travel, the party, overcome with fatigue, camped in a ravine between two mountain ranges. They were jolted awake by a terrifying howl that, according to Mother Joseph's account, "froze the blood in our veins." Sapiel quickly cut wood and circled the camp with fire, since wolves do not ordinarily cross a line of fire. Soon the woods were full of the horrible howls. The travelers knew wolves, which hunt in packs, were now all around them. The horses, tethered inside the ring of fire, were lathered to a frenzy. Trees surrounding the area had been dried by a prior fire, and soon the flames, meant to protect the party, were a serious threat to their safety. Branches and brush around them began to burn, embers cracked and popped menacingly, and great limbs burned and crashed to the ground. The whole night was spent battling burning cinders and blinding smoke, while surrounded by an increasing number of howling wolves. Some provisions were destroyed, the tent had caught fire several times, and the saddles were singed. The dawn's light chased away the wolves, ending a night of trauma and prayer. Exhausted, they fell to the ground with fatigue.

Suddenly, a new sound was heard, that of horses tramping up the trail. Before they could react, a party of Indian warriors with painted faces surrounded the camp. The Indian braves noticed the crosses around their necks and recognized Father Saint-Onge. They immediately offered hand signs of friendship and respect. The Indian people were drawn to Catholicism, the long, dark robes of the priests and nuns, and the symbols of the faith. They trusted the priests far more than the rugged frontiersmen they met in the territory, and the priests often acted as envoys between the tribes and the settlers. The party shared a meal with the Indians, but "cringed before the scalping knives" that hung at their sides.

Another evening while still in the Coeur d'Alene forests of Idaho, Father Saint-Onge spotted tracks while raising the tent. Sapiel identified the tracks as those of a grizzly bear, known to his people as the most dangerous creature in the forest. The only arms the men had against the massive beast were a six-shooter and an ax. The two did not mention the danger to the others, and the night passed without incident.

Early the next morning, Sapiel went to check on the horses. He was horrified to find an enormous grizzly bear attacking one of the horses. The bear, spying Sapiel, jumped the log corral and made straight for him. Sapiel took off running with the grizzly in close pursuit. The bear's claws swiped at the man several times, and he could hear teeth grinding near his head. Sapiel somehow managed to elude the creature's great claws. Suddenly, the bear became distracted by the sound of tinkling bells. A pack train of mules came into sight and the cries of the Mexicans leading the mules, and those of Father Saint-Onge, scared the grizzly off.

"One more adventure before the curtain falls on this unforgettable tour of the Rocky Mountains," Mother Joseph wrote in her chronicles. On a quiet night on the trail, Father Saint-Onge, sleeping under the stars, was awakened by a sensation of something cold gliding up his trouser leg. He knew it was a rattlesnake. With extreme willpower he lay perfectly still so that the reptile would go to sleep near the warmth of his body. After several minutes, which must have seemed an eternity, Father leapt to his feet so the serpent slid away from him. The snake was seen slinking away leaving the poor priest shaken, but unscathed.

The weary travelers arrived back in Vancouver on October 16, 1866, exhausted by the long horseback journey fraught with dangers. The sisters were grateful for the financial success of their tour and for their safe return home.

Many years of contention between the United States and the British Hudson's Bay Company put the sisters' property claim in Vancouver in jeopardy. In 1869, the American government served the mission with an eviction notice, which was later rescinded under protest by the Bishop.

Mother Joseph saw that it was time to consolidate all of their scattered little buildings. Her dream was to construct a magnificent brick convent. With the help of the Bishop's nephew, Mother Joseph negotiated with local businesses for building materials. The nun had developed a reputation as a force with which to be reckoned, even among seasoned salesmen. She could not be pushed around by businessmen who sometimes saw the nuns' works as encroachment and their free labor as unfair competition. It was unusual at the time to find a woman with such will and determination. Her blunt, direct manner sometimes made her seem difficult, even among the sisters.

Mother Joseph's strong work ethic and love of construction made her a taskmaster. She was known to rip apart faulty construction with her own hands, only to rebuild the structures herself. Witnesses recall the black-habited Mother Joseph emerging from beneath a building after checking its foundation, or balancing on a high beam to test its strength. Stories grew of her skill as a carver and woodworker. Many of the convent's statues were carved by Mother Joseph herself.

In 1874, Mother Joseph moved the sisters, the boarders, and the orphans into the House of Providence on Tenth and Reserve Streets in Vancouver. The people of the Pacific Coast cities were amazed at the enormity of the convent, unlike any structure then found in Washington or Oregon. The sisters now had their grand convent; however, they also were in debt $20,000. Once again Mother Joseph set out on a begging tour, this time to the Frasier River country of Canada, raising $10,000, in just three weeks.

For nearly forty-seven years, Mother Joseph of the Sacred Heart continued her work throughout the Northwest. She built schools for Indian children at Tulalip, Colville, and Coeur d'Alene, along with dozens of hospitals and orphanages. Even at age seventy-seven, she answered a call to build an orphanage in British Columbia.

In her last years, Mother Joseph was nearly blinded by a brain tumor and mostly confined to the convent. She died January 19, 1902, of her condition. Her dying words were to remind the sisters to always attend to the care of the poor without regret.

In 1980, the state of Washington named Mother Joseph its most distinguished citizen. A bronze statue of the nun, hammer by her side, was constructed by Felix de Weldon for the Statuary Hall of the House of Representatives in Washington, D.C. Mother Joseph was only the fifth woman, first Catholic nun, and second Washingtonian (joining Dr. Marcus Whitman) to be so honored. Today, the West Coast Lumberman's Association acknowledges Mother Joseph as the first (non-Indian) Northwestern artist to work in the medium of wood. The American Institute of Architects named Mother Joseph the Pacific Northwest's first architect in 1953, fifty-one years after her death. In addition to her wonderful work on behalf of the poor, building schools, hospitals, and orphanages, she designed architecture far ahead of anything in the West at the time.

LIZZIE ORDWAY

1828–1897

MERCER GIRL

Alarge, restless crowd, composed mostly of men, met the ship as
it docked in Elliott Bay. The air was thick with excitement and
anticipation. Seattle's large population of single men, who outnumbered
the women ten to one, eagerly awaited the arrival of Asa Mercer and his
"Mercer Girls."

At the urging of local businessmen, Asa Mercer had ventured east
in search of eligible women willing to relocate to the untamed Pacific
Northwest. Asa Shinn Mercer, the twenty-three-year-old president of
the Territorial University (now known as the University of Washington), saw a solution to the problem of the Northwest's dearth of eligible
females and the abundance of lonely bachelors. On the East Coast, the
situation was reversed. The Civil War had decimated the population of
young men, and young women were faced with bleak prospects regarding marriage and employment.

Though not the first to see the solution, Mercer became the first
to act on the idea of importing New England's women to the Pacific
Northwest. He approached the territorial governor, Pickering, and the
Territorial Legislature. Although they liked the plan, they could not
approve funding, as the territory was not wealthy. Instead, Mercer collected enough money from individual businessmen to fund a trip to Boston to act upon his plan.

In Boston, Mercer advertised the virtues of Puget Sound and met
with interested groups of women—many war widows and orphans. He
detailed the charms of the region and the vast opportunities for employment in this new frontier where women were at a premium. An example
of one such enticing speech follows:

Lizzie Ordway Museum of History and Industry

The climate of Washington Territory is marked by two seasons only, winter and summer. From the first day of April until the middle of November no other spot on this green earth boasts such a mild, equitable and delightful climate as does the valley of Puget Sound. Refreshing showers visit us every few weeks and all nature breathes of purity and healthfulness.

Mercer offered to lead the most worthy candidates to this wonderful new land. Receiving a stack of applications, he chose only women who were of the highest caliber in community standing, education, and moral character. From this choice group, he limited his candidates to those with enough courage and pioneer spirit to brave a long journey to the other end of the continent with virtually no chance of returning home.

In the end, eleven chosen women joined Mercer as he sailed west, including the oldest "Mercer Girl," thirty-five-year-old Elizabeth ("Lizzie") Ordway. Asa Mercer promised the women that they would find careers in the Northwest; he said nothing about marriage. He kept his word, finding mostly teaching positions for them in Seattle and out-lying towns.

The party of twelve left New York aboard a steamer, traveled by train across the Isthmus of Panama, took a steamer from Panama City to San Francisco, before traveling by lumber bark from San Francisco to Port Gamble, and sloop from Port Gamble to Seattle. The sloop *Kidder* arrived in Seattle at midnight, on May 16, 1864. Seattle, expecting the party, was awake to see them land. Carrying lanterns, curious women and respectful young bachelors—washed, combed, and in their newest and cleanest clothes—met the *Kidder* as it docked on Yesler's Wharf.

The arrival of the eleven potential brides from the East on May 16, 1864, was a monumental event in Seattle. Every single man who could afford to purchase a new suit did so; those that could not bought new over-alls. All eligible men were on the dock when the ship arrived. Asa Mercer greeted the men, telling them that these women were of the finest caliber and that if these men desired wives, they must court them in the customary manner. A grand celebration was held in honor of the women. The party lasted from the moment the first passenger walked down the gangplank to well into the early morning hours. A reception was held the next day in the town hall, with the festive mood continuing on through the week.

This first expedition was a success and, as a result, Asa S. Mercer was elected to the Territorial Legislature. Two years later, he made a second trip east with the dream of enticing five hundred women to Seattle. Mercer met with many obstacles and, in the end, only twenty-eight single women landed on Yesler's Wharf.

These refined women left the comforts of modern society in the East for the rugged Pacific Northwest in order to bring New England's culture and refinement to the Northwest. Some were likely lured west by romantic ideas of adventure on a new frontier. The "Mercer Girls" were treated hospitably by Seattleites, who took them into their homes to live until they either married or found employment as milliners, dressmakers, or teachers (the occupations available to women of the day).

Within a year of their arrival, all of the Mercer Girls* remaining in the Northwest had married, except one—thirty-six-year-old Elizabeth "Lizzie" M. Ordway. Miss Ordway never had any intention of marrying at the end of her voyage. Rather, as one of Washington's first career women, Lizzie's goal was, "to carry the educational standards of New England to the new community beyond the Rockies."

✍

The eldest child of a wealthy family, Elizabeth M. Ordway was born July 4, 1828, in Lowell, Massachusetts. Enoch Ordway, Lizzie's father, ran a business that imported cotton. A witty conversant with considerable charm,

---

* One of the Mercer girls died on Whidbey Island, where she taught school, and another returned to Lowell, Massachusetts.

Lizzie moved in high society circles and was a sought-after party guest, although her advanced views were seen as unconventional for the time.

Graduating from the prestigious Ipswich Academy, Lizzie earned a certificate in ancient and modern languages. She was fluent in five modern tongues and knowledgeable about Greek and Roman language and culture. A major influence on Lizzie at the Ipswich Academy was her teacher Gail Hamilton, who wrote under the pen name Mary Abigail Dodge. Hamilton was a noted feminist and author. This influence cultivated Lizzie's feminism and sharpened her skills at bantering with wit and humor. Lizzie was strong in her convictions, very decisive, and willing to act on the strength of her own judgment. Following her graduation from the Academy, Miss Ordway taught school in Lowell, Massachusetts, for twelve years.

In Seattle, Lizzie's first home was with pioneer Henry Yesler and his family, where she and Sarah Yesler concurred on the goals of the suffrage movement—providing equal rights and voting privileges to women. Four months after her arrival, when a fellow Mercer Girl—who was the teacher at Whidbey Island's school—died unexpectedly, Lizzie was asked to take the helm of the school. She moved across Puget Sound to Whidbey Island and taught in Coupeville for the remainder of the 1864 school year.

In 1866, Miss Ordway took command of the Port Madison school on the Kitsap Peninsula. From 1866 until her death in 1897, she was identified as a leader in education for Kitsap County.

Port Madison vied with Seattle as a commercial port in the late nineteenth century due to the extensive lumber business on the peninsula. Mill towns were known for their rough atmosphere, with their schools being no different. Into this environment came the petite, well-bred lady from New England. A tiny, slender, light-haired woman with steel gray eyes, Miss Ordway soon had control of the tough Port Madison school.

Miss Lizzie possessed a pioneer spirit in teaching rough-hewn students under rugged, primitive conditions. Surrounded by the wild

Northwestern woods and enduring isolation and solitude, coarse characters, and apathetic students, she persevered. Without roads, many students paddled to school in canoes or walked along beaches to the schoolhouses. The dangerous Puget Sound currents occasionally caused small vessels to capsize and since some children had drowned in this manner, teachers were advised to watch the tides and dismiss class only when the tides favored water travel.

When Miss Ordway started a school in Port Orchard, the district was the wildest and most unsettled on the Kitsap Peninsula. Teachers were advised against living alone in the "teacherage," or living quarters adjacent to the schoolhouse. A young girl lived with Lizzie and cared for the house while Lizzie was teaching. Lizzie tutored the young girl in the evenings in turn.

As a result of her achievements in Port Madison, Lizzie Ordway was recruited to Seattle to start the city's first public school. Prior to this, Seattle's young had been educated in private, tuition-based classes held in homes, churches, and the university building. Seattle now had a population of twelve hundred citizens who thought more formal education for their children was in order. Together they purchased land and erected a two-story, wood-framed schoolhouse fronting on Third Avenue between Madison and Spring Streets. In August of 1870, Miss Ordway opened Seattle School District Number 1, as the first principal and teacher. The first morning at the new Central School, 125 children showed up in front of one teacher. After welcoming them all warmly, she regretfully told her classroom full of eager faces that she would not be able to keep them all. Then, she sent the youngest would-be pupils home, "to wait a while and to ripen a little." The new teacher reprimanded Seattle's citizens for their lack of forethought. By the second week of school, a second teacher had been hired. Miss Ordway taught at the Central School until she was, once again, summoned to Kitsap County.

Kitsap County officials implored Miss Lizzie to return. She taught again in Port Madison and later in the towns of Port Blakely and Port Orchard. She was uprooted from her position in Port Orchard when district officials needed help with unruly students in Port Gamble, another rough-and-tumble mill town. She won over her classes in Port Gamble, commanding respect and admiration from students and their parents. Of this experience she wrote:

I was sent for to take charge of the school, but, hesitated to do so because its reputation had been that of a school hard to manage. I need not say that I have been agreeably disappointed. The pupils seem to come readily under discipline and I hope I have succeeded in rousing an ambition to redeem themselves, and to feel a love for and an interest in their studies. They have numbered during the past year 39, with an average attendance of 30.

She was remembered by one student at Port Gamble as being, "very small, like a bit of Dresden china, and always beautifully dressed. She made you think of lavender and old lace." The students also knew that Miss Lizzie would not hesitate to use a switch when necessary. Known as a strict disciplinarian, she demanded perfection from her pupils and received it in return.

Elizabeth Ordway believed in women's rights and was deeply involved in the suffrage movement. She served as secretary of the Washington Women's Suffrage Organization. In that capacity, she hosted Susan B. Anthony and Oregon's Abigail Scott Duniway when they visited Washington to lobby the territorial legislature of 1871 for the women's vote. As an officer, she joined Susan B. Anthony on the platform when Miss Anthony addressed Seattle on the suffrage movement. In their fight for the vote and equal rights for women, the suffragettes endured criticism and ridicule from the local male population, as well as the press.

Washington's suffrage bill, which Lizzie Ordway had lobbied for so heartily, was defeated in 1871. In 1883, the Washington Legislature granted the vote to women, but the bill was repealed a few years later in 1887 when the territorial supreme court ruled the law unconstitutional. Washington women were permanently awarded the right to vote in 1910.

Beaten in spirit, Miss Ordway left Washington in 1872, accepting a job at a private girls' school in San Francisco. The climate of San Francisco was not to her liking, so Miss Lizzie returned to her hometown of Lowell, Massachusetts.

The delicate lady from New England now had the Northwest in her blood and after a few months, she returned to the Kitsap Peninsula to teach in Port Madison and in another untamed mill town, Port Blakely. After five years as Port Blakely's teacher, at the urging of local citizens, L. M. Ordway ran for the position of Superintendent of Schools for Kitsap County. As L. M. Ordway, using initials to disguise her sex on the ballot and later in her records, she was elected Superintendent of Schools for Kitsap County in 1881. With her election, Lizzie became one of the first women ever voted into any public office in the Washington Territory.*

An 1881 editorial in the *Seattle Post-Intelligencer* opined, "It may be a good joke to put a woman in nomination, but I do not regard the office of School Superintendent of so little importance as to vote for a woman at the polls. . . ." The majority of Kitsap County's citizens

---

* Antoinette Baker Huntington of Castle Rock was elected Superintendent of Schools for Cowlitz County in 1878 and re-elected in 1880, serving two two-year terms. Antoinette was in the first group of Mercer Girls to arrive in Seattle with Lizzie Ordway. Clara McCarty Wilt, who also had the distinction of being the very first graduate of the University of Washington in 1876, and for whom McCarty Hall is named, was elected to the position of Superintendent of Schools for Pierce County in 1880.

thought otherwise, electing Miss Ordway by 244 votes compared to her male counterpart's 165 votes.

The Office of Superintendent of Kitsap County's Schools had officially existed since 1857; however, no one had ever performed their duties as diligently as Miss Lizzie Ordway. She became the first such official to comply with territorial laws regarding record keeping. In fact, L. M. Ordway was the only superintendent who had ever filed a report with the territorial government as required by law! Her records were meticulously written and organized. In one such report, discussing a teaching contract she noted, "the general rate of pay is $20–$35 a month for three to six months, and does not include board, but the teacher may dig clams on the Director's beach." The Ordway records are still on file at the Kitsap County Courthouse in Port Orchard.

After eight consecutive years as Kitsap County's school superintendent, Miss Ordway stepped down from the job in 1889, at age sixty-one. She remained on the Kitsap County Board of Education, which examined and certified teachers for the district. Miss Lizzie continued to implement ideas ahead of their time. In 1890, she conducted the first County Teacher's Institute. This "in-service" lasted one week and was attended by twenty teachers who traveled to Port Madison to sharpen their skills. When Lizzie resigned from the board of education she was awarded their highest honor, a "First Grade Certification," by her fellow board members for her years of service to the district. Lizzie had witnessed the Kitsap County School District's growth from two districts, in its infancy, to twenty—fourteen of which were created by her.

In 1891, Lizzie retired to Seattle where she lived with sea captain Sylvanus Libby and his wife, Sarah. At age sixty-five, in 1893, Lizzie became the assistant to University of Washington professor Edmond S. Meany in preparing Washington State's education exhibit for the Chicago World's Fair. Her part of the exhibit was to illustrate the quality and availability of good education in the infant state. Easterners were reportedly extremely surprised and pleased to find the high caliber of education in the Pacific Northwest.

Lizzie Ordway died suddenly of cancer on September 22, 1897, at the age of sixty-nine. The Libby family had her buried in their family plot in Lake View Cemetery, where Seattle's pioneers are interred. In 1989, the Bainbridge Island Historical Society nominated Lizzie Ordway to the Washington State Historical Society's Hall of Fame in recognition of her contributions to the Northwest.

Dr. Mary Archer Latham

1844–1917

PHYSICIAN-FUGITIVE

Wanted dead or alive!" So stipulated the warrant issued for the arrest of Dr. Mary A. Latham.

By lying flat in the bed of a wagon, Mary had escaped the detection of the Spokane County sheriff as she was driven out of town. As soon as the wagon passed the city limits, Mary climbed up next to her driver where she remained seated for the rest of the ride to her home in the town of Mead, Washington. Once in Mead, she gathered together a few belongings, hitched up her own horse and buggy, and lit out for the Idaho border, with the sheriff's posse in pursuit.

Dr. Latham's successful escape was due to the aid of countless friends throughout Spokane County and Idaho—friends she had made while practicing medicine in the Inland Northwest for nearly twenty years.

༄

Mary Archer was born November 5, 1844, in New Richmond, Ohio, to Jane (Warren) Archer and English-born James Archer. She was educated at the Claremont Academy in Claremontville, Ohio. On July 28, 1864, Mary Archer married prominent physician Dr. Edward H. Latham. The couple had three sons: Frank, James, and Warren. Like most women of her day, Mary devoted herself to her family as a young wife. As her sons grew, Mary—a woman of high energy—desired more, and following in her husband's footsteps, she entered medical school when she was in her late thirties. At the Miami Medical College in Cincinnati, Ohio, Mary Latham was a member of the first class of women students allowed into the clinical wards of the Cincinnati General Hospital.

Dr. Mary Latham Northwest Room, Spokane Public Library

In 1884, at the age of forty, Mary was granted her medical degree. For three years, she practiced medicine in Cincinnati before she and her husband decided to move west. They had grown tired of the harsh Ohio winters and sought a milder climate in the Pacific Northwest. They migrated west to Spokane from Ohio in late 1887 or early 1888. In Spokane, Mary Latham earned the gratitude not only of her patients for skillful, loving care, but of the entire community for her extensive devotion to civic service.

Dr. Mary Latham's practice in Spokane flourished, as did the ever expanding population of the city. She is believed to be the first woman physician to practice medicine in the state of Washington, although the state did not begin licensing physicians until 1921. Female doctors were a rarity at the time; for those few women that did practice medicine, the acceptable specialty was in the diseases of women and children. Following that convention, Mary began a practice treating women and children. In a January 1, 1892, *Spokane Spokesman* article, Mary's practice is described: ". . . her business has grown with the marvelous growth of the city, and in her special line of work—the diseases of women and children—she has no superior in the State." She was regarded as one of the foremost medical practitioners, male or female, in Washington. For many years Mary had the most lucrative medical practice of any woman in the state.

Mary dedicated her practice to alleviating the pain and suffering of her patients. One of her patients, an author, made the following book dedication to Mary.

I owe this to you for your love shown to me in my sickness and sorrow and despair. Many times when hope had almost vanished you came to me with that sweet womanly sympathy, so cheering and encouraging, and if this book ever proves a blessing to the public or me, we can turn with grateful hearts to you.

Standing five feet six inches tall, erect of carriage, with brown hair, blue eyes, and angular features, Mary exuded dignity, pride, and professionalism. Mary Latham was a consummate female professional in a world that regarded this as a novelty.

Dr. Mary A. Latham's medical skills were widely recognized. She was elected unanimously to a professorship of obstetrics at the innovative new medical school, the Washington Biochemic Medical College, which was established in Spokane by Dr. George W. Carey in 1889. She served as chairman of the Medical Department for the Washington Branch of the Queen Isabelle Association at the World's Columbian Exposition. Described in a newspaper as the "crowning glory of her work" was a women's hospital built for Dr. Latham in Spokane's Lidgerwood District in 1892. Mary not only ran the Lidgerwood Women's Hospital but headed and managed the Spokane Children's Home. However, her compassion was not limited to just humans, as Dr. Latham also acted as secretary and treasurer of Spokane's Humane Society.

Edward and Mary Latham were separated within a few months of their arrival in Spokane, in June of 1888. After thirty-one years of marriage, the couple divorced on July 18, 1895. Dr. Edward Latham left Spokane to serve as a government physician for twenty-five years in Nespelem, on the Colville Indian Reservation. Independently, Mary carried on her practice and community work in Spokane.

Mary Archer Latham was a proud woman, with endless ideas, dedication, and energy directed not only toward her medical profession, but toward many civic activities. Her motto in practicing medicine was "progress." To this end, she was also identified with many progressive movements in the growing city of Spokane.

Dr. Latham was the driving force behind the creation of Spokane's first public library in 1894. Prior to that time, the city harbored a few small private reading libraries, which Mary had helped to found. Mary was also a promoter and director of a reading room owned and operated by Spokane's labor unions. Dr. Latham suggested merging the private libraries and the Union Reading Room to create a larger public facility. To accomplish this, Mary Latham and a handful of others personally rang doorbells throughout the city in an effort to collect books for the new library. The new City Library was also privileged to receive a set of encyclopedias donated by Mary from her own private library.

In her spare time, Mary took up writing. She began by writing stories for local newspapers and magazines. Then she translated a story from German for a leading magazine and eventually published a novel, *A Witch's Wreath,* in the 1890s. One reviewer described the novel as, "written in the author's usually forcible style, [it] is decidedly realistic, and will be a masterpiece of fiction."

This multitalented lady was described in a Spokane daily paper of the early 1890s:

> *In nearly every community there is one who is mediator between wretchedness and wealth, a person whom the affluent respect and the needy love, a person who preserves the rays of summer to dispel the gloom of winter, one who condemns wrong, but pities the wrong-doer, one who has sentiment without sentimentalism, shrewdness without cynicism, dignity without haughtiness, one whose heart pities the suffering, but does not confine that pity to an imaginary field of action, one who believes in human nature, whose nature has not been soured by disappointments, who is too liberal to heartily espouse a creed or sect or religion, who conciliates all doctrines in universal good will to all—such a character is Dr. Mary A. Latham. Probably no woman in all Washington has so many friends as she. Many of the poor into whose lives she has thrown sunshine regard her as their patron saint.*

A fellow doctor said of her, "I believe that Mrs. Latham's career, brilliant as it has been in this city, is only in its beginning, for with her indomitable energy she will go on until the highest success is hers."

So, what happened to the brilliant career of this woman of boundless energy, empathy, and creativity? What could have caused this upstanding doctor to become a fugitive from justice—a convicted felon running from a sheriff's posse to avoid a prison sentence? How does such an outstanding, well-respected community member fall so far?

Mary's troubles began in April of 1903, when her adult son James, who had been living with her, was killed. James, a brakeman for Northern Pacific, was crushed between two train cars he was attempting to uncouple. Additionally, Mary suffered a stroke, which left her partially paralyzed and walking with a pronounced limp.

Like many women of her day, Dr. Latham never cared for living alone. After James's death, Mary deeded a store she had purchased in the town of Mead to James's fiancée, Jennie Johnson, on the condition that Jennie live with Dr. Latham at her home in Mead. When Jennie failed to hold up her end of the contract, Mary felt she was being cheated and attempted to reclaim the title to the store by deeding it to a third party. The end result was a lawsuit that lasted a year and ended in a victory for Miss Johnson. According to witnesses, Dr. Latham stated that Jennie would never possess the store. On May 7, 1905, shortly after the litigation ended, the Mead store was burned to the ground by an act of arson.

Dr. Mary A. Latham was arrested and charged with the crime of arson. She pled not guilty to the charge. A case against her was built from circumstantial evidence, including the fact that she was seen watching the fire burn late at night, that she had moved her possessions from the store prior to the fire, and that she had allegedly attempted to create false alibis for the night in question. Dr. Mary A. Latham was found guilty by a jury of her peers on June 18, 1905.

Before her sentencing, Mary was free on bond. Her son's death, the betrayal of his fiancée, and the civil and criminal trials took their toll on Mary's mental health. On June 30, 1905, days before she was to be sentenced for the arson, Mary had an emotional breakdown in the streets of Spokane. While riding a streetcar through the heart of the city, she began wailing and carrying on about going to meet her deceased son, James. Mary was taken into custody for her own protection and had to be carried into court on a stretcher for her sentencing.

The sentencing for the arson verdict took place before Judge Miles Poindexter on July 20, 1905, after her motion for a trial de novo (a new trial) had been denied. Dr. Mary A. Latham was sentenced to four years in prison and ordered to pay fines and court fees in excess of $1,500. Mary, still proclaiming her innocence, appealed her case to the Washington Supreme Court and remained free on bond pending appeal.

Devastated by the sentence, Mary fled the state of Washington. A *Seattle Post-Intelligencer* headline read, "Dr. Latham Flees in Open Buggy—Sheriff Asked to Catch Spokane Fugitive Either Dead or Alive." The sheriff of Spokane County and his posse pursued a relentless search for the doctor for two weeks before they located and arrested her in the mountains of northern Idaho. The fugitive, Mary Latham, was returned to the confines of the Spokane County Jail until January 9, 1906, when she was transferred to the Washington State Penitentiary at Walla Walla. Her attorney, D. W. Henley, wrote to Governor Mead in July of 1906, asking him to pardon Mary. The petition was denied. Mary Latham served one year and three months of her four-year sentence. On April 1, 1907, Mary was paroled from the State Penitentiary to the supervision of her son, Frank.

During her parole, Mary wrote a letter dated May 22, 1907, asking Walla Walla prison warden, M. F. Kincaid, for permission to resume the practice of medicine:

Many old friends and many new ones are anxious for me to do so. My home of course would be still with my son and everything [would] be in keeping with the conditions of my parole. But I could then be able to cumulate a sum of money, which I very much need as my pretend friends, lawyers et al. have robbed me unmercifully.

The warden's response was, "Tell her she may do so with pleasure."

Dr. Mary A. Latham began practicing medicine once again in an office adjacent to a drugstore owned, in part, by her son. Although her career had been interrupted by her trial and incarceration, Mary was practicing medicine up until the time of her death.

While nursing a twelve-day-old infant stricken with pneumonia, Mary contracted pneumonia herself. The baby and Mary passed away within a day of each other. Dr. Latham died at Sacred Heart Hospital in Spokane on January 20, 1917, at the age of seventy-two.

Remembered as a pioneer woman physician of great civic involvement, Dr. Mary A. Latham is still well respected for her accomplishments and all else seems to have been forgotten.

OLIVE SPORE RYTHER

1849–1934

MOTHER RYTHER—
MOTHER TO THOUSANDS

The small face peeked timidly from behind the humbly dressed man standing in the doorway of the imposing mansion. His sad eyes downcast, hat in his hands, the beaten man had come to ask for help. Would Mother Ryther have room for his son? The boy's mother had died when he was an infant. An elderly grandmother had taken her place, caring for the child while his father worked in a mill on the outskirts of town to support them. Now, the grandmother had died and there was no one to care for the boy. Kindness and empathy radiated from the frail, bent woman, as she urged them into the home that had been a grand manor in its day. The faded wood-paneled entry and stairway hinted at well-worn elegance.

Still clinging tightly to his father's hand, the boy was taken outside to a swing situated on an endless rolling lawn. There, two little girls dressed in their Sunday finest, with ribbons neatly tied in their hair, were swinging. Scooting to the side, the girls patted the seat of the swing and urged the boy to join them. Tempting as this was, the shy child hung back in his father's shadow, refusing their offer.

This plan failing, the elderly matron led the boy and his father to the boys' side of the large yard where groups of youngsters were engaged in a variety of noisy, active games. Although the child became engrossed watching the boys at play, he still refused to let go of his father's hand.

The father and son were then invited to supper. Here they were separated—the boy seated at the children's table, the father with the adults. Still, the boy's eyes never left his father. Following dinner, the children filed out into the large yard and the games began anew. Soon,

Mother Ryther with a few of her charges Special Collections Division, University of Washington Libraries, UW 3641

the shy newcomer was running about the lawn in a game of tag, as his father quietly slipped out the door.

In this manner, like so many before him, the young boy became part of Mother Ryther's family at the Ryther Child Home. Olive Ryther dedicated fifty-one of her eighty-five years to creating a home for orphaned and unfortunate women and children. More than three thousand children were cared for by the legendary Mother Ryther.

Mother Ryther never refused a child or a parent in need, no matter what the circumstances. She asked one dollar per week to board children, but if the parents could not pay, the child stayed anyway. One shabbily clothed mother showed up at the home with her small children in tow—all poorly dressed as well. She pleaded with Mother Ryther to take her young, saying she could not pay for their care. Of course, the children were admitted. A few days later, one of Mother Ryther's matrons spied the same mother, now fashionably dressed, drinking in a saloon downtown. The matron hurried home to inform Mother Ryther. Expecting to elicit a response of ire from Mother Ryther, the matron was stunned to find the anger directed at her when Mother replied, "Well, what of it!" banging her fist on the table for emphasis.

Olive Ryther chose the workers at her home for their need of a job rather than their qualifications. In turn, she received dedicated service from loyal employees. The cook at the home was a grossly overweight woman who had previously worked as the fat lady in the circus. The cook's work could be, at times, sub par, and she was not always gentle with the children, but Mother Ryther overlooked her faults for years because the woman needed the work.

∽

Olive Hannah Spore was born in Iowa on March 15, 1849, the child of Scottish immigrants. On May 7, 1867, at the age of eighteen, Olive married a young carpenter, Noble Ryther. The couple had three daughters: Amy,

Ella, and Mae Bird. Olive ("Ollie") and Noble were dedicated members of the Methodist Church, continually looking for ways to serve the ministry. Inspired to enter missionary service, Noble Ryther, a Civil War veteran, left his family and moved west to the Washington Territory in 1874.

In Seattle, he lived at the City Mission on the waterfront overlooking Elliott Bay. At the same time, he staked a claim on the east side of Lake Washington, north of present-day Kirkland. He divided his time between developing his claim east of the lake and traveling by canoe across Lake Washington to the mission. Building his home proved difficult as he related, "There was plenty of wood out there, but all of it wet."

As a missionary in early Seattle, Noble supplied spiritual guidance, food, clothing, shelter, and sometimes money for indigent men. He also worked clearing land and building homes for others to earn money that, for nine long years, he sent home to his wife and three daughters in Iowa. Seattle was a rough logging town full of saloons and houses of ill repute. Noble did not want to raise his family in this wild city.

After nine years in Seattle, Noble was able to finish building a cabin on a lot in Seattle and he was ready to send for his family. Olive and her three daughters rode the sooty, grimy locomotive west to Seattle in the summer of 1883.

Mrs. Ryther immediately joined her husband, Noble, working at the City Mission on Commercial Street (now First Avenue). The mission lodged homeless and destitute men at a charge of 5 cents a meal, if they could afford it. Olive took over the cooking at the mission where the Rythers and their daughters took their meals with the homeless men.

Within a year of arriving in Seattle, Olive gave birth to the couple's son, Allen. Soon after, she also became mother to four orphaned children. In a dark, dreary cabin on a typical Seattle blustery, wet, winter day, Olive found herself nursing a dying mother. The Long family lived in dire poverty; the woman's absentee husband had last been seen in a waterfront bar. As she lay dying, the feeble mother turned to Olive and pleaded, "What will become of my poor children?" Olive assured the destitute mother that she would take in the children as her own. After their mother's death, the four Long children moved into the simple log home of Olive and Noble Ryther to be raised with their own four children. With their home now bursting at the seams, the Rythers moved to a house at 813 Alder Street, near what is now Harborview Hospital.

While working at the mission, Olive became concerned for the "fallen women," or prostitutes, she saw daily on the streets of Seattle. She began visiting with them, assisting with their problems, and attempting to rescue them from their chosen lives. Olive was very aggressive at asking businessmen and city officials for donations, and she became well known among them for her rescue efforts on behalf of these women. Consequently, the city appointed Olive as women's jail matron. Seattle had no women's jail, so Olive took the prisoners into her own home. The women were barricaded into rooms upstairs where Olive sometimes had to administer morphine in small doses to drug-addicted prisoners.

Next, Olive and Noble founded the City Mission Foundling Home as a haven for girls in trouble. The home quickly filled with unwed pregnant girls and prostitutes, and the babies born to them there. The girls all engaged in household chores, changed diapers, and cared for the infants born at the home as part of their rehabilitation. Many of the babies born to these unfortunate mothers died due to malnutrition and disease. There is a potter's field in south Seattle where most are buried. The babies that survived were nursed to health and cared for lovingly by Olive until good homes could be found for them. The young mothers often stayed on at the Ryther Home, helping with the work and acting as older sisters to the younger ones until they found jobs. Olive Ryther had made many contacts with Seattle businessmen through her fund-raising. These contacts proved useful in finding employment for her girls. Those that showed potential went on to business college. Children were also cared for by Mother Ryther while their young mothers worked.

Olive was so successful at nursing the malnourished babies of fallen women to health, that doctors began sending sick babies to her for care. Word spread of her deeds and, before long, babies and children were dropped off at the home by parents unable to care for them. At one time, Mother Ryther had thirteen babies, all under six months of age, in her care.

When the Florence Crittendon Home for Unwed Mothers opened, Olive changed the focus of her work to sheltering destitute and homeless children. The children were well cared for, given love, and educated, but they were also expected to participate in the work of running the home. Older children were encouraged to mentor and care for younger children, and all were treated as members of a large family. If homes had not been found for the children by their teenage years, they were taught a trade.

Olive worked tirelessly, in a house with no plumbing—cooking, sewing, cleaning, gardening, raising livestock to provide food for the ever-hungry mouths, and caring for a home full of babies and children. Mother Ryther refereed fights, nursed sick and injured feelings and bodies, all while continuously managing the home with wisdom and good humor. Asked once by a newspaper reporter how she did it all, Mother Ryther responded, "Oh, that's easy, I like it."

Olive Ryther was constantly appealing to Seattle's citizens for aid. Farmers brought her excess produce and dairy products, local mills donated cereal and flour, and women's groups made clothing for the children. She was not above visiting local businesses and refusing to leave until she received a check. Once, Mother Ryther entered a Seattle store with twenty-five of her children and addressed the proprietor directly, "These children are staying here until you fit them all with shoes—that'll be your contribution to the Ryther Child Home."

One skill Olive Ryther lacked was record keeping. Mother Ryther kept no receipts, records of expenditures, or donations. She was constantly at odds with the city health department at the turn of the century.

In 1902, city health officials threatened to close the home for not meeting new codes. Laurence Colman, who built Colman Dock, Seattle's ferry terminal, formed a board of citizens to appeal for funds and support the home. As a result of Colman's efforts, the home was renovated and fitted with electricity and indoor plumbing, efforts that brought the home up to city code.

Businesses and citizens continued to contribute money to the home. Noble, often away working on construction projects, sent his salary to Olive. Additionally, Mother Ryther published a small magazine, *The Orphan,* which the children sold as a fund-raiser. Still, there were shortages.

In 1893, the Ryther's daughter Amy was taken by the smallpox epidemic. Then, Mae Bird became crippled with rheumatoid arthritis, and medical bills mounted. In 1905, the mortgage was foreclosed. Laurence Colman came to the rescue again, finding the Rythers a large mansion on Denny Way. The once grand home had fallen into disrepair. Colman was able to secure rent at the rate of $100 a month, due to the condition of the manor. With her large family, Mother Ryther moved to the Denny Way home. After fifteen years in the mansion, the building began to deteriorate hopelessly. No more repairs would fix the leaky roof and faulty plumbing. A campaign was started to gather funds to find a larger, more modern building for Mother Ryther and her children.

Among the fund-raising efforts for the home was a drive to sell bricks to Seattle citizens. These bricks were then used in the construction of the Ryther Home. The money was raised and in May of 1920, the family moved to their new home on Stoneway Avenue. The *Seattle Post-Intelligencer* headline for moving day announced, "Autos Will Transfer Big Family to Its New Home." The home and its occupants were moved in private cars provided by Seattle's caring community.

In 1922, the Ryther Child Home's board pronounced Mother Ryther "too old, dominating, and arbitrary" to run the home. The board members resigned and a new superintendent was appointed to run the Ryther Home. Within three weeks, the superintendent was gone and Mother Ryther back at the helm. Only then did she consent to allowing nurses in to examine and vaccinate the children. Thereafter, several attempts were made to oust Mother Ryther, but the community adored her and staunchly supported her work. In 1930, a reluctant Olive Ryther had to be forced onto a stage at the Pantages Theater to accept an award as "Seattle's Sweetheart."

When she turned eighty in 1929, Mother Ryther was quoted as saying, "I'll never grow old. Most folk grow old as their children grow up. Every time one of my children grows up I have a new youngster to take his place and I have to stay young with my children."

Mother Ryther managed the home on Stoneway for fourteen years until her death at the age of eighty-five on October 2, 1934. Sadly, the once bustling home was silent for an entire year after Mother Ryther's death. The board wanted the Ryther Child Home to continue as a community service to children and sought a way to do so. The next year, in June of 1935, the School of Social Work at the University of Washington conducted a study that resulted in a recommendation that the home be converted into a psychiatric service center for children exhibiting "emotional instability or behavior problems." The home was reopened in 1935, as the Ryther Child Center, to be supported entirely by community funds.

The Ryther Child Center operated at the Stoneway house for twenty years before moving to its present location in North Seattle. Children come to the center with a variety of emotional, psychological, and chemical-addiction problems for which they receive loving care and professional treatment. Mother Ryther's philosophy of recognizing each child as an individual—rather than a naughty, troubled youngster—is still followed. Thus, the legacy of Olive Hannah Spore Ryther lives on in Seattle to this day.

THEA CHRISTIANSEN FOSS

1857–1927

THE ORIGINAL "TUGBOAT ANNIE"

Creak, splash—creak, splash," the rhythmic sound of oars grinding against their locks, then dipping into the waters of the sound caught her attention. The young woman, gutting a fish on the porch of her rough-hewn houseboat, looked up to see a lone rower approaching. Thea had just purchased a salmon from an Indian fisherman on Tacoma's waterfront and was busily at work preparing it for the evening meal. Usually her husband, Andrew, provided fish for the family, but he was across Puget Sound on a carpentry job.

"Hello there," the man called out as he drew near the floating home. "This boat's for sale, would you be interested?"

"How much?" asked the woman in her thick Norwegian accent.

"Ten dollars," came the reply.

Thea considered the offer carefully. Ten dollars was a lot of money to the Foss family. Money was scarce, but she was so tired of hauling heavy buckets of water on foot from the creek that emptied into the bay a quarter mile from her home. "I'll give you five dollars," countered the astute Thea Foss.

"Okay," the rower responded to her amazement, "I'm leaving town anyway and have no further use for the boat."

The rustic appearance of the houseboat must have tipped the seller that money was a rare commodity in the Foss household, and perhaps he took pity on Thea in accepting her offer.

When Andrew Foss returned home two months later, he proudly pulled out his earnings, pouring $32 worth of gold and silver coins onto the kitchen table. Without a word, Thea extracted the contents of her cookie jar, $40. Then, to her dumbfounded husband she remarked in

Thea Foss Foss Maritime Company, Seattle, WA

Norwegian, "I sell and rent rowboats. No matter what time of the day or night people come for them, I am always ready!"

That hot summer night in 1889, Thea's purchase of the rowboat gave birth to the Foss Maritime Company, the largest towing, barging, and marine transportation services operation in the Northwest and one of the largest in the United States. The company motto, coined by Thea Christiansen Foss, is "Always Ready!"

With a remarkably intuitive business sense, Thea knew that there would be a demand for rowboats. She adorned her five-dollar purchase with green and white paint, colors that would become well known in Northwest waters, and sold the boat for a profit. Next, she bought two more boats that she repainted and resold, allowing her to buy four boats. Soon Thea had her own fleet of rowboats, which she rented out to fishermen and duck hunters for 25 to 50 cents a day. Thea Foss's head for business, coupled with her husband's shipbuilding and maritime skills, soon built the Fosses a fleet of two hundred rowboats. Henry Foss, the couple's youngest son, described his parents in a 1966 interview: "Mother was absolutely honest but shrewd. Father was not strong physically, but he was always ready to help anyone out—day or night."

∽

Thea Christiansen was born on June 8, 1857, in Eidsberg, Norway. While visiting her sister, Julia, and brother-in-law, Theodore, in Christiana (now Oslo), Thea met Andrew Olesen, the seafaring brother of Theodore, whose ship happened to be in port. Andrew was attracted to the proud young woman, with her golden braids coiled neatly upon her head. The young mariner could not read or write, but his strong goals and idealistic visions appealed to Thea.

Andrew's dream had always been to sail across the Atlantic Ocean. He and Thea made plans for a future home in the promised land of America. Andrew shipped out, working as a forecastle hand on a vessel bound for Quebec. From Canada, Andrew went south to Saint Paul, Minnesota, drawn by its large Norwegian community. Instead of working with his beloved boats, Andrew found a job building houses and saved every penny to send for his fiancée.

Finally, when he had saved enough for her passage, Andrew sent money to Thea. To his surprise, his brother, Iver, showed up in St. Paul instead. Andrew set to work earning more money to send for his intended. When he had again sent enough money for Thea's trip to America, he was greeted by his sister, Kristina. Frustrated, Andrew now intended to go to Norway and fetch Thea himself! Before he could do this, Thea arrived in Minnesota of her own volition. Determined to pay her own passage to America, she had given the money Andrew sent her to his family members. Thea had worked as an indentured servant to a wealthy family until she had earned enough for her way over. Andrew and Thea were married in St. Paul, Minnesota, in 1882.

St. Paul's Norwegian community already had so many Olesens that Andrew and Thea changed their last name to Olesen-Fossen, the latter meaning waterfall. As the family became more Americanized they shortened their surname to Foss.

During the eight years the Fosses lived in Minnesota, three children were added to the family: Arthur in 1885, Wedell in 1887, and Lillian in 1889. A daughter, Lilly Marie, was also born in Minnesota, but died at age four.

Andrew's love for the sea and strong dislike of cold winters would lead the family west to Tacoma, Washington, on the waters of Commencement Bay in Puget Sound. Leaving his young family, Andrew ventured into the Northwest in 1888. He worked his way west as a carpenter for the Northern Pacific Railroad and, once in Tacoma, became employed as a deck hand for the Tacoma Tugboat Company. In his spare time, Andrew combed beaches for cedar logs with which to build a floating house. Beached logs and salvaged timber were crafted into a simple, one-room floathouse for his family. When finished, the house contained a secondhand stove, beds, a table, and some crude furniture.

After being separated for eight months, Thea and the children traveled aboard an immigrant train to meet Andrew in Tacoma. The end of each railcar held a stove, and the air was thick with greasy smoke from cooking. The train was noisy, sooty, and packed full of immigrant families. Thea arrived in Tacoma in the spring of 1889, near exhaustion from caring for three children—all under the age of five (including one newborn baby)—aboard the crowded, grimy train.

With pride, Andrew brought his young family directly from the train station to their new floating home. A rough-slabbed, wooden structure with a tarpaper roof and stark furnishings floated before her, but seeing her husband's pride, Thea could show no disappointment. She viewed the situation as temporary and accepted her lot even though she would have to haul fresh water to the houseboat every day. Thea could not have imagined then that the family would live on Tacoma's waterfront for nearly a quarter of a century. That first day, both of her young boys added to her apprehension by falling into the bay. Though she harbored a fear of the water, which she never overcame, Andrew's enthusiasm and the natural beauty of their Puget Sound surroundings soon won over Thea Foss.

Once settled into her new home, the young wife's hands were full with housekeeping, washing, and caring for three small children aboard a floating home with no running water. Within three weeks of the family's arrival, Thea became very sick, and for three months she battled typhoid-pneumonia. Andrew begged a local doctor to come to the houseboat and treat his deathly ill wife. The kind doctor paid the houseboat call and provided Thea with medicine at no cost. Although the Fosses could not pay the doctor's fee then, they never forgot the kindness. In more prosperous years, they made substantial donations to Tacoma hospitals. As Thea recovered, Andrew's health began to falter, a fact he blamed on the cold Minnesota winters he had endured.

With Thea expecting a fourth child and Andrew beginning employment anew at a shipyard, the family was forced to move. The city of Tacoma was diverting the Puyallup River to promote industrial development. The Fosses moved their tiny wooden houseboat to "Hallelujah Harbor," named for the Salvation Army shacks dotting the shoreline. Water would still have to be hauled into their home.

In search of more income for his family, Andrew took a construction job on the Kitsap Peninsula across Puget Sound. He would have to be away from his family for two months. It was during this time that Thea launched the family business with the purchase of the five-dollar rowboat. Thea's timing was impeccable; sport boating was extremely popular, thus the business flourished. A sign bearing the slogan, "Always Ready," was posted on the roof of the floathouse. The floating home bustled with activity and thrived as a business. This enabled Andrew to enjoy his chosen vocation, boat building, to add to their fleet.

With the birth of another son, Henry, in 1891, the family now counted six members and had outgrown their tiny floathouse. Andrew and his two oldest sons built a larger houseboat in another saltwater location. This house had a modern amenity—running water! The Foss floating home became a center for Norwegian social activities, as well as for the Foss boating business. Thea was hospitable by nature and loved to entertain the local Norwegian community at "kaffe slaberas" (coffee klatches) in her spacious new home.

Although Thea loved her rowboat rental business, Andrew felt driven to create more. Using the old houseboat as a workshop, he and his brothers salvaged parts from a wrecked steamboat and built a fifty-foot steamer. They lost money on the unsuccessful venture but thought they were on to something.

The young Foss boys spent the majority of their time on the beach. Thea, still deathly afraid of the water, at first tried to keep them away from it. Later, she gave in and let them follow the lure of the sea. Soon the children were venturing forth on the sound by boat. The boys helped build the boats, bailed and cleaned the returned rentals, gave sailing lessons, and collected spilled bait from the rental boats and resold it to fishermen. Thea's enterprising sons even developed their own business by beginning a rescue operation with their powerboat. Using a telescope, they searched for boaters in distress. They did not charge to rescue their own customers, but if the boaters had not rented from the Fosses, they were charged 25 cents.

One day, it dawned on Thea that her boys could run an efficient ship-to-shore delivery service. She purchased a two-horsepower launch, reasoning that the ships anchored in the sound would be better served by the small powerboat than by the rowboats presently bringing them supplies. This acquisition became the first of many powerboats owned by the "Foss Launch Company." Andrew set to work building more boats, and before long they had Foss launches serving every ship in the harbor.

The Foss Launch Company did so well that they were able to buy a fleet of launches from a competitor and ultimately take on the bulk of the harbor service and ship docking on Puget Sound. The Fosses continued to service the anchored ships in Puget Sound, bringing supplies, fresh food, and a water-taxi service to the crews. The boys' tactic was to meet incoming ships with a box of Washington apples and pitch their company's services.

Thea's boys would go on to lifelong careers in boating with the family business. Her daughters would not live to see the family business at its peak. Thea's second to last child, Lela, was stillborn, and her four-year-old, Lilly Marie, had died in Minnesota. In 1914, Thea lost her lovely twenty-five-year-old daughter, Lillian, to tuberculosis. Always accepting, Thea endured Lillian's passing but never recovered fully from the loss. She poured her energy even more fervently into the Foss family business.

Many of Thea's relatives arrived from Norway and became involved in the family business. By the early 1900s, the company had outgrown its headquarters and staff of family members. The Fosses began hiring nonrelated, Scandinavian immigrants, plentiful in the Northwest at the time. Andrew built a dormitory for the growing crew. Thea cooked for twenty-five to thirty men, who dined with the family. She also served as counselor and surrogate mother to the crews. Andrew and Thea insisted the men study for their citizenship tests and become U.S. citizens. The crews rewarded them with loyalty, calling them "Mother and Father Foss."

The Foss general store, run by Thea, supplied ships with food and gear. She stocked the store with fresh eggs, meat, and milk from her own animals, which were kept on an adjacent sandlot. The waterfront store was a popular gathering place among sailors, crews, and dock workers. People were drawn to Thea in spite of her quiet nature. A natural diplomat, this was a woman who had the ability to converse with all of those who frequented the waterfront. These abilities earned her the respect of sea captains, prominent businessmen, dignitaries, and domestic and foreign crews. She ran the boarding house, store, and company office and still had time for her beloved Norwegian Church, as well as for works of charity. She often provided comfort and shelter to young Norwegian immigrant girls. Her philosophy is evident in the following entry of January 19, 1907, from her diary:

The law imprinted in all men's hearts is to love one another. I will look on the whole world as my Country and all men as my brothers. We are made for cooperation and to act against one another is to act contrary to nature. Say not I will love the wise and hate the unwise, you should love all mankind. Let us not love in word and in tongue, but in deed and in truth.

Thea Foss had endless stamina with which to perform the multitude of tasks and businesses she undertook. She also had the ability to organize those around her. Each member of the family had multiple chores—even the cow, Annie, had extra duties. Thea kept forty chickens, several pigs, and the cow (which was fed pancakes through the kitchen window). In addition to providing milk, Annie guided boats in dense Pacific fog. When a captain had trouble navigating Puget Sound waters in the heavy fog, he would blow his horn until Annie met the ship at the end of the Fosses' pier with a resounding "Moooo!" She was then paid by the arriving sea captains who, once safely docked, rewarded her with bovine treats.

The turn of the century brought major changes to the Foss Launch Company. Bicycles became the rage, and pleasure rowing was suddenly out of fashion. Automobiles soon replaced travel by rowing and sailing on Puget Sound, and ships became self-propelled, relegating the Foss rowboats and launches to little use.

The Fosses saw the hills all around the Northwest booming with logging activities. These logs were rafted and towed to local mills around the sound. Seizing another opportunity, the Fosses had their launches begin towing rafts of logs, but they lacked the power to do so efficiently. They decided to invest in more powerful engines for their boats. Key to their success was the fact that Thea and Andrew never borrowed for these upgrades. They saved during prosperous times, for they knew their business was cyclical.

The improved boats were better, but Andrew set out to design a boat just for log towing. Andrew designed his tugs by hand carving prototypes. He fashioned a "teardrop"-shaped boat with a more balanced rudder. His concepts became industry standards, though he never patented any of his inventions, saying they were for the "common good." The tug business grew, along with charter hauling of landfill and war cargo during World War I.

In August of 1919, at the close of the war, Thea's sons sponsored a water sports carnival in her honor. August was chosen as the anniversary of her first rowboat purchase and the founding of Foss Launch and Tug Company. The carnival was held at the family's houseboat along Tacoma's waterfront and was attended by hundreds of spectators.

As Thea and Andrew aged, the boys took command of the company. Together, the family had decided that Arthur would leave school in the eighth grade to assist with the growing family business. They later decided that Wedell should attend law school, and Henry business college. Henry was eventually elected to office as a Washington state senator. Throughout her life, Thea worked tirelessly on behalf of the Foss company. In her later years, she continued to help with the business when she could, telling her children, "Ya, jeg har so mange ting ot gjore." ("Yes, I have so many things to do yet.") Her interest in Foss Launch and Tug never waned. By now, Andrew had built her a grand house on dry land, uptown where Tacoma's "better people" lived. Unfortunately, the new home was out of sight of the family's fleet of tugs and launches, but her boys always kept her up to date on the company. Thea Christiansen Foss passed away on June 7, 1927, one day before her seventieth birthday.

Thea's funeral procession was the largest ever seen in Tacoma. The Foss fleet flew their green and white flags at half-mast as they cruised up Tacoma's waterway. On September 15, 1989, sixty-two years after her death, the Tacoma City Waterway was renamed the Thea Foss Waterway in her honor.

With her son Wedell's assistance, Seattle native Norman Reilly Raine penned a series based on the life of Thea Foss for the *Saturday Evening Post*. Wedell provided the storyline for the first article, published in 1931. The series ran for some time until Raine began to write scripts for the movie industry. Inspired by Thea's life, Raine wrote the script for the film *Tugboat Annie*. The movie, starring Maureen O'Sullivan, Marie Dressler, and Wallace Beery, premiered in 1933. It was shot on Seattle's Lake Union, Elliott Bay, and throughout the Strait of Juan de Fuca. Although pleased by the tribute, Wedell was quick to point out that the raucous Irish character Tugboat Annie was nothing like his quiet, pious, Norwegian mother with her morbid fear of the water.

DR. NETTIE J. CRAIG ASBERRY

1865–1968

DOCTOR OF MUSIC/
CHAMPION OF CIVIL RIGHTS

On the occasion of her one hundredth birthday, Dr. Nettie J. Asberry told reporters that she believed she was the nation's first Black woman to receive a doctoral degree for any subject. If only she could locate her diploma, then she would show it to the reporter. The diploma, a Doctorate of Music, presented to Nettie on June 12, 1883, by the Kansas Conservatory of Music and Elocution in Leavenworth, had been neatly framed but was now missing. The distinguished document had been lost in the large old Tacoma home Nettie had lived in for well over fifty years. It was at this address, 1219 South Thirteenth Street, where Nettie taught piano lessons to generations of Tacoma students. "They were of all colors and walks of life, for this has always been a melting pot area of the city." Mrs. Asberry was one of the best known piano teachers in Tacoma.

⁂

Nettie J. Craig was born at the close of the Civil War on July 15, 1865, in Leavenworth, Kansas, to Violet Craig and William Wallingford. Nettie attended school in Leavenworth, where the pupils were segregated by grade level, not race. She began taking piano lessons at age eight, and even then she showed 3a great aptitude for music.

As a youngster, Nettie had the opportunity to meet Susan B. Anthony, who was in town to visit her brother Daniel R. Anthony, publisher of the *Leavenworth Times*. Nettie remained an admirer and, at age thirteen, became secretary of a women's club, the Susan B. Anthony Club.

Nettie decided to attend college at a time when few women, few Blacks, and even fewer Black women were studying at the university

Nettie Asberry The *News Tribune,* Tacoma, WA

level. It was still the Reconstruction Era in the South, the post–Civil War period lasting from 1865 to 1877, during which the country struggled to reunite. During Reconstruction, new governments in the southern states eliminated racially discriminatory laws and established the first state-supported, free public school systems in the South. The state university was free to all, so Nettie decided to further her education. After she completed her undergraduate work at the University of Kansas, she pursued an advanced degree in music at The Kansas Conservatory of Music and Elocution, a private college in Leavenworth. In 1883, at age eighteen, Nettie Craig received a diploma granting her the "rights, privileges, and dignities" of a doctorate in the teaching of music.

Following college, Nettie J. Craig married Albert Jones. She taught music and performed in church choirs in Kansas City and Denver before moving to the Northwest. News of Seattle's Great Fire in 1889, and the subsequent rebuilding of the city, spread excitement throughout the Midwest about new opportunities in Seattle. Nettie and Albert Jones arrived in Seattle by train in 1890 "amid much bustle and excitement. Trains every day were bringing families from all parts of the country. It was a time of friendship and good neighborliness." Nettie Jones became the organist and musical director for the First AME (African Methodist Episcopal) Church.

After Albert Jones's death, Nettie remarried and moved to Tacoma in 1893. Her new husband, Henry J. Asberry, was the well-known owner of the Tacoma Hotel Barbershop. Henry's clients included not only Tacoma's distinguished citizens, but dignitaries including United States presidents. It was the custom, at the time, for patrons to keep shaving mugs bearing their names on a shelf at the barbershop. When Henry Asberry died in 1939, Nettie donated the collection to the Washington State Historical Museum, along with a lace opera coat she had made for the opening of the Seattle-Yukon-Pacific Exposition World's Fair in 1909.

Nettie Asberry became well known in Tacoma, not only as a music teacher, but for her endless civic involvement. One of her many civic endeavors was to serve as president of the Allen Red Cross in Tacoma.

Many improvement clubs for Black women in Tacoma were begun at Nettie's hand. All of these clubs became charter members of the Washington State Federation of Colored Women's Organizations, which was formed in 1917. Nettie served as an officer and state statistician for the organization. The purpose of the federation is stated in the preamble to their constitution:

We, the colored women of the State of Washington and Jurisdiction, feeling the need of united and systematic effort along moral, physical and intellectual lines, in order to elevate our race, do hereby unite into a State Federation.

Although not officially organized until 1917, the activities of the federation began in 1908, with the preparation for Seattle's Alaska-Yukon-Pacific Exposition World's Fair to be held in 1909. An announcement was made that there would be a women's building for display of handicrafts. Nettie Asberry and a group of Tacoma women became inspired with the idea of displaying the work of the Black women of Tacoma and Pierce County at the exposition. These women formed the Clover Leaf Art Club for just that purpose. They had one year to work! The women applied for space in the Women's Building and set to work on their handicrafts. In May of 1909, articles created by the women of the Clover Leaf Art Club were on display for the fair's opening day. The exhibit consisted of needlework, oil and watercolor paintings, ceramics, and china painting. Three medals were awarded to the Clover Leaf Art Club: a gold medal for the entire exhibit; a silver medal for the Battenburg lace opera coat valued at $500, which had been made by Nettie Asberry; and a bronze medal for the paintings and ceramics of Mrs. Hiram Moore-Baker.

After reading about the National Association for the Advancement of Colored People's (NAACP) work on behalf of Blacks in the East, Dr. Asberry decided, along with others, to found a branch in Tacoma. Nettie Asberry submitted the group's application to the New York office of the NAACP, and the branch received its charter in 1913. The Tacoma Branch of the NAACP was the first branch formed west of Kansas City. Following the founding of the Tacoma Branch of the NAACP in 1913, the group founded branches in Portland, Seattle, Spokane, and other Northwest cities, including cities in Canada and Alaska.

The first official act of the Tacoma Branch of the NAACP was to rally against a measure being considered in the state legislature banning interracial marriages. Someone working in the legislature tipped the group off that this measure was being discussed. Overnight, the Tacoma NAACP Branch organized a caravan of cars including not only Blacks, but whites, Filipinos, and others. They descended on Olympia's powerful Rules Committee and, in a surprise move, defeated the measure.

In 1961, at age ninety-six, Dr. Nettie Asberry was honored for her outstanding achievements in the field of voluntary social service by the Tacoma City Association of Colored Women. The Asberry Cultural Club, one of the women's groups within the City Association, was named for Nettie. On that occasion, Nettie was interviewed by the *Tacoma News Tribune* and was quoted as saying, "I didn't intend to devote my life to teaching, and after I was no longer young, I turned to social work for which there seemed such an endless need." Mrs. Asberry went on to note that early social work was largely done by volunteers such as herself rather than by paid professionals.

At age ninety-six, Nettie still played her piano and walked daily, as well as conducted activities in business and social affairs. She was a devoted member of the Allen African Methodist Episcopal Church, and of the Baha'i Faith. Baha'i is an organization founded in 1863 in Iran that emphasizes the spiritual unity and brotherhood of all mankind. Dr.

Asberry explained that Baha'i includes intelligent people of all colors and classes. All are welcome except for people who belong to groups that maintain color barriers. She belonged to the Baha'i Faith for more than twenty-five years.

During her ninety-sixth birthday interview in 1961, Nettie expressed her views on current events of the time:

> *Courage is the saving grace in this tense world racial situation. Courage of the white people who dare to show their fairness by helping us achieve positions of human dignity, and courage of those of other races who risk insults by quietly asserting their rights as human beings. Money fears are at the base of the prejudice—Ministers, who must believe in our cause if their faith is sincere, are afraid to speak out lest they offend some in their congregations and lose their pulpits; school boards in many places, labor organizations which are afraid to open their doors to colored people lest some white people be put out of work. . . . wherever one goes, it is the same.*

Dr. Asberry also blamed uncensored television for the 1960s youth riots and delinquencies of all races. "Some have estimated that ten years will see the ironing out of most racial difficulties. I believe it will take much longer, and I can scarcely believe that I shall not be here to see it. I keep making long-range plans. I don't think any differently than when I was a young woman."

Nettie J. Craig Jones Asberry died in a Tacoma nursing home on November 17, 1968. At age 103, she was one of Tacoma's oldest residents. Even at her advanced age, Nettie cared for and followed young people as she had in her younger years. In 1902, Dr. Asberry had organized the Mozart Musical Club. This society for young people started with the purpose of broadening their musical culture and knowledge of the lives of great composers. In the year of her death, she donated musical instruments and materials to a library and music hall in Tacoma's Hilltop neighborhood. The Youth Auxiliary of the Asberry Cultural Club built and furnished the room, which was named in her honor. Thomas Simms, an artist residing on McNeil Island, donated a painting of Nettie for the hall. The hall is still located in the Tacoma City Association of Colored Women's Group Clubhouse on South Yakima Avenue.

In 1969, Tacoma's mayor, A. L. Rasmussen, proclaimed May 11, Dr. Nettie Asberry Day. Money was collected for a city memorial in her honor. Events were held on the campuses of The University of Puget Sound and Tahoma High School.

One thing Dr. Asberry failed to do before she died was to locate her precious diploma. Since she had no children, Nettie's possessions were given or sold to friends and relatives after her death. Most of the items were then stored away. In 1976, during the country's bicentennial celebrations, a Tacoma woman was watching a TV show during which they displayed Abraham Lincoln's actual diplomas. Suddenly it occurred to her that she had seen Nettie Asberry's diploma in the possessions she had obtained from the estate. The discovery came at a time when the Asberry Cultural Club was making plans for Tacoma's Black Bicentennial Celebration. The glass frame was broken and the paper brown and crumpled with age, but nevertheless, it was a priceless find. The diploma was displayed during the bicentennial and was hung permanently next to the painting of Dr. Nettie J. Asberry in the Music Room of the Tacoma City Association of Colored Women's Clubhouse.

BERTHA KNIGHT LANDES

1868–1943

MAYOR OF SEATTLE

Winking at the city council president who would be acting mayor in his absence, Mayor Brown instructed her to "keep an eye on the chief of police." Seattle mayor Edwin ("Doc") J. Brown was getting ready to leave town and travel east to the 1924 Democratic National Convention in New York City. Doc Brown, a dentist, had been a tolerance mayor, allowing his chief of police to run the city with a free hand. Gambling, graft, and prostitution flourished during his administration. In contrast, the highly principled president of the city council, Bertha Knight Landes, was a blue-nosed, strong-willed, reform administrator who had been encouraged into civic life by members of the many women's clubs over which she had presided.

As soon as Doc Brown's train was headed east, Mrs. Landes took it upon herself to move her office down the hall from the city council chambers into the mayor's executive suite in the County-City Building. Before moving, she aired the executive office thoroughly, as Doc Brown was a heavy cigar smoker.

Her next act was to charge the police department with corruption. Mrs. Landes wrote to the chief of police, William B. Severyns, stating, "The Police Department has lost the confidence of the people. The innocent men are under the stigma of graft, bootlegging and connivance with crime, as well as the guilty."

She gave Severyns twenty-four hours to do something about the open liquor sales (then illegal), gambling, and vice that was rampant throughout the city.

In an attempt to pacify the acting mayor, Severyns admitted that "about 100 policemen ought to be fired." Bertha then pronounced, in

Bertha Landes Museum of History and Industry

a well-publicized ultimatum, that the chief was to fire the one hundred men or be dismissed himself. Chief Severyns replied smugly, "Well, why don't you do it yourself!" That was all she needed! Bertha Landes issued her General Order Number 1 and assumed control of the Seattle Police Department. She delegated her powers to Ballard police captain Claude Bannick. Bannick had been chief of police during an earlier reform-minded administration and possessed an impeccable reputation for honesty.

The two announced their intentions to dismiss two civil service commissioners and one hundred members of the police department. They proceeded to raid and close down bars, pool and gambling halls, honky-tonks, and speakeasies all over Seattle.

Doc Brown's people at city hall were beside themselves but power-less to stop the acting mayor. They wired Brown to get back to Seattle on the first train west and hatched a scheme to quell Mrs. Landes's enthusiasm for reform.

Brown's secretary, Henry J. Dahlby, sneaked into the mayoral suite before the office opened and put two suitcases on the floor by Mayor Brown's desk. Next, he placed Doc Brown's hat atop the desk, filled the office with cigar smoke, and left a cigar butt in the ashtray. A press release was issued, allegedly by Brown, that he had "no comment to make on the current situation" with the city government.

Whether or not Bertha Landes fell for this act is subject to interpretation. Things did calm down until Mayor Brown's train arrived a day or so after the ruse had been executed. He, of course, immediately rescinded all of acting Mayor Landes's reforms.

This incident may have paved the way for a grand jury investigation and movement in favor of Doc Brown's impeachment.* Bertha Knight Landes ran for mayor of Seattle in 1926 on a platform against sin and vice and in favor of municipal government restructuring. "Rectitude in government, civic decency, and public morality!" was her campaign cry.

Seattle, long known for some of the most corrupt municipal officials in the nation, was ready for a "woman's touch." To Bertha, city government was "but a larger housekeeping."

❧

She was born Bertha Ethel Knight on October 19, 1868, in Ware, Massachusetts, a town west of Boston. Bertha was the youngest of nine children born to Charles Sanford Knight and Cordelia (Cutter) Knight. Charles Knight worked as a painter and real estate agent but was later incapacitated by time-aggravated wounds he had suffered during the Civil War.

In 1891, Bertha Knight graduated with a degree in history from Indiana University, where her sister's husband was the college president. Moving home with her mother, she taught school for three years

---

* A King County grand jury investigated and ultimately criticized Brown's administration but did not find enough evidence to indict or impeach him; they decided to let the voters decide his fate.

before becoming engaged to Henry Landes, a geology student obtaining his graduate degree from Harvard. The two were married on January 2, 1894. A year later, Henry was appointed professor of geology at the University of Washington.

The couple arrived in Seattle in 1895 to a new University of Washington campus. The campus had recently moved from its former downtown Seattle location to one north of Seattle where it is presently located. Their home, where they would live for twenty years, was built on Brooklyn and Forty-fifth Street, where Meany Tower now stands. Very much the faculty wife, Bertha entertained frequently and raised two children as her husband rose to the position of dean of the College of Sciences.

Three children were born to the Landeses: two sons and a daughter. Katherine, the eldest, died at the age of nine of complications resulting from a tonsillectomy. Roger died as an infant. Only Kenneth lived to adulthood, becoming a professor of geology at the University of Michigan. Two years after Katherine's death, Bertha and Henry adopted a nine-year-old daughter, Viola. Bertha also cared for a blind, elderly uncle for some time.

As her children grew older, Bertha became more and more involved in community service groups and women's clubs. Always rising to the top, Bertha served as president of the Congregational Church Women's League, the League of Women Voters, Red Cross Auxiliary, Women's University Club, and Seattle Federation of Women's Clubs. Working in these organizations, Bertha honed her public speaking skills and familiarity with democratic procedure.

As president of the Seattle Federation of Women's Clubs, she was responsible for putting on a weeklong Women's Education Exhibit for Washington manufacturers. Seattle's business community was so impressed with her work that she was lauded by the Seattle Chamber of Commerce and appointed, by the mayor, as the only woman on a five-member commission to study unemployment in the city.

Her success on the commission inspired a fellow member to urge Bertha to run for city council. Bertha Landes had jumped from traditional women's church and community clubs into the world of business, politics, and civic service. She believed that women should raise their families before entering politics and not be dependent on their salary for income; however, she also believed even women with small children at home should be attentive to the outside world. Although she still advocated home and family as a woman's first responsibility, during her 1922 campaign, Bertha stated that the time had come for women to be represented in city government. "It is not only the right, but the privilege and duty, of women to take part in the administration of public affairs."

The campaign for city council was run by five of her fellow club members, all housewives with no previous political experience. The group ran a low-budget campaign without "slush funds"—no paid campaign workers, promised jobs, or obligations to contributors. Her supporters thought it was important for Bertha to enter office "with clean hands," not owing favors to anyone. Henry Landes was his wife's staunchest supporter. This was not a stretch for Henry, long known for his support of women students and faculty at the University of Washington. Both of the Landeses saw public office as a civic duty, not a furtherance of one's own political ambition.

On May 22, 1922, Bertha Knight Landes and Kathryn Miracle were elected to the city council, breaking through an all-male barricade into city government. Bertha was elected by a record margin of 22,000 votes. On the day of her election, Councilman Landes talked to reporters.

> *Our campaign is over. It has been strictly a women's campaign to elect a woman to the city council without entangling alliances, to represent women's thoughts and viewpoints. . . . Our idea was to serve the best interests of the city; not to further the political ambitions of any one woman.*

In fact, fifty-eight-year-old Bertha Landes was quite reluctant to run for mayor in 1926. She changed her mind many times and only filed to run on the last possible day. Bertha eventually decided to run because she believed that she was the only candidate that had a chance of ousting Doc Brown.

Winning by a margin of six thousand votes, Bertha Knight Landes set a new Seattle electoral record and became the first woman mayor of a major city in America. She did not believe that politics had any place in city government and could not be influenced as those who preceded her had been. Bertha's administration was honest and scandal free. The new mayor reorganized city government and cleaned up the streets of Seattle. Qualified professionals were appointed to head city departments. The City Light Department and the Board of Public Works were completely revamped. Seattle's financial mess was ironed out, stricter law enforcement was stressed, the Park Department and recreational programs were expanded, and the railcar system was improved for travel on city streets. One of the first to do so, she advocated a merger between city and county governments.

Insisting on full equality, she disdained the title of councilwoman or mayoress, preferring to be addressed as councilman and mayor. She explained, "Let women who go into politics be the real thing or nothing! Let us, while never forgetting our womanhood, refrain from all emphasis on sex and put it on being public servants."

Bertha enjoyed official ceremonies and was often photographed at groundbreakings, in parades, and with celebrities visiting town, including Will Rogers, Queen Marie of Romania, and Charles Lindbergh. She was quoted in the *Seattle Post-Intelligencer* on October 30, 1927, as saying, "Frankly, I like being Mayor. I haven't seen any reason, since taking office, why a woman can't fill it as well as a man."

As the nation's only major metropolitan woman mayor, she received a great deal of publicity. The *New York Times* and *Sunset Magazine* wrote of her "simple attitude, gentle manner and great poise." She was backed by the national press, women's clubs, and many businessmen. Bertha encouraged more women to seek public office and spoke of government as a "joint man and woman affair."

This national notoriety also worked against Mayor Landes. Easterners wondered if Seattle men were "sissies." Taunts like "the great open space, where men are men and women are mayors" became common. Some local businessmen felt such comments were damaging their images and would hurt business with other cities. Bertha had also made enemies with her liquor raids and stringent reforms. Believing in public utilities, she had clashed with private power companies over both the railcar system and Seattle City Light. Restructuring government had also meant personnel cuts, which were not very popular with city employees.

In 1928, Frank Edwards ran against Mayor Landes on a platform of "No more petticoat government." Edwards was a complete political unknown, with absolutely no record of public service or civic involvement; however, his campaign was heavily financed by private interests. Bertha Knight Landes was defeated by 19,000 votes. Somewhat bitter about her defeat, but stoically and with good humor, she left office.

Still involved in community affairs, she remained active with a busy schedule of lecturing, travel, and continuing community service. In 1933, Dean Landes and Bertha led the first of four university study tours to Asia. Henry Landes became ill on the last trip, developing bronchitis from which he died in Seattle in 1936. As her last public act, Bertha led the next Asian tour alone.

In failing health, she moved to California in 1941, hoping for improvement with the climate. Bertha Knight Landes passed away six weeks after her seventy-fifth birthday, on November 29, 1943, at her son's home in Ann Arbor, Michigan.

The city of Seattle has never elected another woman mayor. Though she was only in office for two years, Bertha attempted efficient management of a major city; strengthened municipal utilities; sought to improve community services and programs; and enforced laws that she considered essential for the health and welfare of Seattle's citizens. By all measures, Bertha Landes was one of the most dedicated, efficient, and some think, the best mayor Seattle has ever known.

FAY FULLER

--- ◈ ---

1869–1958

FIRST LADY OF MOUNT RAINIER

Peppered with a spray of gravel loosened by the climber above, Fay stepped gingerly along the narrow ledge. Each step was a catalyst for a cavalcade of rocks to break loose from above and tumble down the glacial slope. After surmounting one ledge, another—narrower and steeper—would rise to challenge her. Hour after hour, foot by foot, the climb grew more and more treacherous and burdensome as the party approached the great cliff, the most dangerous obstacle of the climb.

Perched carefully on the peaked spines of glacial ridges, the climbers could look down on either side of them and see that one wrong step would plunge them into the icy world below. One of her fellow climbers loosened his pack in an attempt to toss it ahead, across the moat. When he lost his hold, the bundle was sent spiraling downward into a seemingly bottomless black hole. Nothing was said; all among them knew that one wrong step, and they could easily meet the same fate.

The climbers passed the fearsome ridge only to encounter the next obstacle—a face of sheer ice, fifty feet high. Tied together with ropes, the party moved one foot at a time, waiting for each step before them to be carved out by their guide's hatchet. Time became an enemy as the afternoon sun began to melt away the frozen ground beneath their feet, causing sand and gravel to rain down on the person below.

Upon reaching twelve thousand feet above sea level, Fay's breathing became labored. Having conquered the Great Gibraltar Cliff, the party rested before heading upward on great fields of snow and cascades of glacial ice. Fay carefully searched for a toehold while crossing the next bridge of ice. Blue walls of ice, breaking away to reveal caves that seemed without end, surrounded them.

Fay Fuller Washington State Historical Society, Tacoma, WA

At one crevasse, there seemed to be no bridge to cross; the guide probed at the ice with his spike. All steps were probed and tested for strength, lest they lead into hidden crevasses. Chunks of snow broke away, emanating loud crashing sounds as they fell to bottomless depths. One portion seemed stable, but the guide examined it from underneath to be sure before scrambling across. Holding the rope tossed over by their guide, the others followed hand over hand up the great incline framed by endless fissures.

Above a dazzling white expanse of snow, the black rim of the volcano's crater was now within sight. A biting wind burned at Fay's skin, pushed her from side to side, and tore at her clothing. The air became thinner and increasingly difficult to breathe, yet the peak, closer than ever, was within her reach. She toiled upward.

At 4:30 p.m. on August 10, 1890, twenty-year-old Fay Fuller stood on the top of Mount Rainier. The first woman to accomplish this feat, the young school teacher from Yelm had reached an altitude of 14,411 feet.

Fay's climb brought her recognition from far and wide, but not all of it was positive. In an interview with the *Tacoma News Tribune* in 1950, Fay remembered how her fellow Tacomans were shocked at her adventure. "I was very nearly ostracized in Tacoma because of that trip—a lone woman and four men climbing a mountain, and in that immodest costume."

Initially, Fay tried to ignore the negative comments. Speaking only of her feat, she said "I accomplished what I have always dreamed of and feared impossible, and from my experience nothing could be taken."

Shortly after her return, Fay posed for a photographer against a background of faux ice. She modeled the outfit and gear she had worn on the actual climb. The photograph appeared in newspapers and magazines across the country causing both admiration and admonishment. Occasionally, the photograph was used to show the "proper" mountain climbing attire for women in 1890. The caption under one such photo read, "Fay E. Fuller . . . demonstrated the correct mountain climbing costume in 1890." To this Fay replied, "Proper nothing. It was our dressmaker's idea of what I should wear. She designed it. It certainly caused a lot of talk." She further describes her attire in a 1933 letter:

The costume. . .will amuse present-day climbers. I had it made at the time when bloomers were unknown and it was considered quite immodest. How anyone could have scrambled over the rocks thus attired is now inconceivable. There were no boots or heavy shoes available for women at the time and I bought the strongest shoes that were sold to boys. I believe the stock was made by a blacksmith at Yelm from a curved shovel handle.

❧

Fay E. Fuller was born in New Jersey on October 10, 1869, to Ann E. (Morrison) Fuller and Edward N. Fuller. With her family, she moved to Tacoma, Washington Territory, in 1882, where her father became editor of a local newspaper. Following her graduation from high school in Tacoma, Fay took a job teaching school at age fifteen. Her first job was at Rosedale on the Kitsap Peninsula's Henderson Bay. Next, she taught school at the Longfellow School in Tacoma and later in Yelm, a small community south of Tacoma.

On one occasion, Miss Fuller's classroom was visited by Philemon Beecher Van Trump, one of the first climbers to reach Mount Rainier's peak. As Mr. Van Trump told of his exploits, Fay listened, enthralled. She and P. B. Van Trump became friends, and it was this friendship that inspired her great accomplishment.

Always an outdoorswoman, Fay loved the Northwest. She spent many hours riding horseback through tall Northwest timbers. Fay preferred to ride astride the horse like a man, rather than the more proper woman's style of riding sidesaddle. When not in the woods, Fay could be found rowing a boat in the rough Tacoma Narrows' current of Puget Sound. Physical activity was an integral part of her life. For the "healthful benefits of exercise," she performed calisthenics and conducted rifle drills with a group called the Women's Guard.

The daughter and sister of newspaper men, Fay gave up teaching to become a reporter. She began by working for her father, who was the editor of several Tacoma papers. She later became the first woman reporter for the *Tacoma Ledger*. In a 1943 interview, Fay described her job: "I covered the waterfront, equity court, the markets—oh, anything and everything. I walked miles from one end of town to the other, holding my skirts out of the dust and mud."

Captivated by Van Trump's mountain climbing experiences, Fay's desire to challenge the great mountain grew. In 1887, Fay Fuller made her first assault on Mount Rainier, climbing to the 8,500-foot elevation. Though excited by her accomplishment, Fay felt frustration as well. She was certain she could go further, but she did not dare to hope for the peak.

One August day in 1890, the Van Trump family invited Fay to join them on a camping trip to the mountain. The campers included Mr. and Mrs. Van Trump and their ten-year-old daughter, Christine. By horseback, the small party left Yelm on Monday morning, August 4, 1890. A pack horse carried their provisions and tents, and their clothing was packed in saddle bags.

Though she doubted Van Trump would care to climb the mountain again, Fay outfitted herself for the possibility. In Fay's account of her climb, "A Trip to the Summit," which was published in her father's weekly paper, *Every Sunday,* on August 23, 1890, Fay stated she was "dressed in a thick, blue flannel bloomer suit, heavy calfskin boys' shoes, a loose blouse waist with innumerable pockets in the lining, and a small straw hat." She also had packed goggles, had an alpenstock made from a shovel handle with a spike driven into one end, and brought wool blankets, which she tied over her shoulder during the climb.

The party traveled across prairies and through timberlands, over narrow trails, rough wagon roads, and through thick brush. Fay and the Van Trumps spent the first night sleeping on straw in a barn belonging to So-To-Lick, or "Indian Henry," "a smart old Klickitat" who owned a valuable farm on a mountain meadow. It was So-To-Lick who had guided Van Trump's 1883 expedition up the mountain as far as the snow line.

They were joined that night by two other parties, one from Yelm and the other from Seattle. The paths of these groups had crossed several times during their five-day trek to the mountain. When all parties had reached the proximity of Paradise Camp, Miss Fuller paid a visit to the other camps and learned of a planned ascent by a party consisting of the Reverend E. C. Smith, pastor of the Seattle Unitarian Church; W. O. Amsden, Seattle photographer; R. R. Parrish of Portland; Len Longmire of Yelm; and others who were ultimately held back by illness. Longmire invited members of the Van Trump party to join them climbing. Here was her chance! Fay wanted to go, but was afraid if she failed to make the summit one of the men would have to leave the climb to take her back to camp. When Len volunteered to return with Fay, should it become necessary, she joined the four mountain climbers.

This was to be the first of many climbs for Len Longmire, a member of a pioneer, Pierce County family. For the next twenty years, Len guided tourists up Mount Rainier for a fee of one dollar per hiker.

On Saturday morning, August 9 at 11:00 a.m., Fay dressed in her heavy flannels, woolen hose, warm mittens, and goggles. She drove long "caulks and brads" into her boys' shoes, rolled up two blankets containing three-days' provisions and strapped them to her back. To avoid sunburn, she blackened her face with charcoal. For a quick snack, Fay placed chocolates into the pockets of her blouse. As she tells it, "I put a good supply of chocolate in those pockets. You can imagine what happened when the sun came out hot on my back."

As they set out, the sun beamed down on their backs, causing their packs to feel increasingly heavier and hotter. They ascended long steep snowfields, over ledges of rock, and over one small crevasse that afternoon. The group spent the night at Camp Muir, arising at 4:30 a.m. on August 10, 1890, to venture forth into the most difficult part of the climb. Breakfasting only on raisins and prunes, and with no water as the streams had frozen over during the night, they set out up the southeast slope of the mountain.

Twelve hours later, the four men and one woman stood "on the tip top of Mount Tahoma," as Mount Rainier was then called. Fay described the pinnacle moment: "It was a heavenly moment; nothing was said— words cannot describe [the] scenery and beauty, how could they speak for the soul!"

Each of the climbers left a remembrance at the summit. They carved their names in the ice, and deposited hair pins, a sardine can, a brandy flask, and tin cup at the top of Mount Rainier. Fay's hair pins were found by the next party up the mountain, the Hitchcock party. They teased Fay that it proved to them that a woman really had made it to the summit.

Descending, the climbers found they could hardly stand due to the ferocious wind. They found shelter in a crater surrounded by steam jets, "looking as if a row of boiling tea kettles had been placed along the ridge." A fine spray from the steam vents drenched their clothing, forcing them to move their camp to an ice cave. Before resting for the night, each climber bathed their feet in whiskey (yet another scandalous event!). Freezing cold and sickened by exhaustion and sulphur fumes from deep within the dormant volcano, Fay suffered nausea and was unable to sleep during the night. She spent the night listening to the distant roar of avalanches cascading down the mountain's slopes. When she rose, her shoes had frozen stiff and had to be melted over a steam vent. She hated to leave the shelter, finding the wind blowing so fiercely she could barely keep her balance.

The descent had to be made rapidly in order to reach the Great Gibraltar Cliff during the morning hours. Retracing the previous day's path over the snowfield, down the crags, slipping on pumice-covered glacial faces, the party went without water for six hours and ate very little. Once at the Gibraltar Ledges, they found the steps they had carved in the ice were melted by the afternoon sun and had to be re-cut. The steps, cut at intervals easy for a man to reach, were more difficult for the smaller Miss Fuller to span. Descending over the cliff's rock ledge frightened Fay more than climbing up it had.

Slipping and sliding on their backsides down steep slopes like frolicking children, the group reached camp by afternoon. Fay was a sight! Her lips, nose, and other parts of her face were swollen out of proportion by sun and windburn. She suffered burning eyes and peeling wrists, and she found it hard to walk for several days. Her only regret was that she had left her camera at base camp rather than taking it with her to the summit, though she acknowledged it would have proved burdensome to carry. In spite of an accident involving his camera, Amsden was able to take some beautiful photographs, for which he had numerous orders.

After the climb, Fay Fuller and Len Longmire expressed mutual admiration for one another's accomplishment. She said of him that, "dressed in summer clothing and without gloves he was plucky enough to reach the top, a statement that means something even if one is prepared for it." Longmire stated often that Miss Fuller repeatedly refused assistance from the men, even in the most dangerous spots. She emphasized that if she could not reach the top without male help, she did not deserve to make it at all!

Fay's own account of her historic climb was published within weeks of the event in *Every Sunday*. Enthralled with the experience of climbing, Fay published every account she could find about early climbs of Mount Rainier. The publications of such expeditions, and of her own climb, piqued great interest in the sport of mountain climbing.

Fay's second climb, in 1897, proved nearly as historic as her first. A charter member of a Portland-based, mountain climbing club, the Mazamas, Fay joined two hundred members of the group in an assault on the mountain. This was the largest group to ever camp on Mount Rainier to date.

On July 27, 1897, fifty-eight of the Mazamas, including several women, reached the summit, where they burned a red fire on the top of Mount Rainier to signal Tacoma of their successful climb.

Fay Fuller and seven other Mazamas chose to spend the night on the summit. The other fifty descended to Camp Muir. Encouraged by the bright night to continue, some of the hikers left Camp Muir, guided by the light of the moon. Edgar McClure, a chemistry professor from the University of Oregon, began his moonlight descent carrying with him his yard-long, mercurial barometer with which he had calculated the altitude of the mountain at 14,528 feet. McClure slipped and fell to his death without making a sound. His climbing partner believed he had fainted due to cold, fatigue, hunger, and dehydration. McClure's death was the first recorded climbing tragedy on Mount Rainier. Thus, Fay Fuller's second expedition recorded another "first." Two additional climbers nearly met the same fate the next day when they fell into a deep crevasse but survived.

In addition to the *Tacoma Ledger* and her father's papers, Fay wrote for a weekly called the *Stage,* sponsored by a Tacoma theater, and worked for a time in Pendleton, Oregon. In 1900, Fay left Tacoma on an assignment to cover the Chicago World's Fair. When the fair closed, she took a job with the *Chicago Inter-Ocean,* then later took reporting jobs in Washington, D.C., and New York. In 1905, she married Fritz Von Briesen, a prominent New York attorney, and gave up her reporting career. Fay had two children, a son and a daughter and lived for many years in New York. Her last visit to Mount Rainier was in 1950, when at the age of eighty she traveled as high as Paradise Lodge, where she was an honored guest on the mountain.

Fay Fuller Von Briesen passed away on May 27, 1958, in Santa Monica, California, at the age of eighty-eight. Fay predicted that her example would be followed by "a good many women." In fact, there were two women climbers to the summit in 1891, Susan Longmire (Len's thirteen-year-old daughter) and Edith Corbet (whose illness had prevented her from climbing with Fay's party). Fay recommended that all who live within view of the much revered Mount Rainier have the opportunity, and "want to begin life anew might profitably spend a few weeks next summer on its hillside, if they want to fall in love with the world again. The beauty and grandeur and inspiration you will find there will add new life."

KATHLEEN ROCKWELL

1876–1957

KLONDIKE KATE

Hidden on the banks of the roaring river, the young woman dressed in boys' clothing crouched, silently waiting for just the right moment. As the men aboard the vessel released the mooring lines and began to shove off, the lithe figure jumped from shore. She missed the boat deck and splashed into the icy, churning waters. Somehow she managed to get a hand on the boat and clung on desperately as her body surfed the rapids. Coming to her rescue, the burly oarsmen pulled her aboard with little effort.

The ruckus caught the attention of a nearby Mountie on shore who shouted out, "Stop in the name of the Queen!" The Canadian Mountie continued to bellow orders, fuss, and fume as the scow headed toward the rapids, but there was little he could do. Drenched, but victorious, Kathleen waved at him triumphantly, as the square boat proceeded toward the seething froth of the Whitehorse and Five Finger Rapids.

"My trip through Miles Canyon and Whitehorse Rapids was perhaps the most exciting trip I ever made. That man at the giant oar-rudder muscled us through with great, uncanny skill," Kate reminisced.

So began the gold rush adventures of Kathleen Rockwell, "Queen of the Yukon," the dance hall girl from Spokane, Washington, later dubbed "Klondike Kate." From the moment the long-legged beauty with the reddish gold locks walked down the gangplank into Dawson City, she captivated the hearts of the crusty Klondike miners. The large, barnlike dance hall and theater had featured many a pretty girl, but it was Kate who electrified the stage at the Savoy. Her flame dance was a show stopper, during which she twirled yards of bright red chiffon around her limber form and through the air, electrifying the stage.

Kathleen Rockwell Yukon Archives, MacBride Museum Collection

Kate was in her twenties when she made it aboard the ship that was headed north to seek riches, and she quickly became a legend—the darling of the North. Queen of the Klondike, Belle of Dawson, Yukon Queen, Sweetheart of the Sourdoughs—Klondike Kate was wined and dined by rough, tough, free spending prospectors who threw buckskin pouches of gold dust (called pokes) at her feet when she danced.

As a young girl, raised in Spokane, Washington, Kate predicted, "I'm going to see the whole world when I grow up!"

∽

Kathleen Eloisa Rockwell was born in Junction City, Kansas, on October 4, 1876, to Martha Alice (Murphy) Rockwell and John W. Rockwell. As she aged, the year of Kate's birth got later and later, and she commonly cited her birth year as 1880. When Kate was a small child, her parents separated (Kate claimed to have no recollection of her father) and Mrs. Rockwell married her divorce attorney, Frank A. Bettis. Bettis moved his new family, including Kathleen, to Spokane where he was appointed Circuit Court Judge for the State of Washington in Spokane County.

Judge Bettis became a wealthy, political official, well known through-out the Inland Northwest. The Bettis family home was among the largest and grandest manors in the city. Kathleen had a governess, while her mother had a maid and a cook. Kate remembers the cook telling her, "Some day you'll grow up to be a very fine lady like your mother and have a great fine house like this for your own. That is, if you learn to mind your manners, Kathleen."

Judge Bettis adored young Kathleen, known to her family as Kitty, and provided her with every luxury. No one in Spokane would have imagined that this pampered, indulged girl, being groomed to take her place in Spokane's "high society," was destined to become a Yukon dance hall queen!

A gypsy at heart, Kathleen was impulsive and daring. Riding her father's well-bred, trotting horses, she would race them into a frothy lather. Playing hooky from school was a favorite pastime; she bought picnic food on her father's accounts and would treat her friends to outdoor feasts. When her mother caught on and canceled her credit with the merchants, Kate simply changed vendors. Always the showman, Kitty draped lace curtains around herself and danced on the lawn of the great house, performing for her neighbors.

Her good heart also showed at an early age. When their Spokane neighborhood nearly burned to the ground, eight-year-old Kathleen invited her neighbors whose homes had been burned to stay at the Bettis Manor. More than one hundred guests took her up on her offer, filling the house with cots for two weeks.

Since Spokane's upper echelon sent their children to boarding school, Mrs. Bettis decided that would be in Kate's best interest. Kathleen was sent to St. Paul's Academy for Girls in Minnesota. In school, Kathleen enjoyed music, but not mathematics, which she would bribe classmates to do for her. Under strict supervision of the nuns, the lively Kathleen often found herself in trouble. Once during study hall, Kathleen, ever the performer, danced the Highland Fling to the delight of her classmates and dismay of the sisters. The nuns punished her by locking her in the bathroom for the rest of the day. Remembering it was bath day for the nuns, Kate ran the hot water out, so the sisters would have to bathe in cold water. The mischievous girl then removed dirty towels from a hamper and stuffed them down the drain.

When Judge Bettis and Kathleen's mother separated, her heartbroken mother decided to move to New York, where she was unknown, to forget her sorrow. Kathleen and her mother set sail from Seattle on a freighter. Passengers were not allowed on the ship, so the Rockwell women were deemed "stewardesses." Before the Panama Canal was dug, ships sailed around the horn of South America. Mrs. Bettis planned to leave Kathleen with her half-brother who lived in Valparaiso, Chile, while she found a place to live in New York City.

On the exotic cruise, Kathleen saw whales, porpoises, and tropical birds from the ship's deck. When sailors caught the beautiful birds using baited hooks, the tender-hearted Kathleen freed them. Not all was serene though—Kathleen once found herself amidst a drunken sailor's brawl in Valparaiso.

During the trip, Kathleen became engaged to the ship's first officer. Alarmed, her mother placed her in the Sacred Heart Convent when they reached Valparaiso. As a rare "gringa" in Latin America, Kathleen was quite an attraction. Not knowing Spanish, she answered "Si" to all questions and soon found herself with a bevy of suitors. Encouraged, these young Latin lovers threw notes to Kate over the convent's walls. She became particularly enamored with a Spanish attaché and accepted a proposal from the handsome Latino. When her mother heard of the engagement, she quickly sent for Kathleen to join her in New York.

Mrs. Bettis had no concept of money. She had taken the proceeds from the sale of their Spokane house and continued to live in her accustomed manner of luxury until her money ran out. The Rockwell women found themselves penniless and alone in New York City, with $83 between them. Mrs. Bettis went to work in a factory making shirtwaists, while sixteen-year-old Kate began to look for work. Each evening she read the classified ads aloud to her mother in their tiny apartment. One day an ad caught her eye, "Chorus Girls wanted—no experience necessary." Knowing her proper mother would never approve, Kate secretly answered the ad.

Always fond of dancing, she auditioned and was hired by the production company. Her mother was horrified when she heard of her daughter's newfound occupation. Once Mrs. Bettis had calmed down, she accepted Kate's decision but never knowingly let her perform unchaperoned.

When the show opened in Pittsburgh, Kate went with the company without telling her mother. The show flopped, and the company went broke. Stranded, Kate and another girl went to a church and prayed for a way home. Then, the two young dancers stole into a railroad yard and jumped a boxcar to New York. With their last pennies, they purchased stale doughnuts for the ride. In New York, they walked 183 blocks to the room of a friend to clean up before going home. Mrs. Bettis had alerted the police about her missing daughter and was beside herself with worry when Kate finally turned up. She forbade her daughter from the stage, but the chorus girl life was now in Kate's blood. Again defying her mother, Kitty took her next job in Coney Island. Her mother reluctantly agreed but set a curfew. Kate barely had time to dress after her last act and ride the streetcar home by her mother's deadline.

It was a letter from a childhood friend from Spokane that lured Kate Rockwell west again. The friend wrote of high-paying jobs in "continuous vaudeville." There was a job opening, so Kathleen headed west.

Her first night on the job, Kate signed in at the variety theater. Following her stage performance, she returned to her dressing room to wait for her next show. Suddenly her bell rang and she was told to sit in one of the curtained booths or "boxes." An old school friend joined her asking if she would let him buy her a bottle of wine. "Oh, no thank you," the naive Kate replied, "I do not drink wine." The waiter nearly fainted! Crying, she ran to her dressing room where one of the performers explained the role to Kate. Not only were the girls to sing and dance, but between acts they were to flirt with the customers—enticing them into buying expensive bottles of wine. As hostesses, they earned a commission for every bottle they sold. The dancer showed Kate how to pour her glass of wine into the spittoons when the customers were not looking.

She was next booked into the People's Theater in Seattle and a few weeks later, the Savoy in Victoria, British Columbia. Kate became the theater company's starlet, presenting two new flashy songs each week. The owners of the Savoy Theater guarded the virtue of the girls in the company. The performers had a curfew, and every night they were checked into their rooms over the theater. Still, Mrs. Bettis was appalled when she heard of her daughter's employment in variety theaters. Kate appeased her by saying she would send for her mother when she had saved enough money.

Yet it was hard for Kate to save money when she was continuously helping others. When she finally had enough to bring her mother west, she found a girl in her company in need of hospitalization. Generously, Kathleen donated her savings and took up a collection for the sick dancer. A local newspaper reporter heard the story and wrote about Kate's efforts. This was the first of many stories to be written about Kate. Still, her mother was not pleased.

Kate's second write-up was a review of her performance at Seattle's Comique Theater. A reporter wrote that she sang and danced with a "French Flair." Her picture was printed in newspapers and magazines, and she became one of the first pinup girls in the Northwest.

The headline for the Seattle paper the morning of July 17, 1897, changed Kate's life again. The bold type read, "A Ton of Solid Gold—A Rush to the Clondyke [*sic*]—A Rush to the North—All Daft Over Gold." The ship *Portland* had docked in Seattle, bringing gold-toting miners and the beginning of a hysteria that became known as the Klondike Gold Rush. Before long, the towns of Skagway, Dyea, and Dawson City became household words. Everyone knew the path to riches ran over the treacherous White and Chilkoot Passes.

Kate began moving north, taking a job in Bennett, British Columbia, a gold-crazy town where would-be-miners bought their outfits and built scows, or flat riverboats, to take them upriver to the Yukon in search of the precious metal. Kate caught gold fever and longed to go north. The Canadian Mounted Police, or "Mounties," were stopping women from traveling the river to Whitehorse and into Dawson City. Kate concealed her sex beneath boys' clothing and leapt aboard a rickety old scow to travel through the raging Whitehorse Rapids.

A letter was waiting at Whitehorse, inviting Kate to return to Victoria, British Columbia, for a job as a dancer in a large burlesque, musical comedy company that was forming to play in Dawson. Kate returned to British Columbia, auditioned, got the job, and again headed north to Dawson, with the Savoy Theatrical Company. The 173-member company was the largest ever to play the Klondike. The show opened in 1900, featuring dancing girls, as well as a full orchestra.

Kate was initially disappointed to find that the streets of Dawson were not paved with gold and the theater she was to star in was nothing but a big, empty, barnlike structure. Before one week had passed, the Savoy had become the entertainment center of Dawson and all of the Yukon Territory, and Kate was happy to be a part of it all. The cavernous building came alive with the whir of the roulette wheel, clinking of glasses, shuffling of cards, and band music under the glow of coal oil lamps illuminating the room. The girls were always dressed in the finest modern fashions, but the men were wild and wooly—fresh from the gold fields.

As star of the show, Kate was provided a room above the theater. The elegant room, complete with red and gold wallpaper, oak furniture, lace curtains, and a plush red carpet, even provided a view of the river.

Women were scarce on the streets of Dawson and when they appeared on the sidewalks, they attracted the miner's appreciative stares and whistles. There were three types of women in town: the family women who were married to the miners; entertainers, actresses, and dance hall girls like Kate; and the girls across the river who engaged in the world's oldest profession.

Her first year in Dawson was the happiest of young Kate's life. A strange mixture of people came to the Savoy to have fun; the gold-rich millionaires, gamblers, and dance hall girls all mingled to create a festive atmosphere. The show began at 8:30 p.m., and the girls often did not retire until ten in the morning. They knew all the modern dances, and the miners paid handsomely to dance and drink with the girls. The dancers kept half of the dance money and a quarter of the money spent on each drink. The commission on a bottle of champagne was $7.50. On her best night, Kate earned $750, mostly just for rolling cigarettes and talking with lonely prospectors. Dances were a dollar each, and the music stopped frequently. Waiters sold $15 bottles of wine and removed them from the tables when they were still half full. The prospectors had pockets lined with pouches of gold and spent freely, often when they wanted to put aside their loneliness for an evening.

Throughout the frozen winters, the miners lived in isolated, drafty cabins. When the spring thaw came and town was more accessible, they headed for the Savoy looking for company, entertainment, and excitement. When dances pleased the prospectors, they tossed their pokes of gold onto the stage at the dancers' feet. Many came into the Savoy rich and left poor, some men losing as much as $100,000 gambling and free-spending in one night.

Offstage, the girls wore gold nugget jewelry and designer dresses over silk petticoats that rustled when they walked. Kate ordered gowns from Paris, one costing as much as $1,500. Her lingerie was handmade in France. The stage gowns sparkled with rhinestones, seed pearls, spangles, and sequins. Kate always wore tights on stage. Her most daring outfit involved a black satin coat, which she removed to reveal a short, rhinestone-studded costume with pink tights. Risqué in its day, this costume would be considered mild now. Had any of the girls shown a bare leg, the show would have been shut down.

Kate loved the excitement as well as the great outdoors. She kept horses and dogs and mushed dog sleds throughout the icy winters. Even while living the high life of a dance hall queen, Kate cared for others. She housed a pregnant girl with tuberculosis in a cabin near the dance hall. The girl was poor, sick, and had been abandoned by the baby's father. After a performance one evening, Kate slipped out to check on the girl and found her giving birth. The young mother died in childbirth, so Kate took the baby boy under her care. She kept him until he was three years old, at which time she found him foster parents in "the States." Always remaining anonymous, she sent money for the child's college education and followed his career. The man became a successful engineer, but Kathleen refused to ever disclose his identity. Even though he never knew of Klondike Kate's influence on his life, she thought of him as her son. This was the only child Kathleen Rockwell ever "had."

Full of the holiday spirit one Christmas season, the miners crowned Kate "Queen of the Yukon." Cutting her a crown from a tin can and impaling candles on the jagged points, they lit them for her grand coronation. Kate danced in the glow of her lighted crown, adorned in her expensive Paris gown. The men loved the dance, cheering wildly. Her long braids were soon coated with wax that would not wash out. She became the first in town to have "bobbed" hair.

That night, standing in the crowded room watching the luminescent, dancing Klondike Kate, was a quiet Norwegian miner. During the excitement Kate never noticed the silent man. When the chaos subsided, she spotted the blonde Scandinavian watching her. Drawn to him, she approached, took his hand, and asked him to dance. This was the first man she had ever had to ask to dance. Shyly, he answered in his thick Norwegian accent that he had just come to watch. "Yoo are yust beautiful." Finding him sweet, Kate talked for awhile, and he told her he would "vait for her."

It was a slick, handsome, smooth-talking, Greek immigrant though who stole her heart. A natural promoter, Alexander Pantages was a charmer burning with ideas and goals. Most men of the Yukon dressed roughly and usually wore scraggly beards. In sharp contrast, Alex took pains to dress well and was always clean shaven. He was a smooth talker who could also be indifferent or insolent if it didn't suit his needs to be gracious.

When Alex was unemployed, Kate opened her purse strings. She not only supported him, she gave him money so that he could smoke fine cigars, wear imported silk shirts, and dine in elegant restaurants. Kate paid for their room and board as well.

With gold dust gathered from miner's pokes while "giving change," Pantages started his own dance hall, charging miners $12.50 a seat. At its peak, he claimed his theater made $8,000 per day.

In 1901, Alex convinced Kate to leave the Yukon Territory. She purchased a theater in Victoria, British Columbia, but even though it was making money, Pantages told her to sell it. With the money from the sale of her successful theater, Alex bought a theater in Seattle, the Crystal. When the Crystal began to turn a profit, Pantages built theaters in Tacoma, Spokane, Portland, and Vancouver. He became a millionaire from his chain of combination movie/vaudeville theaters.

All the while, Kathleen Rockwell thought herself an equal partner in these ventures. According to her court testimony, Pantages told Kate he needed more money and asked her to travel to Texas where he believed a dance hall girl could still find fortune. In 1903, Kate went to Texas at his insistence. She sent her earnings home to Alex, and he invested them in his emerging theater dynasty. After a year of performing in Texas, Kate returned to Seattle. There she found her "partner" romantically involved with an eighteen-year-old violinist from one of his theaters. Pantages and Lois Mendenhall were married in March of 1905. Four days later Kate learned of the marriage. Despondent, Kathleen sought the company of her mother, who had moved to Seattle and begun operating a successful Seattle real estate firm.

Kate filed suit against Pantages for breach of promise. The *Seattle Times* headline of May 26, 1905, read, "Uses Her Money Then Jilts the Girl." Alexander admitted that he and Kate had lived together but insisted there were no promises of marriage. He also claimed to have little money. A year after her complaint was filed in King County Superior

Court asking for $25,000 in damages, Kate settled the case for $5,000. Heartbroken, she returned to Dawson to attempt a recovery.

With the gold rush over, Dawson was not the same and Kate soon was traveling throughout Alaska and the States with the vaudeville circuit, performing some of her acts on roller skates. Kate's mother, a successful Seattle businesswoman by that time, urged her daughter to quit the stage life and return to Seattle. Compromising, Kate bought "Idlours," a well-known hunting lodge on Hood Canal across Puget Sound from Seattle, using it as a private refuge. She retreated there on many occasions, vacationing from her frantic vaudeville tours.

In 1912, a twisted knee finally forced Kate to retire from life on the stage. Depression set in, and Kate suffered a nervous breakdown. Her doctors ordered a year of rest, so Kate bought a horse, saddle, and six-shooter and rode from Seattle to Medford, Oregon. She wandered central Oregon for a year before returning to Seattle, where in 1914, she met a man who owned a homestead in Bend, Oregon. Her mother traded four acres of Seattle waterfront and some cash for the property. When she went to see what they had purchased, Kate found 320 acres of sage-brush surrounding a tiny, one room shack. In a dress and high heels, she began grubbing sagebrush and piling up rocks. She felt like giving it up many times, but the beauty and desert sunsets always turned her around. For the first time in her life, she was rested and content, and money was not important to Kathleen E. Rockwell.

Kate married Floyd Warner, a handsome young cowboy, in 1915. Her new husband was a jealous man who wanted to fight anyone addressing his bride as "Klondike Kate." Floyd left their homestead to serve in World War I; after the war they drifted apart.

After three unsuccessful years of ranching (she once owned forty-two head of cattle, but they "sort of drifted"), she found herself broke. Kate took a variety of jobs—ran rooming houses, nursed the sick, washed dishes, and ran restaurants. Through all of this, she kept most of her

Yukon gold jewelry. As Kate said in a 1956 interview, "I can remember those queer looks on the faces of customers, seeing me up to my elbows in soap suds, with a thousand dollars worth of diamonds in each ear."

She later returned to Seattle to care for her dying mother. Following her mother's death, Kate continued to take odd jobs throughout Oregon and California. She kept her home in Bend but traveled whenever she had the money. At one point when she was broke in California, she called on her former beau, Alexander Pantages, now a millionaire, for a loan. Alex gave her six dollars.

Later, in 1929, when Alex was accused of attacking a young actress, Kate was called to his defense as a character witness. Pantages's trial ended in a conviction, and he was sentenced to prison for up to fifty years. Three years later, during his appeal, the victim accepted $3,000 to drop the matter, and the case was dismissed.

In 1931, a character from Kate's past read an article about her role in the Pantages Trial in a three-year-old newspaper. Johnny Matson, the shy Norwegian who did not dance, wrote to Kathleen, "I have always been in love with you, Katie, all these years. I never had the courage to tell you before. I have heard that life has not been too good to you. I would like to have the right to take care of you as my wife."

When they met again, Kate, at age fifty-three, told Johnny, "I'm old now." To this he replied, "Yoo look yust the same to me as yoo did years ago, the most beautiful woman a man ever saw." They were married on July 14, 1933, and returned to Dawson on their honeymoon.

With her health no longer up to the Klondike's rugged winters, Kate wintered in Bend while Johnny continued to mine his claim on Matson Creek. Every summer she traveled north to be with him. Twice a year Johnny mushed sixty miles on snowshoes to mail letters to his wife. She went from thinking of Johnny as her "funny little yam and yelly man" to the best man on earth. In 1946, when the letters stopped, Kate sent out an expedition to look for her spouse. Eighty-three-year-old Johnny's frozen body was found on a trail seven miles from his lone cabin. After fifty years in the Yukon, that year was to have been his last, for he had finally promised Kate he'd retire from prospecting in the spring.

At seventy-one, Kate married W. L. Van Duren, an accountant whom she had nursed back to health at her convalescent home in Oregon. The couple wed in Vancouver, Washington, on April 1, 1948. They lived quietly for a number of years until her death.

Several movies based on the life of Klondike Kate were made. While Kate acted as a consultant on some, there were others she disdained. Kate was horrified at Mae West's suggestive performance in *Klondike Annie,* saying, "That picture is a disgrace. Why if any of us girls had acted like Mae West acted on the screen, we would have been handed a blue ticket [fired]."

Kathleen E. Rockwell Warner Matson Van Duren died in Sweet Home, Oregon, on February 21, 1957, at the age of eighty, although her obituaries listed her age as seventy-seven. Kate's ashes were scattered across the central Oregon desert. Forever a "sourdough," Klondike Kate throughout her life lived by her often quoted motto, "Mush on and smile!"

Judge Reah Mary Whitehead

1883–1972

LADY JUSTICE

The frightened young man, hardly more than a boy at age nineteen, stood before the bench accused of kidnapping. His voice quavered as he addressed the judge. The sixteen-year-old "victim" sobbed incessantly in the courtroom galley, as her stern father glowered over her toward the accused.

The judge intuitively sensed there was more to this situation than first met the eye and further interviewed the two youths. They had been trying to elope, when the girl's father intervened, charging his daughter's suitor with kidnapping. Finding no criminal intent, Judge Whitehead then conferred with the girl's mother. The magistrate convinced the mother to sign a consent, so the two lovers could be married. The young couple was then married by the compassionate judge.

Every year, on the anniversary of their wedding, the couple phoned Judge Whitehead and updated her on the chronicles of their family life. These calls continued for over fifty years.

It was in October of 1914 that the young assistant King County prosecutor announced her intention of running for the office of Justice of the Peace for the Precinct of Seattle. Her mother, Mrs. Esther T. Bosley, managed the campaign. With the backing of a number of prominent male lawyers and judges in Seattle, Reah Mary Whitehead beat out the competition of nine men to become the state of Washington's first female judge. She served on the bench in Seattle for nearly twenty-seven years.

⁂

Reah Mary Whitehead was born April 11, 1883, in Kansas City, Missouri, to Stanley and Esther (Gideon) Whitehead. As a youngster, she

Judge Reah Whitehead Reprinted with permission, *Seattle Post-Intelligencer* d/b/a *SeattlePI.com*, an operating unit of Hearst Seattle Media, LLC.

moved with her family to Seattle in 1890. She began her legal career as a stenographer. At age sixteen, Reah took a position in a law office in Skagway, Alaska. Living and working in Alaska for fourteen months, Reah became well known as the youngest court reporter in the Alaska Territory.

After mastering her stenographic skills, she reached the point at which she felt she must either go downhill or move forward. It was then she decided to study law, and she enrolled in the University of Washington's School of Law. At least, she reasoned, she would learn what she was writing about when she copied briefs. During her final year of law school, Reah attended evening classes while working days for a Seattle law firm. Reah graduated from law school at the University of Washington and passed the Washington State Bar exam in May of 1905.

Even after passing the bar, Reah did not work as an attorney for several years. She worked for Judge Thomas Burke and then as chief clerk in the King County Prosecutor's Office under Chief Prosecutor MacKintosh. When George F. Vandervear assumed the office of chief prosecutor on January 12, 1909, he appointed Reah M. Whitehead as the first woman prosecutor for King County, as well as for the state of Washington. An article in the *Seattle Post-Intelligencer* noted her appointment, stating that although she has

> *authority to try cases the same as other deputy prosecutors . . . Miss Whitehead will remain as clerk in the office of the prosecuting attorney and will not draw salary as a deputy prosecuting attorney. She will hold the title, however, and is the first woman to be appointed a deputy prosecuting attorney in this state.*
>
> *Miss Whitehead once prosecuted a cruelty to animals case in the Superior Court and secured a conviction. She will be given an opportunity of handling cases of this character, but for the most part will do office work.*

Her duties, as outlined in the article, were quite reflective of the attitudes of the day. Reah Whitehead had to fight an uphill battle toward receiving equal treatment and the same type of caseloads as male prosecutors. Every case that Reah was given the opportunity to try in superior court she won. On this record and the platform of female magistrates for female "culprits," Reah M. Whitehead was elected justice of the peace for the Seattle District Court for King County, Washington.

Reah was often described in sexist terms. The local newspaper's description of the ceremony swearing in the state's first female judge began with a fashion statement:

Dressed in a simple blue suit, her brown hair arranged in school-girl fashion and her customary rosy cheeks made rosier by the excitement of the occasion, Miss Reah M. Whitehead entered upon her new duties as justice of the peace shortly before noon yesterday morning.

This was hardly a description befitting the decorum of the office! Asked how she liked her new job, she replied, "I will be glad when the novelty of my appearance upon the bench wears off, and I can work like any other justice." A further sign of the times, this article appeared next to an article entitled, "Home Life Regarded as Best for Girls." Even after twenty-seven years of service on the judicial bench, a local columnist interviewing Judge Whitehead asked her for her favorite recipe!

Civil cases tried before Judge Whitehead had a value limitation of $100. Every weekday she presided over cases involving laborers' wage claims, creditors holding unpaid promissory notes, landlords due back rent, and auto collision damage. These actions were not so different from those heard in our small claims courts of today.

In October of 1915, a reporter for the *Seattle Post-Intelligencer* newspaper interviewed Judge Whitehead following her first nine months on the bench. He observed, "She looks more like a debutante. Her cheeks are too pink and she's altogether too pretty for a woman judge." Even though the reporter found that he (like most reporters) "could not reconcile her youthful appearance with the dusty, snuffy technicalities of the court room," Judge Whitehead made profound statements in this interview stating:

> *[y]ou must remember that for years and years and hundreds of years men have made the laws and men have passed on the interpretation of the man-made laws. Until women have an actual hand in the framing of the laws, make their influence felt in the making of laws, the point of view between men and women judges and men and women lawyers will be different: . . . . I believe, of course, that women should have a hand in making the laws and interpreting them.*

Within a year of being sworn in, Judge Whitehead had already heard approximately 1,000 civil cases and 570 criminal cases. Lawyers who practiced before her expressed satisfaction with the "administration of justice by a woman."

Emphasizing the need for women judges, Reah gave an example of a parallel situation. "A few years ago we would not think of having women in police work, yet who would want to go back to that state of things now? They have answered the question of their necessity in the work."

During one of her campaigns for re-election to the bench, Reah further stated:

> *There is no sex in brains.*
>
> *I didn't originate that statement, I simply adopted it in setting forth my belief that a woman is just as mentally capable as a man and that the State of Washington and King County in particular should have a woman superior court judge to even up matters.*

Don't get the idea that I think that I or any other woman
can do judicial work better than a man. That's just the point
at issue. It's that a woman's viewpoint plus a man's viewpoint
equals the human viewpoint. And that is what our courts need.

For a 1926 newspaper article, Reah wrote, "Women are still in their infancy in the practice of law." The first woman to practice law in the United States was Myra Bradwell, in Illinois, in 1869. Subsequently, the federal census gave the number of women lawyers in the United States in 1890, as 208; in 1910, as 558; and, in 1920, as 1,738. Judge Whitehead's article also noted that the 1920 census counted male lawyers, judges, and justices in Washington State as 2,208 while females numbered 29. This worked out to a ratio of one male lawyer for every 220 males in the work force; as opposed to one female lawyer for every 3,200 female workers.

There were six Washington women attorneys in public office in 1926: one state senator, one city attorney, two justices of the peace, one deputy prosecuting attorney, and one police judge. The first three positions listed were elective while the last two were appointive. All, with the exception of one, had received their legal training at the University of Washington.

In the 1920s, statistics showed that five years after entering the legal profession, only 10 to 15 percent of male attorneys remained in the active practice of law. Justice Whitehead believed that, "[m]atrimony seems to exert about an equal pressure upon men and women lawyers in separating them from their profession. A young lawyer with matrimony in view recently announced he was going to procure a divorce from the law on the ground of non-support." Apparently, for men, the practice of law was not always the most lucrative profession they could choose. Women, with limited career choices, found the opposite to be true. Reah reported that two former teachers-turned-lawyers claimed they were earning more money than they had ever earned or could have earned in the teaching profession.

Justice Whitehead was chosen as the representative from Washington State to attend a prestigious meeting of professional women in New York City. The American Women's Association invited one woman from each state and the District of Columbia (a total of forty-nine) to attend the 1926 meeting, planned as a tribute to business and professional women of America. Each state delegate was selected by their congressmen, local newspapers, and women's groups.

At age forty-eight, Reah married retired grocer Frank Sidney Harrison. The June 1931 ceremony was performed by Judge Whitehead's good friend Judge Blanche Funk Miller, a justice of the peace from Tacoma. Reah promised to love and honor her new husband, but the word "obey" was conspicuously absent from the traditional wedding vows. Her announcement that she would continue to use her maiden name for professional reasons met with shock from some in the community. The couple later divorced, and Frank died in 1955.

In 1936, a proposal to reinstate the public whipping post as a means of punishing criminals in Washington State brought strenuous objection from Judge Whitehead. She argued that the whipping post was a testimonial to society's failure to think out problems calmly and clearly, describing the whipping post as an antiquated procedure that does nothing to treat social evils or aid in the correction of criminals. Rather, Justice Whitehead opined, it represented punishment for revenge, with no effort to reduce the cause of crime.

Judge Whitehead served seven terms on the bench in the Precinct of Seattle for King County, Washington. Nearing her retirement, she reflected on the commotion caused by her election in 1914, when, as the newspaper reporter interviewing her noted, "At that time she was pretty nearly the first woman judge in the country, and 'the publicity was terrific.'" Reah laughingly rejected the reporter's suggestion that, in 1941, a woman judge was still a novelty, responding, "[T]here are women sitting on the bench all over the country. I guess it would take the appointment of a woman to the United States Supreme Court to cause a stir any more."[*]

Judge Whitehead was held in high regard by her fellow attorneys. Wisdom, understanding, and common sense prevailed in her judgments. Her manner consisted of quiet judicial dignity, combined with a polite, but businesslike demeanor.

Reah also took an active interest in promoting legislation for the welfare of women and children. Esther Bosley, Reah's mother, was the driving force behind the funding of the Women's Industrial Home and Clinic in Medical Lake, Washington. As a social worker, Esther saw the need for a correctional school for delinquent adult women. Esther organized support for the project from state social welfare agencies, and Reah drafted the bill. The measure was presented to the state legislature where it passed, with funding granted for two years.

With her husband, Frank, Reah lived in a grand old manor, once a rectory, that had been moved during the Denny Regrade, when Seattle's steepest hills were sluiced away. Weekends were spent at her summer cabin on Lake Sammamish. In the summer, she commuted from her lake home, "as much as her work would allow." A frequent walker, Judge Reah Whitehead was known to walk from downtown Seattle to Ballard or up Queen Anne Hill, round trip distances of twelve and eight miles respectively. Rhea loved Seattle, claiming, "the air here is something to be found nowhere else in the world. It's a mixture of the tang of the sea, that rare air from the mountains and earthy smell of cedar and fir."

When she retired on November 10, 1941, citing health reasons, she was replaced by Evangeline Starr, an attorney who had been appointed

---

[*] An event that was not to occur until 1981, when Justice Sandra Day O'Connor was appointed to the U.S. Supreme Court.

divorce proctor for the King County Prosecutor's Office by Chief Prosecutor Warren G. Magnuson. Magnuson ("Maggie") later served six terms in the United States Senate, becoming nationally known for his power and influence.

Judge Reah M. Whitehead passed away at age eighty-nine, on October 13, 1972. She had been residing in California with her niece at the time of her death. Her obituary listed her as one of the first women lawyers in the state and Seattle's first female judge.

Imogen Cunningham

1883–1976

EXPOSED TO THE LIGHT

A resounding "crack" followed by a shower of cascading glass echoed through the Seattle hilltop from the curb next to the quaint, ivy-covered cottage. It must have been a curious sight to see the slender, fair-skinned redhead bent over the garbage breaking the glass-plate negatives apart and tossing the sharp shards into the trash. When Imogen Cunningham left Seattle, years of her professional work were thrown into the garbage container on the street outside of her modest studio. Deciding that the hundreds of negatives made of glass plate were simply too numerous and heavy to be moved, she shattered them into pieces and dumped them out. The glass plate negatives that did survive were only saved to secure stacks of prints for the move to California. Thus was the disposition of seven years of work in her portrait studio on Seattle's First Hill.

But the career of one of the most famous photographers of the twentieth century did begin in Seattle. Imogen Cunningham's career spanned most of the 1900s, lasting nearly three quarters of a century. In a bicentennial edition, titled "Remarkable American Women, 1776–1976," *Life* magazine lauded her as the "best-known woman photographer in America." She was instrumental in elevating photography to an art form, though she once told an interviewer that whether photography should be recognized as art or not was a "useless question," and went on to say that she hoped that, rather than label photography as modern art, artists and critics should be content to "call the work of the camera by its own rightful name of photography."

Imogen Cunningham Imogen Cunningham Trust (self-portrait with camera, 1912)

Imogen Cunningham was born in Portland, Oregon, on April 12, 1883, to Isaac Cunningham and his second wife, Susan. She was the eldest of the six children this couple had together. Her father, a man of Scottish descent, had three children with his first wife, Mary. After her death, he moved from Texas to Portland, Oregon, in 1880, and proposed marriage via correspondence to a widowed single mother. Susan and Isaac Cunningham married in 1882 and their first child, Imogen, was born one year later. Isaac gave his daughter the Celtic name of a princess from *Cymbeline,* one of William Shakespeare's romance plays.

Being a bit of a bohemian, Isaac was in many ways a man ahead of his time. He believed in equality of the sexes, was an independent idealist, a vegetarian, and a self-educated man. He moved his family to a commune on the Olympic Peninsula in Washington State in 1887. The "Puget Sound Co-operative Colony" was located on a bay near the logging town of Port Angeles in Washington's far northwestern corner.

As the utopian community began to lose its luster, Isaac moved his wife and ten children to the city of Seattle in 1889. There the family homesteaded on Queen Anne Hill when the now fashionable neighborhood was a dense forest full of wildlife. Imogen watched her mother and father work hard to support the large family through farming, selling wood and coal, and grading streets. She also observed her mother's role, consumed by childcare and wifely duties, and decided early on that she was interested in a different lifestyle.

A young Imogen began her education at the age of eight, when she trekked through the woods to begin formal schooling in Seattle at the Denny School. Her father encouraged her studies and supplemented her schooling with private art lessons. Imogen graduated from Broadway High School on Seattle's First Hill in 1903 and enrolled at the University of Washington. While a student at the university, Imogen set her career path in motion and took some of her earliest artistic images, including a nude portrait of herself in a remote grassy field on the sprawling campus and a misty platinum print of a swampy area near Lake Washington titled "Marsh, Early Morning."

Cunningham paid her own tuition and was the only one of her siblings to graduate from a university. During her junior year in college, Imogen bought a mail order camera from the American School of Art and Photography in Pennsylvania. With this camera she took her first photographs on the University of Washington's vast, wooded campus including the dew-shrouded photo of the marsh, which she remembered as her first. Isaac built his daughter a crude darkroom in a corner of his woodshed on the family homestead. Here she developed her photographs by candlelight in the rough-hewn, tar-papered shack.

Since there was no Art Department at the university, Imogen inquired of one of her professors as to what course of study she should take to pursue a career as a photographer. He instructed her to study the science of photography through a major in chemistry. In addition to her chemistry studies, she was a member of the German Club, on the Executive Committee for the Woman's League, Vice President of her Freshman Class, Secretary of the Senior Class, a member of Pi Beta Phi sorority, and a photographer for the University of Washington's yearbook the "Tyee." She also worked as a secretary for her chemistry professor and in the botany department making slides, a job that was to influence some of her most legendary later images. Dramatic, cropped, close-ups of plants and flowers are some of Imogen Cunningham's best-remembered photographs.

During her senior year in college, Imogen focused her study on Seattle photographer Edward S. Curtis, famous for his sepia-toned prints documenting the disappearing lives and culture of American Indians. After graduating from the University of Washington in 1907, the young aspiring photographer spent the next two years working for Curtis in his Seattle studio. It was her job to turn the platinum prints on the roof of the building, and this chore was often challenging in Seattle's rainy climate. Though she refined her knowledge of photography through the Curtis Studio, she seldom had contact with the aloof Mr. Curtis whom she described as, "such a big shot in his own mind that he seldom if ever turned up in the studio and if he did, he never spoke to the help."

Her affiliation with Pi Beta Phi sorority proved instrumental in furthering her education and aspirations when, in 1909, the sisterhood granted her a fellowship to study overseas. She added a $250 loan from the Washington Women's Club to her sorority's $500 award and went abroad to study the technical aspects of photography at the Technische Hochschule in Germany. At the institute in Dresden, she studied photochemistry under internationally reputed photo chemist, Robert Luther. Art and art history lessons complemented her photochemistry curriculum with Dr. Luther.

Upon completion of her studies in Dresden in June 1910, Imogen took off for Paris and London documenting her journey through the lens of her camera the entire way. Once back in America she traveled the East Coast, visiting the cities of Philadelphia, New York, and Washington, D.C. Throughout her two-continent travels she met many renowned artists and photographers of the day including Alfred Stieglitz, Gertrude Kasebier, and Alvin Coburn. While she was studying in Germany, her family had moved from Seattle to a farm in Northern California. Imogen visited the Sonoma County homestead before ending the adventure back in Seattle.

Rich with experience, but penniless and homeless, Cunningham set out to become a professional photographer by renting a dilapidated art studio with her few remaining funds. She lived and worked from the tiny, ivy-covered cottage at 1117 Terry Avenue on Seattle's First Hill above the city. In September 1910 the independent young woman hung out her shingle, which simply read, "Imogen Cunningham—Photographs," and began taking expressive portraits of Seattle's citizens. She photographed her subjects in her studio against blue, fabric-draped walls, at their homes, and outdoors taking care to surround her subjects with interesting props as well as to capture the personality and spirit of the sitter.

She made a successful living through portrait photography while deeply involved in the Seattle art community, including the Society of Seattle Artists and as a founding member of the Seattle Fine Arts Society. Three years into her profession, Imogen asserted her feminine independence to a wider audience with an article in her sorority's magazine, the *Arrow*. In "Photography as a Profession for Women," published in January 1913, she heartily advocated a role for women in the arts outside of traditional homemaking crafts. Growing up she had watched her mother toil at such, but expressed the views of her father who supported equality between men and women.

As her career developed Imogen continued to correspond with many notable photographers and artists of the period, and to promote her work across national forums. In 1913 Cunningham was involved in assembling an exhibit featuring the art of Seattle native Roi (George Roy) Partridge for the Seattle Fine Arts Society. Because Partridge was studying in Paris at the time, Imogen arranged the exhibit through a series of letters. Their friendship grew as their correspondence continued. Without ever having met the slim redhead, Roi Partridge professed his love and proposed marriage to Imogen. He had seen her image only in the self-portraits she had sent to him in France. Roi implored Imogen to meet him in Italy, but World War I waylaid the plans, and he came home to his native city in 1914. Imogen Cunningham and George Roy Partridge were married in Seattle on February 11, 1915.

Roi claimed that he received his first real publicity in the Northwest from a provocative photograph that Imogen had taken of him on Mount Rainier early in their marriage. Although he had set up shop in Imogen's cottage studio, the artist preferred to find his subjects in nature and often went on sketching trips around the West. He was drawing on a meadow in the shadow of Mount Rainier when Imogen persuaded her husband to remove his clothes and pose for her against the splendid beauty of the mountain. Roi told of sitting on a cake of ice while being "photographed in the buff." An image from this series titled "The Bather" was published in the *Town Crier,* a regional art magazine, in 1916, creating a sensation in the Seattle press. Her photos were considered immoral and scandalous by polite society. The *Argus,* another local publication, professed shock to see nudes against a mountain backdrop, claiming the photos a "portrayal of shame." Ironically, Imogen was later praised as one of the first women photographers to include nude male figures in her portfolio, but the negative publicity at the time caused her to pack away the nude study and not bring out the images again until fifty years had passed.

When her first child was born in 1915, Imogen found herself saddled with domestic chores, which hampered the time she had to spend on her craft. Her creative instincts were stifled by the duties of motherhood, while her husband continued to sojourn into the wilds to pursue his nature drawings, leaving the young mother alone with her small son, Gryffyd. A frustrated Cunningham described herself as having "one hand in the dishpan, the other in the darkroom." So, expressing herself with her camera meant taking pictures of subjects in and around her home, mainly her son and her garden, "finding beauty in the commonest things."

Roi was absent again on one of his sketching trips while Imogen suffered the ill effects of her second pregnancy. During this time there had been three fires in the cottage studio caused, perhaps, by a girl she had hired to help with her domestic chores. The last fire all but destroyed the darkroom and glass-plate negative collection. Sick and discouraged, she wrote to her husband that she was moving to California to be near her mother and father who could assist in caring for the growing family. Roi expressed annoyance at his wife's unilateral decision but it did not dissuade Imogen, who packed up her home and studio and shattered the glass-plate negatives that had survived the fire so that she would not have to move them. In 1917 she left Seattle for San Francisco where her husband begrudgingly joined her. Here she gave birth to twin sons, Rondal and Padraic.

Leaving Seattle meant giving up her own studio and darkroom, but Imogen continued to shoot her surroundings all the while caring for three little boys. She famously stated that she "was not willing to sacrifice her skill with the camera to maternity." Roi worked as a designer and taught art courses at Mills College in Oakland. Before long the couple had befriended many in the state's sizeable art community including photographer Dorothea Lange. Although she shot portraits of college girls for pay at times, she continued to study light, the human form, and plant life through the lens of her camera. Her magnified images of magnolias and calla lilies brought her international acclaim and are considered classics. Ten of her platinum plant prints were shown at the prestigious 1929 "Film and Foto" exhibition in Stuttgart, Germany, when she was nominated as an "outstanding American photographer" by Edward Weston.

With a group of like-minded, San Francisco-area photographers such as Ansel Adams, Imogen formed "Group f/64." Group members sought to advance and promote clear, honest, sharply defined photography. One of the earliest works depicting f/64's ideals of visual purity and expression was Cunningham's "Magnolia Blossom." But, Imogen did not confine herself to one artistic genre, preferring to explore many subjects and photographic techniques over her long career. The *New York Times* said of her in a 1970 article, "She had just gone on doing anything that pleases her."

In 1931 Imogen's photographs of legendary dancer Martha Graham appeared in the magazine *Vanity Fair,* beginning her storied association with the publication. She was later hired by the magazine to shoot some of the era's greatest movie stars, an assignment she only agreed to if she could take the portraits without glamour or pretense, a novel concept at the time. The association with *Vanity Fair* proved to be the catalyst that ended Roi and Imogen's marriage in 1934. By now Imogen's images were admired internationally and had brought her fame across many audiences. *Vanity Fair* had asked her to work in New York City, while her husband requested that she wait until he could travel with her. She refused to postpone her assignment and set off for New York. Roi's response to his increasingly independent, ambitious spouse was to file for divorce.

Cunningham returned to the Puget Sound area many times for exhibitions and to photograph such Northwest notables as artist Morris Graves. Imogen traveled to Seattle in 1935 to produce a catalogue for the Cornish Art School founded by her friend Nellie Cornish. She borrowed the Seattle darkroom and studio of her former employer's brother, famed western photographer Asahel Curtis, to produce a unique brochure filled with young dancers and artists from the school.

As Imogen's freedom to explore and take innovative images grew, she chose subjects ranging from street people to presidents. She claimed she photographed "anything that can be exposed to light." Always expanding her horizons and changing with the times, in the 1960s Imogen could be seen wearing a peace symbol medallion over her long black cape while documenting college protests, civil rights marches, and hippies in Haight Ashbury.

In her eighties, Imogen set out to preserve her life's worth of images. The Guggenheim Foundation awarded her a grant of $5,000 in 1970 so that she could spend a year preserving and cataloging her collection. While sorting through her images she rediscovered the glass plate negatives of Roi posing nude at Mount Rainier. Once, when interviewed about her life's work, she was asked about the "erotic content" of some of her photos to which she responded, "Young man, I don't take erotic pictures." Further concerned with her legacy, she donated documents to the Smithsonian Institution and in 1975 founded The Imogen Cunningham Trust. To this day the Trust manages, publicizes, and displays the collection.

She continued to experiment through her lens into her nineties, creating a series titled "After Ninety." Cunningham had turned ninety in 1973, revered as a celebrity, with exhibits of her work shown from coast to coast. By this milestone, she had often been interviewed, filmed, or appeared on television. In 1970 she had a day named after her in San Francisco. As a living legend, her opinions and advice were constantly sought, which she found to be inconvenient and a disruption of her work.

Following a brief illness, Imogen Cunningham passed away in San Francisco at the age of ninety-three on June 23, 1976. Upon her death she was hailed worldwide as a pioneering visionary. In her hometown, the University of Washington Press, which had previously published other bodies of her work, released a book of her "After Ninety" series. Her alma mater had awarded Imogen Cunningham the title of *Alumna Summa Laude Dignata* in 1974 and in December 1999 named her as one of 100 Alumni of the Century. But, the most tangible honor bestowed by her school was Cunningham Hall. The edifice had been constructed as the Women's Building for Seattle's 1909 World's Fair, *The Alaska Yukon Pacific Exhibition*. After years of stagnation, the building was remodeled, rejuvenated, reopened, and renamed as Cunningham Hall in 1983, where it houses the university's Women's Center. It was moved across campus in 2009 to preserve it as one of the last buildings remaining from the world's fair. Cunningham Hall stands today as a lasting monument to this fiercely independent, original woman whose "Everything Under the Sun" exhibition at the Seattle Art Museum was held a century after this pioneer photographer set up her studio in the city.

Isabel Friedlander Arcasa

1889–1992

CUSTODIAN OF COLVILLE HERITAGE

Hunting deep in the forests of the Cascade Mountains, the band of Native people froze in their tracks and stared in amazement. There in the clearing, standing just where they had last seen him exactly one year ago, was their fellow Wenatchee tribesman. He stood with his arms folded over his chest, staring straight ahead as if in a trance. A strange dog was by his side. The dog barked once at the approaching hunters, then sat silently next to his master.

Eventually, they were able to rouse the man from his trance-like state. He told of being captured and held prisoner by a band of Sasquatches—the mammoth, hair-covered creatures also known as Bigfoot. For one year he had lived in their cedar bark shelters and shared their food as an equal. The Sasquatches were great hunters who were able to scamper up steep inclines and shoulder heavy loads of game. They hunted by night, leaving their crude bark houses and returning early in the morning with game. The Indian learned the signals with which the band communicated. Their sounds were much like the hooting of owls. After he lived with them for one year, the Sasquatches brought the man back to the exact spot where they found him. They hypnotized him and left a dog with him for protection.

That Wenatchee tribesman was Isabel Friedlander Arcasa's great-great-great grandfather. "The reports of the big foot prints are nothing new. We Indian people know all about those dark people even if we have never seen them." This story had been passed down through Isabel's family for generations and was regarded not as legend, but as family heritage.

Isabel Friedlander Arcasa was well known and respected for her great storytelling ability. Through Isabel, tribal lore and traditions going

Isabel Arcasa (left) and her mother "Elizabeth" Father Tom Connolly, S.J., Sacred Heart Mission, De Smet, Idaho

back thousands of years were kept and passed on to today's generations. For all of her 102 years, Isabel remained sharp witted and maintained a wonderful sense of humor. She loved to share her tales with everyone around her.

In the Indian way, Isabel had many names throughout her long life. The first girl born after five boys, her mother called her "Kee-arna," meaning "little girl." When her brother Bill could not pronounce the word, the family shortened her name to "Wana." As she grew older her mother gave her the name of her Skokomish great-grandmother, "Ti-men-wy."

Then while visiting her grandmother, she met an old woman of the San Poil Tribe to whom her grandmother had given shelter. One day the feeble old woman called young Isabel to her bedside and whispered to her, "I do not have long to live. When I die, I want you to carry on my name, 'K-new-teet-kw.' I want you to have my things and keep my name alive." The old woman then handed Isabel a long string of copper, Hudson's Bay beads, a necklace of blue and white glass beads, and two ceremonial pipes. Finally, most Indians at this time had

English names as well as Indian names. She was baptized "Isabel" by a Catholic priest.

The Wenatchee, Chelan, and Entiat Tribes accepted Catholicism around 1870 when Father Urban Grassi founded his mission in the area. Isabel's grandfather, Chief Tsil-hoo-sas-ket of the "En-tee-etkw," or Entiat Tribe, was baptized Catholic but balked when Father Grassi told him he must give up one of his two wives. Chief Tsil-hoo-sas-ket was married to Isabel's grandmother Sts-kul-nas-ket, as well as to her younger sister, La-mee-iy. Being a good Catholic, Sts-kul-nas-ket, christened Suzanne, told her husband that she would leave him so that he could marry La-mee-iy, or Rosalie, in the Catholic Church. Suzanne's children were grown, but Rosalie still had a small baby. Suzanne left her husband and returned to the camp of her father. Rosalie and Chief Tsil-hoo-sas-ket were then married in the church. Not satisfied with this arrangement, the chief rode into Suzanne's camp one day and asked her to return with him. She refused, but he would not leave. That night, saying she was going to the river to take a bath, Suzanne left camp. She escaped by paddling her canoe and swimming her horse across the Columbia River. Suzanne hid from Tsil-hoo-sas-ket until, after several days waiting, he gave up and returned to his village of Entiat. Chief Tsil-hoo-sas-ket and his brother, Wapato John, became staunch Catholics, building churches for their people in Entiat and Manson, near Lake Chelan.

❧

Isabel Friedlander was born on the banks of the Columbia River on November 22, 1889, the year Washington became a state. She was the daughter of an Entiat Indian mother and white Jewish father. Though the mixing of white men and Indian women was not uncommon in the American West, the story Isabel tells of how she became a Friedlander is truly unique and fascinating.

Isabel's mother was Skn-wheulks, later christened Elizabeth. Elizabeth's father was Tsil-hoo-sas-ket, chief of the Entiat Tribe. His father and grandfather, also named Tsil-hoo-sas-ket, had all been chiefs of the Entiat Tribe. His mother was a member of the Skokomish Tribe from western Washington. Elizabeth's mother, Sts-kul-nas-ket, or Suzanne, was descended from the Wenatchee and San Poil Tribes.*

When Elizabeth grew older, Chief Tsil-hoo-sas-ket made arrangements with the Moses Band of the Columbia Tribe for his daughter to be married to Chief Moses's younger brother, Tser-men-tsoot. In those days, the Indians arranged trades to find brides for their young men. The Moses people gave Elizabeth's father horses and possessions for his daughter.

Tser-men-tsoot was already married to a woman by the name of In-ha-noomt, who later left her husband. Elizabeth had three children by Tser-men-tsoot; only one, a baby named Mary, lived. One fall, when Mary was two years old, all of the Moses Band camped near Vantage, on the Columbia River, for their horse races. During the races, Elizabeth's husband, Tser-men-tsoot, was killed. It was the custom of these tribes that when a woman was widowed, the deceased husband's brother would become her husband. It was then the brother's obligation to provide for and watch out for the widow and her children.

All of the band went into mourning, and they buried Tser-men-tsoot. Chief Moses, Tser-men-tsoot's older brother, attended the funeral, but after it was over, he told his people it was time to move on. Chief Moses took all of Tser-men-tsoot's many racehorses and valuable belongings away with him. He even took with him a small pony belonging to the baby, Mary. In his wake, Elizabeth was left stranded with her baby and a few in-laws. Without possessions, Elizabeth stayed at the Vantage camp throughout the harsh winter.

---

* In 1872, the U.S. government established the Colville Reservation, eventually combining twelve separate tribes: the Colville, Arrow Lakes, Columbia, Chelan, Entiat, Wenatchee, Okanogan, San Poil, Methow, Nespelem, Palus, and Joseph Band of Nez Perce.

In the spring, an old woman asked Elizabeth if she wanted to return to her people. The desperate Elizabeth eagerly accepted the invitation. The elder woman gave the young widow a riding horse and a pack horse so she could return with baby Mary to her father's camp.

Elizabeth wasted no time traveling to her family's village in Entiat. Later that fall, Elizabeth went with her aunt and Uncle Louie to a little trading post across from the mouth of Lake Chelan. A soldier from Camp Chelan was running the trading post. His name was Herman Friedlander, but the Indian people called him "Peranik."

Elizabeth was a handsome woman, and Herman Friedlander could not take his eyes off her. Peranik questioned Uncle Louie about Elizabeth. "Gee, that's sure a beautiful woman! I sure would like to have her for my wife." Uncle Louie replied, "Oh, you can't have anything to do with her; she is just a widow." The soldier was undaunted, "Well, you tell her if she ever wants to get married, that I'd sure like to marry her!" Uncle Louie told Elizabeth of the conversation during the trip home.

While Elizabeth and her aunt and uncle were in Chelan, Chief Moses arrived at the camp of Elizabeth's father, Chief Tsil-hoo-sas-ket. Moses exclaimed, "I am going to come and get my little niece and my brother's wife to marry now. I will bring you some horses, saddles, blankets and valuables." Tsil-hoo-sas-ket agreed, following the Indian custom that a man could marry his deceased brother's wife and eager to obtain horses, saddles, and blankets from the other chief.

Upon returning from the trip to the trading post in Chelan, Elizabeth's father told her of Moses's visit. Elizabeth was furious when she heard of Moses's intentions. She was angry at the way Chief Moses had left her all alone with no horses in Vantage. Elizabeth declared, "I would never marry Moses, even if he was the last man on earth! Does he not realize what he has done to us? What he did to his little niece, when he took everything away from us and left us stranded? If it had not been for some good people, we would have been lost."

Elizabeth told her Uncle Louie, "You just take me back to the Chelan Trading Post tomorrow. I will marry that white man!"

The next day Elizabeth and her Uncle Louie traveled to the trading post in Chelan. Elizabeth spoke no English, so her Uncle Louie explained to Herman Friedlander the situation with Chief Moses. "She says she doesn't want him. She says she'll marry you." Herman Friedlander found the nearest justice of the peace and they were married that day!

A few weeks later, Chief Moses rode into Entiat with his string of horses for Chief Tsil-hoo-sas-ket. Elizabeth's father had to decline the horses, telling Moses, "I'm sorry, but your sister-in-law went to Chelan and got married to that white man, Peranik." With that, Moses became enraged. "I am going over there, and I'm going to kill him for taking my wife." So he left his string of horses right there and rode to the trading post.

In Chelan, Elizabeth and Herman were living in a square, canvas soldier's tent. The couple heard a rider approaching at a frantic pace. Herman took his gun outside to greet the rider. As he rode up, Moses hollered, "You took my wife! I am going to kill you! She is my wife!"

"No!" exclaimed Herman, "She is my wife. We were married by a justice of the peace."

Moses insisted, "She was my brother's wife, so now she is my wife. I am going to kill you!"

"Well, go ahead and shoot," said Herman as he leveled his rifle directly at the chief.

When Moses saw the rifle pointing at him, he became silent. He turned his horse around and rode off, never to return.

For the first few years of their marriage, Herman and Elizabeth lived in Chelan where he ran a small store and saloon. Herman Friedlander had been born into a wealthy East Coast family, but his father disowned him for marrying a full-blooded Indian woman. Herman's two brothers,

Frank and Sam, also came west and founded jewelry stores bearing their name in Seattle and Portland.

From Chelan, Elizabeth, Herman, and Mary moved up the Columbia River to Lincoln, across from the San Poil Tribe's Village of White Stone, where Elizabeth's family lived. Herman bought a farm with an orchard and ran a store in the nearby town of Wilbur. The Friedlanders lived happily and had seven children together: Louie, Sam, Herman, Bill, Isabel, Millie, and Ed. Elizabeth and Herman never spoke the same language, though they probably both spoke some Chinook jargon. The children spoke the languages of both their parents and they grew up paddling canoes back and forth across the river between their farm and the San Poil village of cabins and tepees, where their grandparents lived.

Herman Friedlander died of a heart ailment when Isabel was only eight years old. Elizabeth eventually sold the farm and store and moved to the White Stone Village with her parents. In those days, many generations lived under one roof so houses were full with beds covering every inch of the floor at night. Elizabeth later married an Indian man, Charlie Comedale, who died within a year of their marriage.

At the age of six, Isabel and her brothers were sent to the Indian boarding school in Tonasket. When the school burned, Isabel was transferred to the mission schools in Omak and Ward. At just seven years old, Isabel took her five-year-old sister, Millie, and ran away from school. Her older brother found the sisters and returned them to the school.

The nuns at the mission schools punished the students when they spoke their Native Indian languages. After three years of such treatment, the children could barely understand their aunt when she came to take them home. Once home, they regained fluency in their language quickly. Isabel was then sent to school at Fort Spokane where she remained until she was fifteen.

Arranged marriages were still common among Indian people when Isabel was a young girl. Trading horses and cattle with Isabel's stepfather, a man arranged a marriage between fourteen-year-old Isabel and his son. Despite her mother and aunt's objections and Isabel's cries, the two youngsters were married by a priest. Upon leaving the church, other children teased Isabel and in anger, she threw her wedding ring into the dirt and ran off. The two never lived together as husband and wife.

When she was eighteen, a man from the Umatilla Tribe named Julius LaCourse asked for her hand. Worried about the validity of her first marriage, Isabel consulted a priest who told her he would have to write a letter to the Pope. A month later, the papal letter arrived and dictated, "This woman is not an animal that can be sold. Her parents cannot accept presents and sell her like an animal. Her first marriage is annulled."

Isabel married Julius LaCourse and they moved to Pendleton, Oregon. Five children were born to them: Herman, Melvin, Maybelle, and two babies that died in infancy. The family moved where there was work—living in Pendleton, Nespelem, Quincy, Taholah, and Seattle. All of the family worked as migrants, following the crops during the summer, then settling in so the children could attend school in the fall. When her daughter, Maybelle, became sick with tuberculosis, Isabel took a job at Cushman Hospital in Tacoma to be near her.

Julius was a talented musician. He played violin, with Isabel who played piano, in a dance band that played for grange hall dances on weekends. With their children lying beside them on a mattress they brought from home, Isabel and Julius played late into the night.

After twenty-three years of marriage, Isabel gave Julius an ultimatum— he had to quit drinking or she would leave him. When he refused to give up the bottle, she left, divorcing him, although she remained a practicing Catholic. She met her next husband, Marcel Arcasa, while she was working at a youth camp on the Colville Reservation.

Isabel knew a lifetime of hard labor, working as both a cook and waitress. She plowed fields, worked farms, nursed the sick, and acted as a midwife. As a midwife she brought twenty-eight babies into the world and saved the lives of two of their mothers.

Besides raising her own three children, she raised five orphans. In her eighties, she took in her three-year-old great-grandson when his parents were killed.

For her tireless work on behalf of the church and community, Isabel received a papal blessing and Pro Ecclesia Et Pontifice award from the Catholic Church. Always looking after those in need, she canned fruits and vegetables to give hungry families to tide them over through the winters. Young priests were taken under her wing as soon as they moved to her town of Nespelem.

In 1989, Isabel celebrated her one hundredth birthday, the same year the state of Washington celebrated its centennial. The Eastern Washington Historical Society awarded her the honor of "Pioneer of the Year." Along with other centenarians, Isabel was invited to an honorary dinner at the State Capitol. Seated next to Governor Booth Gardner, she entertained him with stories of capturing and racing wild horses in her youth. She was not afraid of the wild ones she explained, it was the tame horses that always bucked her off!

Though most of her prized possessions (including woven baskets, beaded bags, moccasins, dresses, and two tepees) burned in a house fire, Isabel was rich in family and friends. She had grandchildren, great-grandchildren, and even great-great-grandchildren at the time of her death, not to mention her countless nieces and nephews. Many accomplished women can be counted among Isabel's descendants, including her niece Lucy Friedlander Covington, who was a Colville tribal council-woman of great renown. A tireless champion of Indian rights, it has been said that without Lucy's efforts, the Colville Reservation might have been lost to the Termination Bills of the 1960s. Isabel's granddaughter, Anita Dupris, is an attorney, who has worked for years as a judge in the Colville tribal court system.

Isabel passed away on April 24, 1992, at the age of 102. As a legacy to her people, Isabel left behind many stories and legends in the form of manuscripts and tapes of interviews she gave in her twilight years. Always happy to be interviewed, she told her friend, Father Tom Connolly, as he prepared audiotapes of her histories, "I don't care if anyone hears my voice after I'm gone. That's the only way I can haunt you folks!"

MAUDE C. LILLIE BOLIN

1891–1966

YAKAMA COWGIRL AVIATOR

Fingers tightly clenching the plane's doorway as her clothing was whipped about by the wind, the dark-haired, young woman summoned up her courage and leapt from the airplane. Free falling downward toward the earth, Maude pulled at her parachute cord. The chute opened, stopping her plunge with an abrupt jerk. She then enjoyed the pleasant experience of drifting through space to the ground. "I don't think I'll take another jump soon unless it becomes necessary, but I certainly enjoyed the sensation of the two trial jumps," Maude assessed.

Maude made two such parachute jumps as a prerequisite to receiving her pilot's license. Learning to fly in 1927, just nine years after Amelia Earhart began flying, Maude was one of Washington State's early female aviators. She was one of only two women living in the Yakima Valley to pilot a plane solo, and the first American Indian woman (a member of the Yakama Tribe) in the state, and probably the country, to fly.

Her first attempt to fly solo was one of Maude's biggest thrills. She described how difficult it was for a beginner to hold a plane steady but, finally, she learned to handle the control stick. Making a good landing was her hardest problem. Still, she persevered until she was able to bring her plane to earth without serious jolts or "zooms."

Maude loved flying, participating in air shows and cross-country flights. In 1928, Maude made her first cross-country flight. With another pilot, she flew across the country dropping campaign literature for Senator C. C. Dill. A charter member of the Yakima Lady Birds, a woman's aviation club formed in 1928, she endeavored to make women of the Yakima Valley more flight minded.

Maude Bolin Lowell Evans, Toppenish, WA

In 1930, after receiving her solo pilot's license, Maude traveled with the Pacific Northwest Air Tour. Forty planes started out on the tour of sixteen Northwest cities and towns. Maude's plane was one of the few that actually completed the circuit, making all of the sixteen scheduled stops. The Pacific Northwest Air Tour had great educational value for the visitors at local airports, as well as for the pilots. Maude claimed that participating had greatly increased her confidence in her solo flying skills.

The next year, in 1931, while en route to an air meet in Cleveland, Ohio, Maude's plane was involved in a collision. She was one of four pilots traveling from Seattle to Cleveland as part of the Pacific Northwest Air Tour. Maude's plane was the first of the four to land. Minutes after landing her plane at an airstrip in Montana, it was hit by a Seattle plane attempting to land. The Seattle pilot had entered a crosscurrent of wind as he attempted his landing, causing it to collide with Maude's plane on the landing strip. Both planes were demolished; only the engine and propeller were salvaged from Maude's plane. She received some compensation from the other pilot and expected to be able to buy a new plane. Her husband, Charles Bolin, drove to Montana from their home in Toppenish to retrieve his wife.

While flying, problems Maude encountered included inclement weather, poor visibility, and overheating radiators—all inherent dangers to a solo Northwest pilot. On another occasion Maude's biplane struck a tractor during a landing, shearing off a wing.

Flying airplanes was just Maude's latest venture in feminine independence. Her earlier career as a cowgirl and rodeo performer also required a great deal of courage, skill, and endurance. Maude performed with the Spain Brothers' rodeo shows throughout the West. A daredevil, she often raced horses in rodeos such as the Pendleton Round-Up, Ellensburg Rodeo, and Toppenish Pow Wow.

She frequently competed in the women's relay race, a top feature in Northwest rodeos. In the relays, one person holds the string of tough-mouthed, relay ponies, while the rider makes the quick change of mount needed for the race. Riders were to run three laps on three different mounts, changing horses after each lap. The races were treacherous, requiring bravery and expert riding skills. Well into her thirties, Maude still rode in the relays during the Toppenish Pow Wow, although she admitted that participating in the contest without practice was now difficult.

∞

Maude's roots were in the Northwest's earliest pioneer days. Her father was the first white settler on the Yakama* Indian Reservation, in the Yakima Valley. Her mother was a member of the Yakama Indian Tribal Nation, as was Maude. The Yakama Reservation was created by treaty

---

* Recently the Yakama Tribe resumed the traditional spelling of their name, rather than using "Yakima" as the city and valley do.

in 1855, which was ratified by Congress in 1858. White men were not allowed to enter the reservation without the tribe's permission and the approval of the Indian Agency.

Nevada Lillie, Maude's father, had crossed the plains to settle in the Washington Territory. He drove stagecoaches throughout central Washington. Nevada was a pioneer with a large interest of livestock. He contributed substantially to the development of the Yakima Valley. In addition to ranching and driving stage, Nevada served for many years as a United States deputy marshal. Josephine (Bowzer) Lillie, Maude's mother, earned the title of "Mother of Toppenish," because forty of her eighty acres of Indian allotment land was platted to become the business district for the town of Toppenish.

Congress passed the Allotment Act of 1887 with the idea of turning Indians into farmers by allotting them from 40 to 160 acres of land in their own names instead of the tribe's. The 1912 census showed 4,548 allotments had been issued to Yakama tribal members, with each man, woman, and child receiving a typical tract of eighty acres. Unlike reservation land, the allotments (with the granting of a fee patent approved by the Department of Indian Affairs) could become deeded land vested in the owner's name and sold to white settlers. The results of the act were sometimes disastrous, as individual Indians who were uninterested in farming sold or lost their land to taxes. By the time the act was repealed fifty years later, Indian land holdings in the United States had dropped from 136 million acres to only fifty million acres.

No one took advantage of Josephine Lillie, a progressive, forward-looking woman, vitally interested in community affairs. Josie filed her plat with the Yakima County Commission on April 4, 1905. The platted land became the business district of Toppenish. Toppenish is the Yakama term for "sloping and spreading" and describes the sloping plains of the west end of the reservation's valley. The town boomed, and lots within the forty acres sold like hotcakes. This became the first deeded land on the Yakama Reservation.

A trading post license was granted to the Lillies by the government in 1890. They erected a small building and opened a store and post office. Josephine served as the town's postmistress and operated the first store. Maude Claire Lillie, born on July 25, 1891, was the fifth of eight children born to the Lillies.

Nevada and Josie Lillie separated in 1898, and Josephine, seeking a better education for her children, moved them to Portland, Oregon. Maude studied drama, elocution, and millinery at the Western Academy of Elocution and Dramatics. In a 1929 newspaper interview, Maude stated her original goals,

> *I wanted to be an actress always, but though I studied for a career on the stage my mother would never give her sanction to such "wild" plans. I served six months' apprentice as a beauty parlor worker once and again I learned the millinery trade by serving a six months' apprenticeship there.*

On August 1, 1911, Maude Claire Lillie married Charles F. Bolin, a prominent attorney, cowboy, and Yakima Valley baseball star. The Bolins built a grand manor in Toppenish, the finest home located on the Yakama Indian Reservation. Their mansion was centered on an eighty-acre ranch including Maude's allotment, adjoining the town of Toppenish. Although the couple had no children of their own, for a time they raised two children belonging to Maude's sister.

Maude became an experienced rodeo performer and ran her own round-up business in Toppenish. At their ranch, Maude and Charley Bolin organized the first Indian Fair and Round Up in Toppenish, later taking their show on the road. In these shows, Maude performed with many notable rodeo cowboys and cowgirls of the day. Maude's Yakama

Indian ancestors were known as accomplished horse riders. When Lewis and Clark explored the Northwest in 1805, the Yakamas had been horsemen for seventy-five years.

Her career as a professional rodeo rider began with the Spain Brothers' Western Show. John Spain, the handsome gentleman cowboy, was a renowned bronc rider in his day. As a young man, John won the title in the World Championship Saddle Broncbusting Contest at the second Pendleton Round-Up, held in 1911. In the famous incident, after a last-go-around, one judge's vote settled a three-way-tie between John, George Fletcher (the famous Black cowboy), and Jackson Sundown (a noted Nez Perce bronc rider). John continued to win rodeo purses even after losing his hand in a roping accident.

Maude, a pretty, dark-eyed brunette, was also a sought-after singer who was often featured at important Toppenish weddings, funerals, and social affairs. The talented lady might one day be found daintily pouring tea at a social affair, and the next day be seen clad in soiled coveralls at the airport.

Using her dramatic and musical training, Maude directed young members of her tribe in a gala production of *Hiawatha's Wedding Feast*, performed for the community in 1936. It was the first time a Northwest production had used Indian actors and actresses exclusively in a production about Indians. Maude took great satisfaction in helping the Yakama actors, mostly high-school students or younger, achieve success with the production. She was proud of the youngsters, feeling many of them had voices that with training would far surpass the ordinary. Maude reported,

> *There was not a trained voice among them. As for the dances—well, of course, they did not need training for them. They were dances every Indian child knows from the time he can stand and walk and run. They didn't rehearse those—they just did them. The dances were outstanding features to the pageant.*

To make the most of the limited time permitted for practice before the performance, Maude said she repeatedly summoned to their minds the stately memory of their grandparents, and they responded by fitting their actions to that memory.

Maude again directed young Yakamas in a presentation of *Sacajawea,* performed at the 1948 Toppenish Pow Wow. *Sacajawea* had a cast of 120 people, mostly tribal members. The pageant was performed on three successive nights at the Toppenish Pow Wow and was host to most of the population of the Yakima Valley. Maude's goal was to put on a show using young Native American performers that was historically accurate as well as emotionally appealing. This endeavor was a great success.

An asset to her community, Maude was called upon to lead a wide variety of community projects. In 1942, she headed the local United China Relief Committee, which succeeded in raising more than the Toppenish quota of contributions for Chinese war relief during World War II. She appealed to the citizens of Toppenish stating, "Contributions will help to maintain Chinese morale at this supreme hour of crisis and keep open our one unbroken fighting front in the Far East."

In 1946, the town of Toppenish sponsored a drive to have its own general hospital. Maude generously contributed three quarters of an acre of land for the site of the Central Memorial Hospital, now known as Providence Hospital, which opened its doors in 1951.

In 1950, Maude, with the assistance of the city of Toppenish and the Chamber of Commerce, appealed to the Commissioner of Indian Affairs in Washington, D.C., for a fee patent on her allotted land in order to deed it over to the city of Toppenish. The allotted land was held in trust for Maude as a member of the Yakama Tribe and could not be deeded to a non-Indian without permission of the Department of Indian Affairs. The trust land lay across several streets within city limits, and the land was needed to extend the city limits and ensure the continued growth of the town of Toppenish. The patent was approved, and Maude's land was annexed to the city, becoming "Bolin's Green Addition."

Another act of Maude's generosity was to offer to donate her home to the town of Toppenish as a museum for the purpose of preserving antiques, historical relics, and art of both the Yakama people and the settlers. The gracious Bolin mansion, built in 1911, shortly after Maude's marriage to Charles Bolin, was a focal point in Toppenish. Mrs. Bolin stated, "I want to donate my home as a memorial to my mother, the mother of Toppenish. All of the wonderful handcrafts and arts of the Indians and the history of this reservation town should be preserved for posterity." Unfortunately, the city, fearing a lack of funds would prevent them from maintaining the home, refused the offer. The city did accept Maude's donation of land for a city park. The park was named Pioneer Park and dedicated to the memory of local pioneers.

In 1959, she was sent as a local representative from Region V to a White House Conference on Children and Youth. The Toppenish Pow Wow named July 2, 1960, Maude Bolin Day, in honor of all that she had contributed to the Pow Wow and to her town. Maude passed away just six years later, on February 17, 1966, at the age of seventy-four.

Professional cowgirl, singer, aviator, drama coach, community leader—all of this comprised the multifaceted character of Maude Bolin. As a role model for the community and for her Yakama Tribe, Maude modeled independence, courage, and diversity at a time when women were expected to find fulfillment solely in the home.

PANG YEE CHING

1892–1992
JOURNEY TO "GAM SAAN"

Bags packed, ready to disembark, the young Chinese bride listened to the hustle and bustle of the passengers on the upper decks shuffling their luggage about as they prepared to leave the ship. The ship, SS *Mongolia,* was now docked in San Francisco Bay, and the first- and second-class passengers were disembarking. Soon, thought Yee Ching, her family would be free to enter "Gam Saan," the golden hills of America, to pursue their dream of building a new life.

Yee Ching, five months pregnant with her first child, had already endured nearly two months of difficult ocean travel in the ship's crowded, lowest-class quarters. Not only had she been confined to the underbelly of the ship during most of the voyage, but she and her husband had been housed next to the boiler room throughout the trip. Now, the journey had ended; she could not wait to begin life in America with her husband of just one year.

Yee Ching and her husband, Lee Je Yuen, found their excitement to be short lived. The couple now had to wait in what seemed an endless line for their papers to be inspected by U.S. immigration officials. "Do not worry," Je Yuen assured his young wife, "Our papers are in order, there will be no problem." What was happening? The Lees watched as some well-dressed Chinese people were directed off the ship, but others were sent toward a smaller boat waiting on the pier.

Finally, an immigration official examined their papers and asked Je Yuen questions, which he answered in broken English. When the official had finished questioning the couple, the official pointed to the waiting boat, "That way." Confused and frightened, the couple followed directions. The Lees now found themselves aboard a small boat bound for an

Pang Yee Ching Lucile Lill

isolated island in San Francisco Bay where they were told there would be more questions. The Lees, like most Chinese immigrants from 1910 to 1940, were being sent to Angel Island to face an intimidating immigration process.

When they arrived at Angel Island,* Yee Ching felt her heart drop as she was directed to a building on one side of the camp and her husband to another. She was led to a long barracks that contained about one hundred metal-framed beds with dingy bedding. Guards locked the doors to the barracks behind her. Yee Ching was separated from her husband for the next few weeks; she was assigned a number, fed boiled meat and vegetables that often made her and the others sick, and subjected to humiliating physical examinations and terrifying interrogations.

The interrogations consisted of a series of mundane, irrelevant questions about the immigrants themselves, their families, and their villages in China. If the interrogators detected any inconsistencies in the immigrants' answers, they were sent back to their barracks to await further questioning on another day. Many Chinese immigrants failed to satisfy the interrogators due to their fear and nervousness at being grilled and confined in such a manner.

The Chinese Exclusion Act, prohibiting Chinese laborers from immigrating and denying citizenship to newly arrived Chinese, was passed in 1882. Merchants, teachers, students, and visitors were exempt from this law but still could not become U.S. citizens. The Angel Island Immigration Compound was built to enforce the Chinese Exclusion Act. For the first time in American history, a group of people were denied entry into the country based solely on their race. The Chinese Exclusion Act was not repealed until 1943. Some Chinese were detained for

---

* The description of the Lees' stay on Angel Island is based on a compilation of Chinese immigrants' experiences, rather than on specific memories described by Yee Ching.

months, or even years. The Lees were quarantined on Angel Island for two weeks before being allowed to enter the country.

∽

The third of seven children, Pang Yee Ching was born to Pang Shu Kaui and Chung Chow Ying on December 30, 1892, in Fa Yuen, Gow Yuen Chong Village in Canton, China. The Gow Yuen Chong Village in Fa Yuen, Canton, was populated by one hundred people, all members of the Pang family, who spoke the "Hack Ga" dialect. Most in the village were hard-working farmers who grew vegetables, sugar cane, sweet potatoes, and taro root. Extended families lived under the same roof where grandparents cared for the children while both mothers and fathers worked in the fields. The village centered around a large pond in which fish were raised both to feed the villagers and for market.

At age three, Yee Ching moved with her family to Hong Kong. Her father, Pang Shu Kuai, had worked as a jade cutter in his native village, but in hope of a brighter future, he moved his family to Hong Kong where he took a job as a custodian and messenger for the American Wellesley Presbyterian Church. As part of his compensation, the family was provided living quarters at the rear of the church. Though cramped, these accommodations were modern by comparison to their windowless, tile-roofed village home constructed of bricks mixed with clay, mud, rice, and wheat. In Hong Kong his children were educated by the Presbyterian missionaries. It was here that Pang Shu Kuai and his family converted from Buddhism to Christianity.

Even though it was unusual for Chinese families to educate their daughters, Yee Ching and her older sister, Tai Yee, were sent to boarding school in Canton. At eleven years of age, Yee Ching and her sister set out on a three-day boat trip before arriving at the Sok Ching Elementary School in Canton. The family paid one dollar per month for tuition, room, and board for each student.

After six years of study at Sok Ching, Yee Ching, an exemplary student, was asked by the school's principal to teach school. The principal secured special permission from Yee Ching's parents and then hired the sixteen-year-old to teach grades one through three. She sent for her younger sister, Yee Paw, and supported her on a meager teaching salary. At first, Yee Ching found teaching school difficult because of her young age and lack of teaching experience. Many days she was reduced to tears of frustration. Still, she continued teaching at Sok Ching for three more years.

While teaching in the Hoy San District, Yee Ching met her husband, Lee Je Yuen. Lee Je Yuen had graduated from the Presbyterian Theological Seminary in Canton, China, on January 12, 1911. At that time in China, arranged marriages were the norm, but Yee Ching and Je Yuen fell in love. Observing tradition, Yee Ching's father took "hom toy," or salted greens, to the Lee family village as a gift prior to the wedding.

Pang Yee Ching and Lee Je Yuen were married in a Presbyterian church in Canton on January 1, 1914. Yee Ching wore a light blue silk dress and a white veil. She and her bridesmaid were carried to the church in a traditional bridal chair shouldered by two attendants.

After her marriage, Yee Ching continued to teach while Je Yuen attended school in Canton to learn English. The couple dreamed of coming to America. Je Yuen applied to the American Consulate in Hong Kong for the papers needed to go to America. In addition, he took a test to ensure he had the proper qualifications to teach in the United States. Using borrowed money for their passage, the young couple boarded the SS *Mongolia* for America in 1915.

Following their two-week detention on Angel Island, the Lees settled in Los Angeles's Chinatown where they were hired to teach Chinese to young residents. The school was adjacent to a church, and the Lees were given living quarters in half of the school building. They later moved into Je Yuen's brother's home. Both Yee Ching and her husband became ill with tuberculosis during their first few years in Los Angeles. Yee Ching was sent to a sanitarium for recovery.

When his friend, Lee Yick Soo, retired as minister of Los Angeles's Chinese Presbyterian Church, Je Yuen was called upon to be the church's pastor. An integral part of the church, Yee Ching taught Sunday school, worked with the Women's Association, and was the church pianist. Yee Ching had learned to play the organ at the school in China simply by watching the organist. She not only played the old piano at the back of the church for her family as a girl, but taught her younger siblings to play.

Both Yee Ching and Je Yuen continued their work as teachers at the Chinese school. During this ten-year period, the couple was blessed with three children, whom they taught to speak their father's native Hoy San dialect. The children also attended classes at the church school where their parents taught.

After his contract with the church expired in 1925, Je Yuen decided to return to China to continue his ministry. He proceeded to apply for passage to China for his entire family. With China in the throes of constant political and economic turmoil, Yee Ching vehemently opposed returning the family to their native land. Her staunch argument was that, not only was the timing bad, but they could not ignore the fact that America offered far superior, unlimited educational opportunities for the growth of their children. In a surprising display of independence for a Chinese wife, she told her husband that if he returned to China, she would not go with him.

While all of this was being considered, a family friend, Tom Foo Yuen, convinced Je Yuen to move with him to Spokane, Washington, to run an herb shop he had purchased. The pregnant Yee Ching and her children moved in with a cousin while her husband traveled to Washington to start the business. That fall of 1926, Yee Ching gave birth to her fourth child.

When her husband sent for her in 1927, Yee Ching and her four children traveled three days by train to a new, unknown western city, Spokane. Tom Foo Yuen and Lee Je Yuen formed a partnership and named their business Foo Yuen Herb Company. Tom taught Je Yuen and Yee Ching the herbal profession, passing on an art that had been passed from generation to generation for five thousand years. The partners hired a Chinese herb pharmacist to help with the business, but within two years of the shop's inception, the hired pharmacist left the company, and Mr. Tom retired. This left Yee Ching as her husband's sole professional assistant in his business. The children helped out with the business, performing clerical and custodial duties at early ages, just as Yee Ching had helped her family earn their living in China.

Due to the Lee family's hard work, the business endured although the herb shop's first years of operation were slow. Yee Ching's innovations aided in the business's eventual prosperity. The Foo Yuen Herb Company was located over the Manning Cafe in downtown Spokane. When she heard the cafe's proprietors talking about obtaining new kitchen appliances, Yee Ching marched into the restaurant and asked them what they were planning to do with their old electric coffee grinder. Surprised, the proprietors presented Yee Ching with the grinder for a small fee. The Lees were then able to grind their precious imported Chinese herbs more efficiently and with less effort than the old mortar and pestle had required.

The Foo Yuen Herb Company sold nothing but Chinese herbs, gathered wild in the mountains of China. During World War II, importing became difficult and exorbitantly expensive. Fortunately, the Lees had had the foresight to stockpile Chinese herbs before the war began and had enough herbs saved to avoid the high prices of importing during the war years. Without these efforts, the Foo Yuen Herb Company might not have survived World War II.

Upon entering the herb shop, customers were greeted by a tangy, pungent, spicy aroma. Glass cases contained a variety of barks, roots, leaves, and shoots waiting to be ground, steeped, and used as remedies for rheumatism, nervous disorders, weakness, stomach pains, colds, and flu. Patients often sought out the Lees for treatment as a last resort for curing their ails. Most of their customers were Caucasians, rather than Chinese, and more European immigrants than Americans sought treatment. Germans especially believed in the Chinese herbal treatments.

In addition to riding the cable cars into downtown Spokane to work at the herb company, Yee Ching raised her seven children in their humble wood- and coal-heated home. She grew her own vegetables and herbs, as proper Chinese vegetables could not be found in Spokane. Using her clothesline, Yee Ching hung bunches of greens out to dry and made traditional hom toy. In the hot summer, she canned fruits and jams over her wood-fueled range. Her Maytag washing machine was a blessing compared to the hand-carved bamboo washboards she had used in China. Even with this modern convenience, she rinsed her laundry in the upstairs bathtub in order to preserve the soapy water for multiple loads of wash.

The Lees purchased their first home in America in Spokane near St. Luke's Hospital. The location of their house proved useful, as Yee Ching walked to the hospital for the delivery of her next three babies, twin boys and a girl. Even with the addition of a third bedroom, which Yee Ching had insisted her husband have built, the family—now with seven children—was crowded in their small home. During her early years in China, Yee Ching had been raised in a small dirt-floored house that had been home to her family for generations. Many family members shared the home with each other, as well as with village chickens, pigs, and cows. When thinking back to her childhood, this small house in Spokane, though crowded, must have seemed very modern with its running water and indoor bathroom.

There were very few Chinese people in Spokane in the early twentieth century. At one time, the Chinese community in and around Spokane had been much larger. A *Spokesman-Review* reporter estimated the Chinese population in 1888 at approximately six hundred. These were mostly young men brought over in the 1860s to build the railroads. Prior to that, Chinese prospectors mined for gold with dreams of making a fortune and returning to China. It was not legal for any of these workers to bring wives into the United States. Only American-born Chinese, Chinese dignitaries, and a few merchants were allowed to do so. By the 1940s, Spokane's Chinese population had dwindled to approximately one hundred. As a result, for the first four decades of this century, there were very few Chinese women in Spokane and Yeé Ching had little female companionship. This was in sharp contrast to her Los Angeles days, when she worked in the Chinese church surrounded by many lady members and friends.

Although Yee Ching missed this aspect of her life, the dual role she now had of being a working mother did not leave her much leisure time. She pushed aside thoughts of loneliness and concentrated on her priority of being a good mother, centering her leisure moments around her children. She homeschooled the four youngest children in Chinese, teaching them the fundamentals of reading and writing, along with Chinese prayers, songs, and rhymes. They, in turn, helped her gain proficiency reading English.

Through her creativity and resourcefulness, Yee Ching enhanced their playtimes too. She helped her children make newspaper kites; race cars from empty thread spools, wax, and rubber bands; wooden guns with strips of old inner tubes for ammunition; slingshots from tree branches; and wooden scooters with cast-off roller skate wheels. She genuinely enjoyed playing along with her children. In her later years, she played mahjong and American and Chinese checkers with her friends and family, but she also enjoyed more active endeavors. She relished the games of pool and ping-pong and liked to hit golf and tennis balls. At age eighty-eight, Yee Ching fell and broke her hip while playing badminton!

The Foo Yuen Herb Company operated in Spokane from 1925 to 1957, when the Lees retired and returned to Hong Kong for a visit while their new house was being built in Spokane. Mr. Lee died in 1971, following complications from a stroke. His obituary lauded Lee Je Yuen as a revered leader in Spokane's Chinese community. Je Yuen was head of the Kuo Min Tang, a Chinese political organization founded by Generalissimo Chiang K'ai-shek. The Tang (not to be confused with a Tong, or Chinese secret society) was the main avenue for money sent to buy supplies for the Chinese Army to defend China against the invading Japanese Army during World War II. The Lees were responsible for supervising Spokane's collections for Chinese war relief. Like other Chinese-Americans, the Lees were required to wear buttons identifying them as Chinese, rather than Japanese, during World War II.

Je Yuen and Yee Ching held church services in their home, with Yee Ching playing the piano and directing hymn singing. In her later years, Mrs. Lee was often called upon to say eulogies for deceased members of the Chinese community, whether she knew them or not.

When invited to participate in planning a formal Chinese church in Spokane, Yee Ching, then a widow, enthusiastically agreed. She opened up her home for meetings and worship services. Finally, the Chinese Baptist Church of Spokane was established in the early 1970s. The Chinese community in Spokane had grown considerably by this time and church attendance was promising. Yee Ching was very proud to be a founding member of the church. Until her death, she was a loyal supporter of the church and enjoyed involvement in all of its activities. Once again, she had found a home in a Chinese church and the fellowship and camaraderie she had been deprived of in her early years of living in eastern Washington.

A long anticipated visit occurred when Yee Paw, Yee Ching's sister, arrived for a visit from Hong Kong. Yee Paw, or Fifth Auntie as the children called her, was the sister Yee Ching had supported in Hong Kong with her small teaching salary. Both sisters, now well into their eighties, were hard of hearing, so they communicated by writing notes to each other in Chinese. Yee Ching, eighty-four, took her younger sister rowing on Hayden Lake, and the two enjoyed many mahjong games together before Yee Paw returned to Hong Kong.

Yee Ching's eldest daughter, a retired public school teacher, began tutoring several Chinese immigrants from Hong Kong and Taiwan who were eager to learn English. They met in the daughter's home, gathering around the breakfast nook. Yee Ching, who was living with her daughter, was then in her eighties. Whenever students came, Yee Ching joined in the class with enthusiasm! Her interest was twofold; not only did she relish the opportunity to improve her own English, but she knew she could help in teaching. When her daughter could not get an explanation across to her students in either Cantonese or fumbling Mandarin, Yee Ching would bridge the gap and write in Chinese characters, since the written characters are exactly the same, irrespective of spoken dialects. Indeed, she still had the knack of teaching!

Though she raised her children in a mostly Caucasian community, with no support system and little English, Lee Yee Ching's seven children were all exceptional students who went on to become class officers and valedictorians. Three of Yee Ching's sons became doctors, one became a dentist, and the fourth son and two daughters became educators.

When one of her daughters agonized over the decision to marry a Caucasian, Yee Ching strongly and convincingly encouraged her, showing a wisdom and tolerance uncommon for older Chinese in the early 1950s. As she often told her children, "We are all made out of the same dough, when God put us in the oven to bake, some just came out a little browner, and with different features." Yee Ching was right, America—"Gam Saan"—did offer her children golden opportunities. She and her husband were very proud of their children's educational achievements, their military and professional careers, and their subsequent marriages and families.

Yee Ching Lee died on December 31, 1992, one day after her one hundredth birthday. A teacher, pastor's wife, business owner, founding member of Spokane's Chinese Baptist Church, mother, grandmother, and great-grandmother—Yee Ching Lee had been an inspiration to those who knew her throughout her one hundred years.

HAZEL WOLF

1898–2000

CITIZEN OF THREE CENTURIES

When the two INS agents entered the downtown Seattle office, they found the foreign-born subversive they were seeking, flashed their badges, and announced their intention to arrest the alien worker. The tiny figure continued to tie up the transcripts she had been preparing to send to a client, and told the men that they would have to wait until she had finished. She could barely hide her trembling hands as she bound together the bunch of legal transcripts and called the messenger service to come pick it up. She pushed the office intercom to tell her boss that she was being arrested before allowing the agents to take her away.

The Immigration and Naturalization Service detained the middle-aged legal secretary at an Immigration Detention Center where she was placed in a cell with two young Canadian women. The teens, a waitress and a nursing student, asked the reason for their cellmate's arrest, to which she replied, "I've been accused of trying to overthrow the government by force and violence." Thinking the girls would be amused, she was surprised at their reply: "The government ought to be overthrown!" Not long after that, reporters showed up at the jail and were turned away, only to persist until they got their quote, "The American people will see to it that I'm not deported." The quote was picked up and run by the Seattle press under headlines like "Red Secretary."

Hazel Wolf did not spend more than half a day in jail before her friends paid her $500 bail. After living as a legal, resident-alien in the United States for twenty-four years, and involvement with labor unions and Communists, Mrs. Wolf told the papers that she wasn't sure why she was targeted that day for arrest. In her traditional manner of taking

Hazel Wolf Gary Braasch Photography

up causes, and advocating for others, she made sure that the two Canadian girls received assistance from a Travelers' Aid group who took them safely home to Vancouver, British Columbia. Hazel's advocacy on behalf of immigrants would become a lifelong endeavor. As for her own case, it would take nearly fifteen years of litigation, including hearings before the U.S. Supreme Court, before her deportation order was canceled.

Mrs. Wolf had been swept up as part of the anti-Communist hysteria during the McCarthy Era of the 1950s, one of many people identified in investigations supposedly meant to uncover disloyalty to the country and subversive political activity. Though she had severed her ties with the local Communist Party years before her arrest, she never tried to deny her party membership. It was just one chapter in the long history of social and environmental activism that defined this woman's 101 years.

How did this lifelong activist come to join the Communist Party? Quite by accident she happened to meet a man with a petition while waiting in line for a food voucher. It was 1934 during the Great Depression, when jobs were scarce and unemployment insurance and Social Security were nonexistent. The man told Hazel that the intent of the petition was to ask the Washington Legislature to give unemployment benefits to the jobless. Intrigued, Hazel decided to attend one of the group's meetings. When she showed up at the home where the meeting was to be held, she found an eviction in progress. The sheriff and his men were carrying the family's furniture out of the home, so party members took action, picking up the family's belongings and returning them to the house through the back door. The sheriff finally gave up on the eviction and left. During her days as a Communist, Hazel fought for food and shelter for the underprivileged, for women's rights, and against racism. As the Depression wound down, these needs seemed less urgent and Hazel lost interest in the party in the early 1940s. Years later she was arrested as an alien who had once been a member of a subversive organization.

Ironically, Hazel Anna Cummings Anderson had been born under an American flag in a hotel in Victoria, British Columbia, on March 10, 1898. Her mother, an American, had left Tacoma two weeks earlier so that her husband's family could assist with the birth while he, a sergeant in the Merchant Marines, was away at sea. Because Mrs. Anderson was dismayed at having her child born on foreign soil, she hung the American flag over the birthing bed, even though she had lost her own citizenship for marrying a Scottish-Canadian.

During the long deportation process, the United States attempted to send Hazel to Canada, but that country refused to accept her because she had been married to an American. The Immigration Service next tried to deport her to England since her father was originally from Scotland. The British Parliament declined to take her in part because she had once been institutionalized for tuberculosis. Attorneys for whom she worked, Barry Hatten and John Caughlan, argued her case for over fourteen years. As his legal secretary Hazel often debated with John about who actually worked for whom. Eventually, the 9th Circuit Court of Appeals stayed the deportation order and remanded the case to an administrative panel. In the end the Immigration and Naturalization Service finally gave up, dismissing her deportation order in December 1963. At some point in the struggle, Hazel decided not to worry about something that may or may not ever happen and set about to fight other battles—for the environment, wildlife, clean air and water, open spaces in cities, and wilderness preservation. As she told high school students at Rainier Beach High School in 1990, she fought for "many issues that we face today due to the destruction of so much of the earth on which we live."

Hazel Wolf, who gave herself the nickname "Leo" as a child, grew up poor in a rundown British Columbia neighborhood. Her Merchant

Marine father had been injured at sea and spent many years in a wheel-chair while his wife struggled to support him and their three children. He died of his injuries when Hazel was ten years old. Though poor, young Hazel was happy, athletic, and spent most of her time outdoors—swimming, boating, and playing with the local boys.

Leo came to activism and organizing early in life, challenging her eighth-grade principal to let girls play basketball. He agreed to provide the field and equipment if she could organize two teams. When she succeeded in forming the teams, the principal had to allow girls' basketball. She described the incident as being her first experience organizing on behalf of women's liberation.

Hazel did not go on to high school because she had to work to help support her family. At fifteen she enrolled in a business college for a six-month secretarial training class. This set her path as a secretary, a career she held from age sixteen to sixty-seven, mostly working for law firms.

After a failed marriage, the young, single mother came to Seattle in 1921 when work for women had become scarce in Canada. She wanted to be a nurse but was denied employment in Victoria hospitals because she was married with a child. Leaving her daughter, Nydia, with her mother, she went to Seattle to pose as a single woman with the goal of training to become a nurse.

Hazel held a series of odd jobs in Seattle, including waiting tables and working for a novelty company, before becoming homesick and returning to Victoria. There she found the job market still difficult and returned to Seattle in 1923. Never finding enough money for nursing school, she settled into a career as a legal secretary and brought her daughter to the States. The two lived with nuns at St. James Cathedral for eight years. Her siblings had moved to Port Angeles by 1928 when Hazel married her second husband, a timber worker on the Olympic Peninsula named Herb Wolf. With few law offices in Port Angeles, Hazel came back to Seattle to work the next year. At the urging of her boss, she went to the INS offices to apply for citizenship, but left when she witnessed immigrants being treated rudely by agents. Her boss prodded her to pursue it, but a car accident delayed her citizenship hearing in 1930. She was denied her second attempt in 1939 for failing to establish good moral character based on her living arrangements at the time.

At age thirty-five she completed her high school education by taking night classes at Broadway High School. While on welfare to support her daughter, she went on to study social work at the University of Washington for two years. Her experiences with social workers and the chance meeting with a Communist Party petitioner in the welfare line caused her to change her course from becoming a social worker to becoming a social activist. Hazel felt she could do her best work among her peers, doing real social work and lobbying the government for change, so she gave up on school.

During the New Deal, formed to put the Depression Era population to work, Hazel was taken off welfare and employed in various Civil Works and Works Progress Administration jobs, where she became involved with labor unions as a secretary for teachers and government employee groups. After World War II, she came to work for a civil rights law firm in Seattle's only skyscraper, the Smith Tower. However, her legal career was interrupted for several years with a bout of tuberculosis for which she was sent to a sanitarium at Firland, north of Seattle.

Wolf was already known as a labor and union organizer when she again applied for citizenship in the late 1940s. This attempt at becoming an American citizen led to her arrest as a Communist and a long battle with the INS. Hazel Wolf finally became a U.S. citizen on her third attempt in 1974. By then she had been retired from the law firm for nine years and had begun her historic association with the Audubon Society.

At the urging of a friend, Hazel reluctantly joined the Audubon Society and went on a bird-watching trip to West Seattle's Lincoln Park, where she became entranced observing a tiny brown creeper laboring for food. Hazel later told audiences that she knew the bird was female because it appeared to be so intelligent and told of her epiphany saying, "This little bird works hard for a living, just as I do." The observation led to her passionate involvement in the Seattle Audubon Society, where she spent thirty-five years as their secretary, helping to found twenty-two Northwest chapters of the National Audubon Society. On her one hundredth birthday she spoke of the work that the Audubon Society had accomplished in saving bird habitat by protecting "ancient forests, rivers and seashores." Working with other environmental groups, the Sierra Club, Greenpeace, and the Earth Island Institute, they helped to protect the food supply by urging a ban on dangerous chemicals and pesticides like DDT. As a lifelong nature enthusiast and onetime president, she edited the *Outdoors West* newsletter for the Federation of Western Outdoor Clubs until the last day of her 101 years.

In a quest to join environmental groups with Washington Indian tribes, Wolf and a friend drove her old Chevy to fifteen reservations in the state and three in Canada to convince them to collaborate with environmental groups and work toward preservation of forests and fish habitat. Tribal representatives were invited to attend the first "Indian-Conservationist Conference" at Seattle's Daybreak Star Indian Cultural Center in 1979. She continued working with tribal leaders to defeat the Northern Tier Pipeline proposed to carry oil from Alaska through the Northwest to market in the Great Plains. The Audubon Society, Sierra Club, and Northwest tribes sued to stop the project, which was eventually vetoed by Governor John Spellman, who later told Hazel that he had been a member of the Junior Audubon Society. In addition to helping to halt the Northern Tier Pipeline, she lobbied against big Columbia Basin irrigation projects, campaigned for a nuclear weapons freeze, and as president of the Hanford Oversight Committee led a group against dumping high-level, radioactive waste at the Hanford Nuclear Reservation.

Always an advocate for the poor and minorities, she fought for the cleanup of the Duwamish River, believing that the polluted waterway was most dangerous to those living in low-income housing near its banks. With funding from the EPA and the American Lung Association, the Community Coalition for Environmental Justice proved that asthma rates were very high among children living in the vicinity of the river. The coalition was founded to help fight industrial pollution and clean up the area for the poor living in these south Seattle neighborhoods.

Beginning in the mid-1980s, Hazel made a series of trips to Nicaragua. She admired the government's stand on labor, and environmental issues, protecting its rain forests, and banning poisonous chemicals from farming. Like such dignitaries as Jimmy Carter, Hazel went to observe the 1990 elections in Nicaragua to ensure fair reporting on their voting process. At her ninetieth birthday party Mrs. Wolf asked her guests to contribute to a collection to ship medical supplies to a Nicaraguan women and children's hospital.

A *USA Today* photograph of the great grandmother in her nineties paddling her kayak on Lake Washington secured her celebrity status. The picture so intrigued elementary students in Alabama that they wrote to the avid outdoorswoman, who responded by flying to Decatur, Alabama, and speaking at their school. The rest of the country was learning of Hazel Wolf, Northwest treasure, outdoor enthusiast, author, and activist. She became an even more sought after speaker, promoting social justice, environmental concerns, and telling the world of her incredible life. When interviewed about his profile of her in his book, *Coming of Age,* author Studs Terkel described Wolf as one of the ingredients that made Seattle special saying, "You have the Mariners, and you have Hazel Wolf."

King County honored Hazel Wolf on the occasion of her one hundredth birthday by naming a 116-acre marsh in East King County the "Hazel Wolf Wetlands Preserve." Seven hundred guests came to her centennial birthday celebration, and she, in turn, asked her guests to donate to a fund for her "Kids for the Environment" program created to teach environmental stewardship and appreciation to schoolchildren. Her groups pledged to raise $300,000 to establish these clubs.

The next year Hazel tried to convince her friends to break her out of Providence Hospital so that she could join in the massive protests during Seattle's World Trade Organization Conference. If only she hadn't been hospitalized for hip replacement surgery, she surely would have been front and center during the WTO protests that overwhelmed city streets in 1999.

A self-described streak in her caused Hazel to see needs, look for others who might be interested, and band them together. Her strength was in organizing and inspiring others to act, but she always did so with good humor. She had the ability to act without making enemies, saying, "sooner or later I make them laugh." Once at a banquet she sat down next to a timber company executive and asked him how he was coming along with the destruction of our national forests. Another member of the timber industry told her, "You say the most offensive things in an inoffensive way." Wolf even convinced Boise Cascade company officials to preserve an old logging camp, which became the 3,000-acre Hazel Wolf Bird Sanctuary at Wenas Creek, site of the yearly Audubon Memorial Day campout and home to 200 bird species.

At age 101, she told students at Hazel Wolf High School on its opening day that she was able to go on, year after year, fighting the establishment for pure water laws, sustainable forest management, and a chemical-free food supply without suffering burnout by leaving the city turmoil occasionally. Taking trips into the wilderness for bird-watching, hiking, and kayaking was her way of changing direction and resting her body and mind. "We need to refresh ourselves by touching our mother earth from time to time," advised Wolf, but she went on to say that she would only live in a city, as that is where the action is.

Her name has graced wetlands, a bird sanctuary, a private high school, a children's endowment fund, and a film festival; her honors were numerous including being named the Audubon Society's Conservationist of the Year in 1985, a Chevron Conservation Award given at the Smithsonian, and the National Audubon Medal of Excellence in Environmental Achievement, both bestowed upon her at age ninety-nine. Seattle University granted her an honorary Ph.D. in the Humanities, and she in turn inspired the 1997 graduating class with a witty speech at their commencement ceremony. Washington State gave her an Environmental Excellence Award, the City of Seattle its Spirit of America Award, and Governor Mike Lowry declared her ninety-eighth birthday to be Hazel Wolf Day.

A ninety-five-year-old when Studs Terkel wrote of her in his *Coming of Age* book, she told the author, "I was born in 1898. I'm going to live till the year 2000, so I can have been in three centuries. Then I'm going." Hazel Wolf died January 19, 2000, after urging her granddaughter to complete her newsletter *Outdoors West* that day, living just long enough to continue her work into the twenty-first century.

SUSIE REVELS CAYTON

1870–1943

JOURNALIST WHO BELIEVED IN EQUALITY

When the *Seattle Times* noted that a competing newspaper, the *Seattle Republican*, had never missed a printing in its existence, it added that the paper's success may have been "partially due to the fact that Susie Revels Cayton has been associate editor and publisher."

Soon after, in a cover story titled "Good Woman's Helping Hand," her husband, *Republican* editor and publisher Horace Cayton, clarified: "Not partially due, but we ourselves sometimes think wholly due to that fact, for bless her heart, she has for all these years stood like a stone wall by our side and sometimes when the battle for existence was so severe that to live through it seemed more than human, she never wavered."

Horace continued:

The woman who works on and on amid privation not only for herself but for her little ones and yet always sees victory ahead is the woman that not only makes husbands men in the true sense of the word, but who makes the men and women of tomorrow. The woman who can jot down a note or an article while the baby is soothed to sleep or while the dinner cooks and thereby hold up her end, and at the same time always having a stock of love and tenderness for the discouraged man, is the woman that rules the world.

Susie may not have ruled the world, but she helped lead one of Seattle's most prominent businesses, steer one of its most influential families, and shape her community.

Susie Revels Cayton Seattle Republican

Susan Sumner Revels was born in Natchez, Mississippi, in 1870, the fourth of six daughters of Phoebe and Hiram Revels. She was descended from a long line of free Black people on both sides as well as some white ancestors. Her father, Hiram Rhoades Revels, was a minister in the African Methodist Episcopal (AME) Church and the president of Alcorn University, the first publicly funded university for Black people in Mississippi.

It was an optimistic time. The Civil War was over, Reconstruction was rebuilding the South, and Black Americans were looking forward to forging better lives.

Susie's father rode that wave of optimism to become the nation's first Black senator, elected by the Mississippi legislature in 1870. His victory was symbolic: He was chosen for the seat previously held by Jefferson Davis, who had left it at the start of the Civil War to take up the presidency of the Confederacy. (Davis thought so highly of Hiram Revels that he gave the family a mantel clock that eventually took pride of place at Susie's Seattle home.)

Hiram Revels was an example of civic-mindedness. He had preached throughout the eastern United States before the Civil War, aiding freed slaves when he could. He helped set up Union regiments of Black soldiers during the war, and after the war he dedicated his efforts to educating Black people. But he also believed in striving for harmony between the races, a value Susie would embrace.

Susie spent her childhood enveloped in a warm and intellectually stimulating atmosphere of life on a college campus. Hiram retired from Alcorn and moved to Holly Springs to resume work as a pastor but was soon teaching again, this time at Rust College. Susie was writing short stories by the time she was ten or eleven, and she studied journalism as well as nursing at Rust, graduating with honors in 1893 and teaching there for three years.

Horace Cayton had met Hiram Revels when the young man enrolled at Alcorn in 1872, studying to become a teacher. Horace had been born into slavery shortly before the start of the Civil War and attended a Freedmen's school before going to Alcorn.

By the late 1880s, the tide had turned against formerly enslaved people in the South. With the end of Reconstruction came the hammer of Jim Crow laws and overt discrimination. Black men feared being lynched for simply looking the wrong way at a white woman. Deciding the South was no place for a Black man with education and ambition, Horace headed to the West, where he developed a reputation as a sharp-witted newspaperman who didn't back down from in-print arguments with his white counterparts.

Horace moved to Seattle in 1889 and worked as a reporter for newspapers including the *Seattle Post-Intelligencer* before starting his own weekly newspaper, the *Seattle Republican*, in 1894. He sent Hiram Revels copies of the *Seattle Republican*, and Susie's father, in turn, dictated letters to Susie to send back. Susie soon began adding her own thoughts and sending those along, too. For two people so passionate about the written word, getting to know one another by letter was a fitting way to build a relationship. Susie traveled to Seattle to marry Horace in 1896.

Like others in Seattle, the Caytons were riding the wave of cash that flowed into the city from supplying miners in the late-1890s Alaska Gold Rush. Horace himself made money by loaning a miner money to stake a claim in Alaska that paid off when the man instead opened a successful barbershop. The city's growing and increasingly diverse population fueled many businesses, including the *Republican*. Writing had drawn Susie and Horace together, and it was what would make their living and reputation in Seattle.

By the early 20th century, the family was living in a nice house in the exclusive Capitol Hill neighborhood, surrounded by white neighbors (some of whom complained that the Black family in their midst was driving down their property values). At one time, they had a Japanese servant and a Swedish maid. They socialized with the brightest lights of Seattle society, Black and white. Their views that races should work together for the benefit of all, along with Horace's steadfast support for the powerful Republican Party, earned them a level of respect among white peers.

As Richard S. Hobbs writes in his book about the family, *The Cayton Legacy*, "Horace Sr. and Susie emerged as adults with an unswerving devotion to fighting injustice, which was to carry them through four decades of life and work in Seattle."

In Seattle, the Caytons hoped to find a community where people of all backgrounds could talk politics and progress. It was on this hope that the *Seattle Republican* was built. Horace and Susie were working to create a rare thing for the time: a news outlet aimed at people of all races. As Horace wrote of his newspaper: "It stands for right and champions the cause of the oppressed as it sees it, whether that oppressed be black or white."

The *Republican* soon became the most popular and successful Black-owned newspaper in the city, and both Black- and white-owned businesses took out ads.

Susie had started writing for the *Republican* even before she came to Seattle; and after she arrived, Horace made her the paper's associate editor. She was a prolific contributor even as she held down duties of a wife and mother to their growing family. As well as opinion pieces, features, and newsy tidbits about goings-on around town, she wrote short fiction.

She also wrote fiction for other publications and was likely the first Black woman published in the *Seattle Post-Intelligencer*. Her stories tugged at readers' emotions, reminding them about the struggles of the poor and unloved and showing how big a difference people could make in one another's lives. When Horace was away, she oversaw the

Republican's production and distribution, which earned the respect of Horace and even the *Seattle Times*.

In accordance with her social stature, Susie held herself with dignity. As her son Horace Jr. wrote in his autobiography, *Long Old Road*: "She was a handsome, perhaps a beautiful woman, tall and of stately bearing. Her complexion was a light olive, and her dark brown hair and eyes enhanced the attractiveness of her oval face. She had the cultivated grace which was characteristic of many southern women who had been reared in gentle homes."

As many prosperous Black Americans have done through history, the Caytons felt compelled to lift up fellow Black people. If the white community wouldn't recognize Black progress and Black excellence, they would. In 1907, the *Republican* published a special edition featuring stories about prominent African American leaders, following that up with another one in 1909. That year, Booker T. Washington stayed with the Caytons when he visited Seattle for the Alaska-Yukon-Pacific Exposition.

The Caytons also created and joined organizations to fill gaps in education and the social safety net. They were regulars in the Sunday Forum, a civic group dedicated to enhancing lives of Black Seattleites and discussing the issues of the day. Through the group, Black citizens joined forces to demand that businesses hire Black workers and serve Black customers.

"We each get a certain amount of enthusiasm from what the other one says and we go away the better for having been here," Susie wrote in 1906. "It is exceedingly pleasant to see the leading men of the city coming into this hall to consult together for the good of the race and he or she who does not come is the worse for not doing so. I sometimes wish that I were seven or eight men that I could be present at all of such meetings and help enthuse the race along better lines."

In 1906, Susie founded the Dorcas Charity Club, partly to care for poor or sick Black children whose families couldn't afford to take care of them, and was chosen as its president in 1908. One of the club's lasting contributions: ensuring that the newly founded Seattle Children's Hospital adopted a policy of not discriminating based on race, religion, or financial status.

She was a sought-after public speaker, especially for African American groups. In one of her speeches, she noted the lack of Black dolls and encouraged the community to make sure their children had access to dolls that looked like them, even if that meant making the dolls themselves.

In public, the Caytons were reserved and genteel. Horace saved his most pointed barbs for the paper (where he often let loose with a sharp and unsparing wit). Even as they moved comfortably in both Black and white society, the Caytons were well aware that for Black people, one false step could risk the esteem of both the Black and white communities. They acted accordingly, portraying a dignity that their place in society required. Some saw the couple as "snobs" trying to gain the approval of influential white people.

As Horace Jr. wrote of his mother: "Though her general disposition was gentle and amicable, at times she showed a hard streak in her personality; she was a curious mixture of the warm earthiness of my Methodist grandfather and the tight primness of my Quaker grandmother. If we ran afoul of what she called her principles—her Quaker beliefs—we would feel the full weight of her towering disapproval."

By this time, the Caytons had four school-age children—Ruth, Madge, Horace Jr., and Hiram Revels (another child, Lillie, was born in in 1914, when Susie was forty-four)—and were also raising Emma, the daughter of Susie's sister Lillie, who died in 1900. Every day, they sent the children to school with the words "Go out and achieve." They wanted their children to follow the family legacy of scholarship and civic engagement. The children took music lessons, filling the house with the sound of the family orchestra. Susie introduced them to the opera and

Shakespeare plays. As their Japanese servant, Nish, learned English, she had him teach her Japanese.

But the Cayton family's fortunes were about to take a turn for the worse. Declining newspaper revenues and investments that didn't work out forced the family out of their Capitol Hill home into a less affluent neighborhood.

By 1913, the *Republican* was caught up in economic hard times as well as a local and national disintegration of race relations. An influx of migrants upset the delicate balance that had existed twenty years earlier—Seattle's white settlers had been tolerant of people of color as long as there weren't many of them—and now the lines between races hardened. Businesses that previously served everyone started excluding Black customers. The *Republican* was caught in the middle, considered too Black for white readers and too white for Black ones.

Some historians have speculated the decline in readership may have been because white readers were put off by the Caytons' reporting on lynchings of Black people in the South. The paper refused to sugarcoat the facts, and it pointed out the hypocrisy of white men's willingness to kill to defend white women's honor even as they besmirched the honor of so many Black women. The *Republican*'s white-owned counterparts railed against the Caytons' stance with racist insults.

After Horace lost a high-profile lawsuit that he filed against a cafeteria that refused to serve him, advertising dried up even more. The newspaper closed, and Horace scraped by managing an apartment building they owned on Jackson Street, in what would become known as the Central District, and asking friends to hire him to write for their papers.

"My father and his paper had been the victims of the changing pattern of race relations in the city. . . . There was no longer a place for an in-between group, and everyone became identified as either Negro or white. We were, to my knowledge, the only Negro family to feel so dramatically the impact of these social forces, and our fall from our unique position was swift and, for us, painful," Horace Jr. later wrote.

The Caytons eventually saved up to start a new paper, *Cayton's Weekly*, focusing on the Black community—a tough sell in a city that by this time had other periodicals aimed at Black readers. In 1919, a decline in revenue forced the Caytons to sell their house and move into their apartment building. Even worse, their eldest daughter, twenty-two-year-old Ruth, died. Susie and Horace took in Ruth's baby daughter, Susan; and Madge, a student at the University of Washington, took on some household responsibilities as well as a waitressing job.

As the *Republican* had before it, *Cayton's Weekly* reported on the atrocities facing Black people in the South. In October 1919, the paper produced an issue devoted entirely to the lynchings that were by this time happening in much of the country, especially the South. Horace also took white newspapers to task for framing resulting protests as Black "uprisings." His words did not endear him to the establishment or potential advertisers.

In 1920, *Cayton's Weekly* closed. To earn extra money, Susie and the children spent the summer picking raspberries, living on-site in near poverty. Horace tried various other publishing ventures over the years—a monthly magazine, one-off books and pamphlets—but never with much success.

As Jim Crow took hold in the South, whites in the North, including in Seattle, clamped down on Black opportunity in their own ways, by passing redlining laws that restricted where people of color could live and denying even the most educated Black people jobs and social opportunities.

When Susie tried to find work, she discovered that no one wanted to hire a college-educated Black woman. The vast majority of Black women of the time worked in domestic service—an option Susie eventually had to take.

In 1931, as the Great Depression set in, the family lost their apartment building to foreclosure and moved to a small house. Susie and Horace, now older and without much income, joined many others who took public assistance to stay alive.

Susie and Horace reacted to their circumstances in different ways. He pinned hopes on using his old networks to succeed, a strategy that worked less and less over time. Meanwhile, Susie's views grew increasingly radical. She had always been "a free thinker," and was always a game participant in the family's kitchen-table debates over social, legal, and political matters. She came to believe that trying to appeal to wealthy white citizens wasn't working, and this belief brought her to the second act of her life. The sympathy for working class people she had felt before found a home in the socialist movement.

Her son Hiram Revels (who went by Revels) was an avid participant in labor movements and, later, the Communist Party, organizing protests and marches throughout the West. Susie was intrigued, and she, too, joined in, eventually becoming secretary of the Skid Road Unemployed Council and vice president of the Negro Workers Council.

As Quintard Taylor writes in *The Forging of a Black Community: Seattle's Central District from 1870 through the Civil Rights Era*, "The daughter of Hiram Revels of Mississippi, the first black U.S. senator, and wife of Horace Cayton, Sr., who remained an active Republican until his death in 1940, she would seem an unlikely supporter of the cause of socialism, but Susie Cayton was an unusual woman."

She was a rare sight, a sixty-something Black woman surrounded by young, mostly white, male activists. They came to see this warm and intellectually gifted woman as a grandmotherly figure, calling her "Mother Cayton." While the now-elderly Horace was retreating from public life, Susie was having a renaissance as a figure of renown, locally and beyond.

Returning to her heyday as a public figure, Susie put her skills to use speaking to union groups, workers' clubs, Black activist groups, and even the PTA. "I'm having the time of my life and at the same time making some contribution to the working class I hope," she wrote in a letter to Madge, who had moved to Chicago.

Black luminaries found a welcoming atmosphere at the Cayton house. The renowned actor, singer, and activist Paul Robeson met with Susie when he stopped in during a concert tour; they became good friends. He even spoke to her sewing club. As Taylor notes, "Of course, with Susie as its leader, this was no ordinary sewing club. To Susie, piecing quilts together for the needy provided a good rationale for gathering a dozen women together to discuss social and political issues."

Horace died of cancer in 1940. Susie kept her calendar full until her diabetes worsened and she went to live with Madge in Chicago; Horace Jr. and Susan were also living there.

Susie's children were keeping their parents' scholarship and social contributions alive. After graduating from the University of Washington, Horace Jr. studied sociology at the University of Chicago and rose to prominence in that field. Among his friends were author Richard Wright and poet Langston Hughes, both of whom visited Susie in Chicago and listened avidly to her tales of everything from growing up as Hiram Revels's daughter to her work with the Communist Party.

Madge, a social worker, devoted much of her life to caring for family members facing illness and aging. Revels moved to San Francisco and gained a reputation as a savvy workers' rights activist. He worked with Robeson, by this time a good friend, to improve African American lives. Lillie became an advocate for people with alcoholism, and Susan befriended and promoted Chicago Black Renaissance artists and writers.

Susie died in Chicago in 1943. Long in the shadow of her famous husband and sons, she has gained recognition in her own right in recent years. She is a representative of a small but notable group: Black women pioneers who succeeded against high odds and now stand as models and inspiration for those who come after them.

EMMA SMITH DEVOE

1848–1927

"GOOD-NATURED AND CHEERFUL"
FIGHTER FOR THE VOTE

O ther women seeking the vote had marched to demand the vote. They had threatened. They had protested. Washington suffrage leader Emma Smith DeVoe had a different idea: a cookbook.

The pages of the *Washington Women's Cookbook* were filled with homespun recipes, many of them specific to the region—clams feature prominently, and there's a section on recipes for sailors (the tail of a shark: "Good eating. Boil it with plenty of spice and serve with a cream sauce."). The Mountaineers, a recreational club founded in 1906 with nearly equal numbers of men and women, contributed a chapter on "Cooking in Camp." The book also includes beauty tips, plus instructions for making soap and getting laundry clean—all subtle reminders of women's expertise in the home.

But amid the recipes were stirring declarations supporting women's suffrage and brief essays about, for example, the fact that women's interest in cooking for their families would lead them to push for better food-safety laws when they could vote.

The cookbook raised funds and public awareness, but it also reminded people that women who wanted the vote were still women—still interested in domestic duties and caring for their families.

Later, Emma would say: "We had two ideas in view in this. One was, of course, the money and the other was the vindication of the slur put upon suffragists that they have no domestic traits."

In many ways, Emma DeVoe was the perfect figurehead for Washington's women's suffrage movement. She was attractive, well-spoken,

Emma Smith DeVoe Photo by James & Bushnell, Seattle. Retrieved from the Library of Congress, www.loc.gov/item/mnwp000362/.

and musically talented. She was the kind of woman men thought women should be—even as she sometimes clashed with fellow women.

Emma Smith was born in Roseville, Illinois, in 1848. A talented musician, she studied music and taught music lessons in Illinois, where she lived for much of her young adulthood.

Music introduced her to John Henry DeVoe, a fellow music lover; the two met while she was singing with a choir. They married in 1880, then moved to the Dakota Territory in 1881 before moving back to the Chicago area. In both places, Emma set about creating clubs advocating for women's voting rights, a goal she had steadfastly supported from an early age. As a girl, she had heard Susan B. Anthony speak, and the encounter with the suffrage movement leader left a lasting impression.

She and Henry were active in the temperance movement, which often overlapped with the women's suffrage movement and brought many women into political life for the first time. The movement gave Emma an education in organizing, public speaking, fundraising, and organizing supporters.

Anthony, president of the National American Woman Suffrage Association (NAWSA), lived with the DeVoes while she tried to bring women's suffrage to South Dakota, and Emma learned from her and others even as the campaign failed to produce voting rights.

Henry was beside her in the fight, even performing with Emma at meetings and writing songs in support of the movement. As Jennifer Ross-Nazzal writes in her comprehensive biography of Emma, *Winning the West for Women: The Life of Suffragist Emma Smith DeVoe*: "Just as they had influenced the South Dakota suffrage campaign, the DeVoes continued to encourage reformers to sing their way into the hearts of voters."

Along with her mentor Carrie Chapman Catt, a prominent figure in the NAWSA, Emma helped organize regional clubs and conferences for suffrage groups. Catt praised Emma in one of the women's-suffrage-focused newspapers of the time: "Mrs. DeVoe has a species of grit which I wish were more common with our workers." By the mid-1890s, Emma was traveling through the Midwest, earning money on the speaking circuit to supplement Henry's uncertain income from ambitious but often unsuccessful business ventures.

Women in the western United States tended to have more power than in most parts of the country, and suffrage leaders came to pin their hopes on getting the vote there first. Western territories had long offered rights to lure more women settlers. Women in the Oregon Territory (which originally included what is now Washington) got the right to own land in 1850, before many of their counterparts elsewhere in America. In 1881, the Washington Territorial Legislature gave women the right to own and sell property, sign contracts, and file lawsuits.

So, it's not surprising that western territories, starting with Wyoming in 1869, were the first to grant women the vote.

Emma's first foray to the West was to Montana and Idaho as an organizer for NAWSA. Some of the women there were offended by the idea that an outsider could succeed better than locals could. But national organizers felt that they needed someone experienced in attracting "the right people." And Emma, with her good looks, good taste, and savvy social skills, was that woman.

Arriving in towns where she knew no one, Emma charmed her way into churches, farmers' granges, and women's groups and formed local suffrage chapters. With her pleasant voice and her obvious passion, she developed a reputation as a skilled speaker. One newspaper called her a "stunner in persuasiveness."

Emma carefully dressed and styled her masses of dark, wavy hair for her public appearances, crafting a persona that was somehow both electrifying and unthreatening. One reporter described her as "a tall, capable-looking woman of middle age, vital, comely and strong, and of a friendly Western cheerfulness and confidence of manner."

She was, in some ways, a bundle of contradictions that managed to work together. Even as she courted support from "the right sort of people"—often newspaper publishers, preachers, and businessmen—her message focused on the ties between women's rights and economic advancement for farmers and other working-class folk. Her demeanor was refined, but she knew how to talk to people who worked with their hands. Her ability to forge bonds with farmers and laborers was key to her success.

The contradictions extended to her personal life. She loved her husband, but her work for the movement meant she had little to give him. Her best friends were activists, and she traveled so much that she spent more time with them than she did at home.

Underneath her carefully cultivated exterior, Emma could be hotheaded, stubborn, and demanding, and she often tangled with even the best of her friends. They almost always mended their relationships for the good of the cause, but the push and pull of strong personalities was a constant in her life.

With her husband in ill health, Emma quit organizing in 1898. When Henry did not improve, they decided to move west for a change of climate. He took a Washington-based job with a railroad, and almost as soon as they arrived in Tacoma, she resumed organizing.

In Washington, the fight for women's right to vote had a tumultuous beginning that foreshadowed a long and difficult road to success. In 1854, a proposal to grant adult women citizens the right to vote lost in the Washington Territorial Legislature by a single vote, eight to nine.

In 1871, the state's first women's suffrage convention drew hundreds of participants, who formed the Washington Territory Woman Suffrage Association (WTWSA). Lawmakers responded negatively to pressure from the WTWSA, passing a law saying that women in Washington could not get the vote until Congress passed a federal law allowing it. Clearly, some in the legislature not only didn't want to give women the vote but also wanted to stop hearing about it. Over subsequent years, pro-suffrage legislators raised the issue multiple times, only to face defeat.

(It should be noted that these women were specifically fighting for the rights of white women—and, in fact, to gain support they often compared themselves favorably to the "heathen Chinese" and "squalid" Native people.)

In 1883, supporters finally got a bill passed that said the word "men" in laws also applied to women, and women began voting. But in 1887, the territorial Supreme Court declared that the 1883 law did not overtly give women the right to vote. The blow felt all the worse for the taste of equal voting rights the women enjoyed in the intervening years.

A new women's suffrage bill passed in 1888 went again to the territorial Supreme Court. There, with impressively convoluted reasoning, the justices declared that the United States did not fully consider women to be worthy of the full rights of citizenship, and therefore any state law giving them such rights was invalid. The word "citizen," they said, "then meant and still signifies male citizenship and must be so construed."

Some women wanted to take the case to the US Supreme Court but were persuaded not to because such fights might hurt Washington's chances for statehood. With some male leaders promising that women's suffrage would be enshrined in the state constitution once the territory gained statehood, women withdrew the case.

But when it came time to approve a state constitution in 1889, voters said no to giving women the vote and yes to laws that specified that only men were eligible. Rather than guaranteeing their rights, the constitution had just made women's task more difficult than ever: Amending it would require approval from not only two-thirds of legislators but also a statewide majority of voters.

Legislators voted to add women's suffrage to the state constitution in 1896, but the effort to get at least half of the state's voters to approve it was defeated. Opponents of women's suffrage said giving women too many rights would lure them out of their homes, disrupting family life and eroding the very ground on which the American family stood.

In 1905, Emma helped run a convention in Oregon that brought suffragists together to capitalize on the centennial of the Lewis and Clark Expedition and celebrations of Sacajawea's role in it. When she returned to Washington, she brought the Washington Equal Suffrage Association (WESA) into the NAWSA club fold. She used her husband's railroad benefits to travel around the state organizing for the cause.

In 1906, WESA elected Emma as its president, a role she would also be elected to for each of the next three years. These would be the most crucial years yet for winning women the vote in Washington, and Emma would build on the work of the women before her.

Having won and lost this fight so many times before, suffrage movement leaders knew that any but the most well-planned and disciplined of efforts would fail. But years of trying had given women experience at honing their tactics and organizing themselves into clubs and committees, holding and publicizing meetings, and lobbying elected officials. After years of discouragement, they were fired up again. They were angry—but they were organized.

Leaning on one another, women encouraged each other to raise money, attend and participate in debates, and pressure civic leaders. Women's clubs helped by raising money and arranging speaking engagements.

They communicated gently yet persistently, combining soft pressure with creative methods of getting the word out. Basing her strategies on those honed by Carrie Chapman Catt, Emma devised ten "Principles for Guidance in Suffrage Campaigns." They were:

1. Keep the issue single. Be for nothing but suffrage; against nothing but anti-suffrage.

2. Pin your faith to the justice of your cause. It carries conviction.

3. Rely upon facts rather than arguments.

4. Plead affirmative arguments always. Put your opponents on the defensive.

5. Convert the indifferent: There are thousands of them. Let the incorrigible alone; there are only a few.

6. Avoid big meetings; they arouse your enemies.

7. Avoid antagonizing big business but get the labor vote quietly.

8. Be confident of winning.

9. Try to have every voter in the state asked by some woman to vote for the amendment; this will carry it.

10. Always be good-natured and cheerful.

"Good-natured and cheerful" was a hallmark of Emma's style. She hid her unbending will beneath a polite and genial exterior. The combination of pleasant and persistent was a winner. Some men saw women's suffrage activists as unladylike loudmouths who didn't respect their rightful place. Emma's demeanor and rhetoric eased those fears. She reminded her listeners of women's roles as wives and mothers, and she said that they should have the vote not despite those roles but because of them.

Emma preferred the "still hunt" method of working one-on-one rather than hosting large rallies that could alarm tradition-minded members of society. As she once told another woman, Lucy B. Johnston, "We did *not fight* for suffrage, we *worked* for it."

By the 1909 legislative session, a coalition of women had gathered ten thousand signatures from men and women around the state in support of women's suffrage. WESA members rented a house by the capitol, with Emma working full-time there in charge of the lobbying effort. She deputized women from suffrage groups across the state to talk to individual legislators, and she helped draft legislation to amend the state's voting laws.

According to one account in a woman's newspaper, "Relays of bright and clever women visited the capital by turns. Letters and telegrams were poured incessantly in upon the members by their constituents in the field."

Some suffragists, and especially firebrand May Arkwright Hutton of Spokane, objected to Emma's approach. They wanted to demand their rights more loudly. They also felt women shouldn't have to emphasize their differences from men or promise, overtly or not, that voting power wouldn't inspire them to move beyond their traditional spheres. But Emma reasoned that in order to win men over, it was better to be pleasant than militant.

Emma's tactics won out. Rather than publicize the vote for the amendment, the women focused on pressuring individual legislators, with an eye toward turning their attention to individual voters once it passed.

The bill passed both the House and Senate, and acting Governor Marion Hay signed it on February 25, 1909, before handing Emma the pen he used.

But the push had just begun. A statewide vote on the amendment was set for November 1910. Hundreds of women throughout the state turned their attention toward convincing their husbands, brothers, friends, and civic leaders to vote for women's suffrage.

Women argued that voting was not only a matter of justice and dignity but that voting for women's rights would show men at their best. Echoing the sentiments Emma and her colleagues used with legislators, the *Votes for Women* newspaper opined, "The women of Washington want political equality with their brothers, not because they have been badly treated, but because they have been well treated."

Two coinciding events brought the Washington suffrage battle to the forefront: the 1909 Alaska-Yukon-Pacific Exposition (AYPE) and the NAWSA national meeting. Emma invited prominent suffragists from all over the country and dubbed the train they rode into Seattle the "Suffrage Special." Here, in front of the world press and visitors from all over, women could press their cause, with the Washington vote as a centerpiece.

At the AYPE, state and national women's groups distributed information, staffed booths, and helped with exhibits. It was a chance to introduce their campaign to a wide audience. They even held a "Woman Suffrage Day" on July 9, and volunteers handed out "Votes for Women" ribbons.

While they were united behind a common cause, it was inevitable that differences would arise, as they had in previous social movements (and would in later ones).

As the members of the national organization converged on Seattle, the occasion fanned flames of division among Washington's suffrage campaigners. Hutton and a group of like-minded women, branding themselves "the insurgents," arrived at the WESA state convention and objected to Emma's continued leadership, which they saw as dictatorial, and her paid position with the group. The WESA refused to seat them. Pandemonium erupted, complete with shouted insults and some insurgents being locked in a room before they were ousted.

For this, the NAWSA fired Emma. The infighting splintered the movement into multiple suffrage groups.

But Washington women's differences weren't enough to make them drop their common goal. They had come this far; they weren't going to lose focus now. Although women chose different groups to affiliate with, they kept up the positive but single-minded pressure on the men around them.

Always looking for positive publicity, women printed posters and penned articles and opinion columns for their local newspapers.

Dr. Cora Smith Eaton, a medical doctor and good friend of Emma's, unfurled a "Votes for Women" banner when she climbed to the top of Mt. Rainier. They stayed "on message," not wavering from the positive and upbeat emphasis on the justness of their cause. *Washington Women's Cookbook* was one of the WESA's most creative projects, and it got them welcome attention in the local press.

The work paid off: In November, the amendment passed with nearly two-thirds of the vote. Washington became the fifth state to adopt women's suffrage, joining Wyoming, Colorado, Utah, and Idaho. Partly riding the wave of the first suffrage victory since 1896 (when Utah and Idaho women got the right to vote), ten other states would follow before the Nineteenth Amendment took effect in 1920.

Emma carried lessons learned in Washington to other states. She helped create the National Council of Women Voters (NCWV), set up to educate voters in the "free states," improve conditions for women and children, and make the case for suffrage in other states and nationally. At its first meeting, Emma was named president. This elicited dismay from those who thought she already had too much power and was too much a politician, willing to switch alliances to suit her purposes.

NCWV members met with members of Congress and gathered signatures for petitions. They explained that women voters hadn't made the sky fall politically since their enfranchisement but instead had worked to make their states better places for all.

In 1915, Carrie Chapman Catt took over as president of the NAWSA, and Emma and her old friend renewed their friendship. They presented a united front as their organizations worked together for both national and state women's suffrage.

Over time, Emma and her colleagues updated their methods, combining the "still hunt" with publicity campaigns and carefully crafted speeches. In 1914, Emma and other Washington state suffragists participated in a National Day of Demonstrations asking Congress to consider the so-called "Anthony Amendment" giving women the right to vote. Congress brought the matter out of committee, but it didn't pass. That year, though, thanks partly to the NCWV's efforts, suffrage passed in Nevada and Montana.

Between her trips around the West and to Washington, DC, Emma spent time at the Parkland home she and Henry owned, called Villa DeVoe. In 1917, when the United States entered World War I, Emma and Henry became officers at their local Red Cross. Despite all of her time away, and no matter where her career took her, he was her touchstone of encouragement at home.

When the war ended, Catt proposed founding a new organization, the League of Women Voters, a national organization free of some of the baggage attached to older groups. Emma agreed to merge the NCWV with the new league in 1919.

The combination of suffragists' unyielding efforts and women's contributions during World War I spurred the passage of the Nineteenth Amendment in 1919. As with the change to the Washington state constitution, ratification would be the real test. Emma once again toured the country rallying supporters until the amendment was ratified in 1920.

Emma had gained her greatest desire. Now in her seventies, she could have been forgiven for spending the rest of her days basking in her achievements. But she had energy left, and she devoted it to becoming a powerhouse in Washington's Republican party. While she had eschewed partisanship during her push for the vote, she now used her organizing skills to bring supporters into the Republican fold.

She impressed male party leaders the same way she had when she was fighting for the vote, and they agreed to appoint her an elector in the 1920 election. She rose to become an associate member of the Republican National Committee and attended meetings in Washington, DC.

In her later years, she slowed a bit, and in 1927, she developed bladder cancer, which caused her death on September 3 of that year in Tacoma. Henry survived her, having been her greatest supporter all the way to the end. Built on a foundation of work by others before her, Emma's accomplishments are hard to quantify. But evidence of them is visible every time a woman casts a vote.

Kara Matsushita Kondo

1916–2005

COMMITTED TO JUSTICE AND COMMUNITY

In June of 1942, as Japanese American families gathered to be loaded onto trains and carried to an uncertain future, a soldier among those overseeing the families asked a young woman named Kara Matsushita to take a walk with him.

Kara would recall: "The first thing he said as we were out of earshot of the people milling around the station was, 'Why are you letting them do this to you?!'"

"What do you mean?" she replied.

"Taking you away and putting into camps."

When she could only laugh, thinking he must have been joking, he replied, "This is no laughing matter. We're trained to assess people and situations; to make judgments on subversives. I see nothing, absolutely nothing that justifies this evacuation. When we go into a community, we check police records, go to school to check on students, and make every assessment as to the nature and character of the people we have to deal with. We find nothing! The Japanese students are tops in their classes. Citizenship is flawless. We couldn't find any delinquency. There's nothing on the police records." He couldn't understand why the US government would do this to innocent people.

"I was speechless," Kara recalled. "If he didn't know, what answer could I give? Many a night when I was finally alone, I had wept over the same question . . . Why? Not so much that it was happening to me, but that it was happening at all."

It was a question she would never stop asking. And while she had no way of escaping her fate in 1942, she never let others forget what

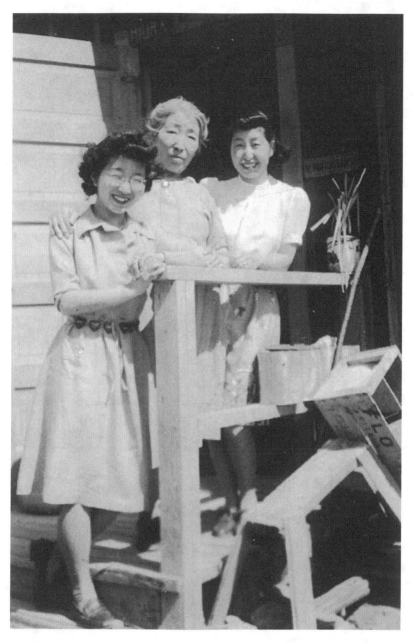

Kara Kondo (left), her mother, Kiyoko, and her younger sister, Marjorie Courtesy of the
Yakima Valley Museum

happened. Most of all, she wanted to make sure nothing like it would ever happen again.

She kept that pledge as she made a life for herself in rural Washington, winning friends even as she spoke of uncomfortable truths and committing herself to a community that had once rejected people like her.

Kara grew up in Wapato, Washington, in the Yakima Valley. Her father, Yasutaro, settled in the valley in 1905 after immigrating from Japan. Her mother, Kiyoko, soon joined him. Kara and her older sister, Amy, and her younger sister, Marjorie, grew up on farmland their father leased. Family friends visited often, and the girls grew up listening to their stories. Kara's parents instilled in her a love of reading and learning as well as Japanese culture.

Japanese immigrants came to America for the same reasons most immigrants do: to forge a better life. Discrimination prevented many Issei (first-generation immigrants from Japan) from taking lucrative jobs once they arrived in the United States. In the cities, they often opened small businesses such as stores and restaurants. Others settled in farming areas south and west of Seattle. Japanese farmers were so successful that by about 1915, they were operating 70 percent of the stalls at Seattle's Pike Place Market.

Non-Japanese farmers, unhappy about the competition, helped persuade the government to pass a law in 1921 forbidding Japanese immigrants from buying or leasing land. Many Issei moved to cities and opened businesses, but others found a way around the law and kept farming, often by subleasing land from white farmers, which added to their expenses. Sometimes prejudice was even more personal; Japanese Americans were required to sit in the balcony at the Yakima movie theater.

By the early 1930s, about 1,500 Japanese Americans lived in the Yakima Valley, with their lives centered around "Japanese Town" in Wapato. "We had our own social, athletic, and religious activities, a thriving subculture, a community within a community. The size of the Japanese population was small enough so that everyone know each other. There was a distinct feeling of being a part of an extended family," Kara recalled. They celebrated Japanese festivals, learned judo and kendo martial arts, and had their own baseball league. They also befriended Native Americans and recent immigrants from other countries.

As a young adult, Kara went to design school in Seattle and worked as a nanny, returning to the Yakima Valley in the summer to help farm and sell produce. World War II would cut her education short.

As Japan took over more and more territory in the Pacific, and especially after the bombing of Pearl Harbor on December 7, 1941, a cloud of suspicion fell over the West Coast, home to more than 110,000 people of Japanese descent. Many people supported forcibly removing Japanese immigrants and their families away from the coast. Radio programs and newspapers fanned flames of prejudice.

The military decreed the removal of all Japanese Americans a necessity, even as it incarcerated only a few German or Italian nationals and no American citizens of German or Italian heritage. The fact that no American residents of Japanese descent were ever found to have committed espionage or sabotage didn't matter.

On February 19, 1942, President Franklin Roosevelt signed Executive Order 9066, allowing the US government to forcibly move Japanese Americans out of their homes. The government created a new agency, the War Relocation Authority, to build and oversee "relocation centers" away from the coast. On March 30, a group of Japanese Americans from Bainbridge Island near Seattle was the first to be "evacuated."

About one-third of the people removed were Issei, while about two-thirds were Nisei—second-generation immigrants like Kara, born on American soil and thus American citizens.

Families were taken to hastily constructed and often primitive "assembly centers" for weeks or months before being sent to one of the more permanent "relocation centers." For the people taken from their homes, the process was chaotic, unpredictable, and traumatic.

At first, Japanese Americans were only displaced from "military exclusion areas" that comprised the western half of West Coast states. "Removed from the west coast by 150 miles or so, fairly isolated, agricultural, we were led to believe that evacuation would not take place," Kara later said. "True, our Japanese community leaders were picked up immediately following Pearl Harbor, and all aliens had to register. Travel and curfew orders trickled down to affect us but were told to continue all other normal activity. Indeed, all farmers were urged to enlarge their operations; to contribute to the war effort."

And so that spring, Japanese American farmers in the Yakima Valley planted their crops, hoping for the best. Kara said, "The Japanese farmers worked harder than ever, as if the evacuation edict could be stayed by their performance. Diligently and lovingly they tended the growing things. Perhaps deep down they were saying farewell to the land that nurtured them and the only life they knew."

Even as they did, they noticed Caucasian people in trucks passing by, evaluating their farms, preparing for the time when they would be able to take over.

When the order came for Yakima Valley families, they scrambled to sell what they could, bury or throw out heirlooms that could make them look too "pro-Japan," and give away much of the rest. While a few of their neighbors spoke up in their defense, and more locals quietly supported them, Japanese Americans could never be sure who their true friends were and who couldn't wait to see them leave town.

Because Amy had married and moved out by then, Kara, in her mid-twenties and a fluent English speaker, handled arrangements for her family. She tried to make her aging parents' lives as comfortable as possible.

As families gathered near the trains that would take them away, soldiers took down their details. Kara helped translate for her

Kara Kondo Courtesy of the Yakima Valley Museum

Japanese-speaking neighbors and ensure that the soldiers spelled names correctly. She was one of the last to board. As they pulled away, she watched her father's face as he sat gripping the arms of his seat. Recalling it later, Kara said, "You could see the shadow of Mt. Adams and the sun behind it. And looking at his face I could just feel that he was saying goodbye to the place that he'd known so well."

Kara and her family were taken to an assembly center set up at the grounds of the Pacific International Livestock Exposition Center (now the Portland Expo Center), where windowless stalls that normally held cattle were converted into primitive living quarters. Plywood floors were placed directly on top of years' worth of built-up dirt and manure. Walls stopped well short of the ceiling, giving little privacy. At night, everyone could hear the wails of babies and the snoring of other inmates. Kara never forgot the sound the gate to the outside made as it clanged shut behind them.

Even in their three months at the assembly center, with no idea what lay ahead, Japanese Americans tried to keep up some feeling of normality. Having written articles for local newspapers before the war, Kara contributed to the center newsletter. Families quickly set up makeshift classes for children. But they all knew what they had lost.

In mid-September, Kara and her family were moved to the Heart Mountain Relocation Center in Wyoming. At its height, it had almost eleven thousand prisoners, making it the third largest city in Wyoming at the time. Like other relocation camps, Heart Mountain was set in an inhospitable landscape. Winter temperatures dropped to well below zero. Wind blew dust in through cracks in the walls of their hastily built wooden barracks. Everyone had to do their washing and showering in a communal central block.

"It's amazing what physical things you become accustomed to," Kara said later. "It's the mental part of you that somehow goes through the kinds of emotions and leaves an imprint on your attitudes and feelings later."

Surrounded by barbed wire, the camps were patrolled by armed guards. The prisoners were sometimes forced to do unpaid labor. Anyone objecting to being held, or to the poor conditions, was swiftly punished with anything from denial of medical care to physical violence. Those deemed "rebellious" were taken to remote "isolation centers."

But there were some happy moments. At Christmas, they got caring letters and small gifts from church groups and schoolchildren. Kara and other young women went around the camp singing carols, even to a guard in one of the watchtowers. Although they didn't think their gesture would mean much to the guard, they heard a voice almost choking with tears say, "Well, thank you." It made a kindhearted Kara think about how lonely he must have been.

Keeping up her journalism, Kara wrote about the camp's social activities for its newspaper, the *Heart Mountain Sentinel*. She reported on dances, marriages, and dinner parties.

She wrote about a Halloween dance in 1942:

With the slower tempo of a waltz, couples again crowded the floor. Bobbing black heads jostling closely together.

A tall youth danced with a pretty girl.

"Say, this is some party. Pretty nice . . . I almost forget where I am."

The smiling face of his partner became thoughtful, a look of sadness crept into her eyes—

"I can't forget. I never do."

Kara and other prisoners took classes in creative writing and traditional Japanese poetry styles, such as haiku, senryu, and tanka, carrying on a poetry tradition that had existed in the Yakima Valley before internment. The busier they could stay, the less time they would have to think about what they were missing.

One of her poems reads:

Hoping the day of our freedom
May come soon
I wait for the sunrise
This New Year dawn

Kara had dated a handsome pharmacy student named Tak Kondo before the war, and because he had been drafted into the military before Pearl Harbor, she was able to leave Heart Mountain to marry him in 1943. She moved with him to bases in Kentucky, Pennsylvania, and Missouri, going to college and working as a newspaper reporter as he continued the medical training he had started in Seattle.

Even as the war raged on, she spoke out about what was happening in the internment camps. In one speech to a group of businessmen, she told the story of her "evacuation," ending by saying that even though their incarceration was unjust and illegal, the Nikkei (Americans of Japanese descent) were going along with it, because cooperation "is the very best way to prove our loyalty and to our country." When she finished, the men sat without saying a word, and she thought her speech had been a dud. She later heard that the businessmen had simply been too stunned to respond.

Released at the end of the war, many of the Yakima Valley's Nikkei, knowing there was little waiting for them in their former community, found new opportunities around the country. For years, many formerly imprisoned people refused to even talk about their experiences. Wherever they went, they found hurtful reminders of having been considered potential traitors despite any evidence to the contrary.

Kara's family did return to Wapato, where Tak's family owned land and where he got a job working at a pharmacy. The thriving community she had known before was gone. When they returned, "Every business in Wapato had 'No Japs Wanted' signs, and there was a distinct feeling of hostility," Kara recalled.

But over the years, relationships first thawed, then warmed. In the late 1940s, the couple bought a house in Yakima's Terrace Heights neighborhood, where some neighbors initially rejected them but others were more kind. Kara's warm, witty, and welcoming personality helped. Anyone looking through her family photos would see that no matter her age or the situation, she's wearing an enormous smile in all of them.

After Tak served in the Korean War, the couple adopted a child, Elaine, who had been born in Japan. Kara busied herself with motherhood. Ten years later, she and Tak adopted a son, Lance.

But she also threw energy into community involvement, having realized that was what it took to make a difference. She joined the Yakima County League of Women Voters in the 1950s and almost immediately joined its board. She would serve as its president twice during her many decades of service. She was appointed to the mayor's committee on human rights and felt compelled to march in the local Martin Luther King Day parades to show support for others who were often marginalized.

"I didn't think I was a community activist, but I've often been labeled that," Kara said in an interview. "And undergirding that is my experience in the camps, too, because you can point out in many ways how it can happen to people. . . you feel obligated, really, as a duty, somewhat, to keep the . . . issue alive, because it applies not only to us as Japanese Americans having experienced it, but what is happening to other groups as well."

Later in life, she would support the fight for more rights for Latino workers, even as she understood why some people wouldn't stick their necks out to support those marginalized groups, as they hadn't for Japanese Americans.

She eventually grew interested in environmental issues, too, going to conferences and educating herself about land and water issues, serving for twenty-two years on the Yakima Urban Area Regional Planning Commission and statewide advisory committees relating to planning and water use. Her diverse interests made her as excited to discuss the latest Mariners baseball game as well as new government regulations.

She also kept alive memories of the community she remembered from the old days. In 1973, she helped organize a reunion of families that had lived in the Yakima area before the war. Afterward, she compiled a booklet listing all of the information she could find about them.

It was during the 1970s that a movement toward recognition of, and reparations for, formerly incarcerated Japanese Americans gained momentum. With her political and civic experience, Kara felt she had to help push the work forward. She started putting pressure on elected officials and collecting petition signatures.

When a group of former internees met in Seattle to talk about their experiences, it was the first time many had spoken openly of their pain and hardship. Understandably, many were reluctant to testify about their incarceration, not wanting to air their private stories or relive dark memories. Those at the meeting were preparing to testify to the Commission on Wartime Relocation and Internment of Civilians, which started its work in 1980.

Kara was one who worked up the courage to speak out, and she didn't hold back. She spoke on behalf of families who couldn't be at the meeting because it was harvest season, reminding the panel about their contributions to the area's farming heritage. At one point during her testimony, she noted that "Supreme Court Justice William Douglas is also a Yakima product," but added with characteristic wit, "I'm afraid he was not helpful insofar as the Evacuation/Internment Court cases were concerned."

Ultimately, the commission determined that the causes of the incarceration programs were "race prejudice, war hysteria and a failure of political leadership." The resulting Civil Rights Act of 1988 declared that "a grave injustice was done to citizens and permanent resident aliens of Japanese ancestry by the evacuation, relocation, and internment of civilians during World War II" and that restitution was in order. In 1990, the US government sent payments of $20,000 to formerly imprisoned people. Kara gave part of her check to the local Heritage University, which still gives a scholarship in her name.

When a group of Japanese Americans in Seattle created Denshō: The Japanese American Legacy Project to commit incarcerated peoples' memories to permanent history, Kara was one of the people who agreed to be interviewed. Her detailed interview with them, like her writing, gives an idea of her intelligence, dedication, and sense of humor.

She also spoke to generations of school groups and civic organizations, bringing her trauma to light over and over in hopes of ensuring others would never have to experience anything like it. She helped create educational materials to use in teaching about the era. She connected historians with other Japanese Americans in the community to make sure their important stories could also be told.

Kara died at her home in 2005, at age eighty-nine. In some ways, her legacy after her death has grown beyond her own life. The Yakima League of Women Voters named its annual luncheon for her, in honor of her service to the organization. The Kara Kondo Dryland Garden at the Yakima Area Arboretum pays testament to her concern for water issues and love of helping living things grow.

One unique legacy came in 2012, when the Yakima Valley Museum hired opera singer and composer Sarah Mattox to compose a new work. Drawing on artifacts from a 2010 exhibition the museum produced about the incarceration of Japanese Americans during the war, Mattox noticed that one woman had written some of the exhibition's most compelling words: Kara Kondo. Mattox asked Kara's daughter, Elaine, for a copy of Kara's camp diaries, and Mattox's opera, *Heart Mountain*, is based on Kara's life. Selections from the new chamber opera have been performed around the region, helping even more people get to know the woman whose words so eloquently depicted both injustice and hope.

BIBLIOGRAPHY

NARCISSA PRENTISS WHITMAN

Barto, Harold E., and Catherine Bullard. *History of the State of Washington.* Boston: D. C. Heath and Company, 1947.

Beaver, Lowell J. "Historic Memories from Monuments and Plaques of Western Washington." *Historic Memories,* 1960.

Bennett, Robert A. *We'll All Go Home in the Spring.* Walla Walla, WA: Pioneer Press Books, 1984.

Dodd, Lawrence. *Narcissa Whitman on the Oregon Trail.* Fairfield, WA: Ye Galleon Press, 1986.

Nixon, Oliver W. *How Marcus Whitman Saved Oregon.* Chicago: Star Publishing Company, 1895.

Sager, Catherine, Elizabeth Sager, and Matilda Sager. *The Whitman Massacre of 1847.* Fairfield, WA: Ye Galleon Press, 1986.

Whitman, Narcissa. *The Letters of Narcissa Whitman 1836–1847.* Fairfield, WA: Ye Galleon Press, 1986

Whitman, Narcissa Prentiss. *My Journal.* Fairfield, WA: Ye Galleon Press, 1982.

Special thanks to Glen Adams and Ye Galleon Press.

KICK-IS-OM-LO (PRINCESS ANGELINE)

"Angeline Is Non-committal." *The Seattle Press-Times,* October 21, 1891.

"Battle of Seattle." *The Seattle Press-Times,* January 30, 1892.

Conover, C. T. "Just Cogitating: Angeline Wanted to Be Buried among Tillicums." *The Seattle Times,* December 21, 1958.

———. "Just Cogitating: Angeline Was Best-Known of Chief Seattle's Children." *The Seattle Times,* December 15, 1957.

———. "Just Cogitating: Princess Angeline Was Familiar Figure in Seattle," *The Seattle Times,* November 11, 1956.

———. "Just Cogitating: Princess Angeline Was Noted Sight in Old Seattle." *The Seattle Times,* July 19, 1959.

Dorpat, Paul. "Princess Angeline's Shack." *The Seattle Times,* May 13, 1984.

Duncan, Don. "Gentle Reign of Angeline." Don Duncan's Driftwood Diary, *The Seattle Times,* June 28, 1970.

"Gift Recalls Local History." *Capitol Hill Times,* September 17, 1958.

Chief Seattle and Angeline. Kitsap County History. Silverdale, WA: The Kitsap County Historical Society Book Committee, 1977.

"Poor Old Angeline, Only Living Child of the Great War Chief Seattle." *Seattle Post-Intelligencer,* August 2, 1891.

"Princess Angeline." Obituary. *Seattle Post-Intelligencer,* May 31, 1896.

"'Princess Angeline' to Be Given Friday Afternoon in Frederick & Nelson Store
    Auditorium." *The Seattle Times,* May 8, 1930.
"A Princess Prophecies." *The Seattle Press-Times,* March 31, 1892.
Riley, Lori Jackson. "Grandmother and Princess Angeline." In *Incidents in the Life
    of a Pioneer Woman.* The State Association of the Daughters of the Pioneers of
    Washington, 1976.
"The Royal Family." *The Seattle Press-Times,* April 7, 1892.
Sayre, J. Willis. *This City of Ours.* Seattle: Seattle School District No. 1, 1936.
"Seattle's Princess." *Seattle Mail & Herald,* October 26, 1901.
"She Was Very Ancient." *The Seattle Press-Times,* October 21, 1891.

MARY ANN BOREN DENNY

Atkins, Frank R. "Schooner 'Exact' Brought Settlers to Alki Landing." Costello
    Scrapbook. Seattle Public Library.
Bagley, Clarence B. *Pioneer Seattle and Its Pioneers.* Seattle: Argus Press, 1928.
Beaver, Lowell J. *Historic Memories from Monuments and Plaques of Western
    Washington.* Trademark Historic Memories, 1960.
Buerge, David M. "Seattle's Pioneer Women." In *Washingtonians.* Seattle: Sasquatch
    Publishing, 1989.
Crowley, Veryle Morehouse. "The First Christmas at Alki Point." In *Incidents in the
    Life of a Pioneer Woman.* The State Association of the Daughters of the Pioneers
    of Washington, 1976.
Denny, Arthur. *Pioneer Days on Puget Sound.* Seattle: C. B. Bagley Printer, 1888/
    Seattle: The Alice Harriman Company, 1908.
"Dennys Celebrate: Its Wedding Day & Birthday Fete." *The Seattle Times,* September
    2, 1933.
"Denny Family 'Stitch in Time' Is Historical." *The Seattle Times,* December 11, 1932.
Hanford, Cornelius. *Seattle and Environs.* Seattle: Pioneer Historical Publishing Co.,
    1924.
Kamb, Lewis. "Aiding Seattle's First People." *Seattle Post-Intelligencer,* August 9,
    2004.
"Mrs. Arthur A. Denny Dead: Woman Founder of City Passes Away." *The Seattle Daily
    Times,* December 30, 1910.
Newell, Gordon. *Westward to Alki: The Story of David and Louisa Denny.* Seattle:
    Superior Publishing Company, 1977.
"Rolland Denny's Life of Integrity Spanned Era of City's Development." *Seattle Star,*
    December 21, 1947.
Sketches of Washingtonians. Seattle: Wellington C. Wolfe & Co., 1906.
*A Volume of Memoirs and Genealogy of Representative Citizens of the City of Seattle
    and King County Washington.* New York and Chicago: The Lewis Publishing
    Company, 1903.

Watt, Roberta Frye. *Four Wagons West: The Story of Seattle.* Portland, OR: Binford & Mort, 1931.

Special thanks to Denny descendants Amy Johnson and Andrew Harris.

MOTHER JOSEPH

Acceptance of the Statue of Mother Joseph. Presented by the state of Washington, May 1, 1980. Washington, D.C.: U.S. Government Printing Office, 1980.

Archives of the Sisters of Providence—Sacred Heart Province:

Letters from Mother Joseph to:

Mother Caron, November 16, 1856; Mother Caron, December 4, 1856; Mother Caron, December 21, 1856; Bishop Bourget, December 29, 1856; Father Truteau, April 19, 1857; Mother Caron, May 1857; Mother Caron, June 1857; Bishop Larocque, August 15, 1857; Bishop Bourget, December 27, 1857; Bishop Bourget, December 18, 1858; Bishop Bourget, January 30, 1861; Bishop Larocque, March 3, 1862; Father Brouillet, V.G., January 2, 1863.

Annals of Providence Academy: Mother Joseph—December 26, 1843—Entrance, p. 372

Annals of Sisters of Providence:

1861—pp. 142, 145, 147

Collections in The Mines of Idaho and Montana, 1866—pp. 207, 210, 222

Begging Tours: 1867—p. 224; 1873—p. 303

House of Providence Building: 1873—p. 327, 1874—pp. 329, 370–371; 1877—pp. 230, 235, 274

Diary written on The Sea Voyage, November 2, 1856—translated by Sister Martin, and Sister Mary Barbara.

"Chronicles of Saint Joseph Hospital," Vancouver, Wash., Vol. 8, 1858–1952. Translated by Sister Dorothy Lentz, S.P., 1978.

"The Institute of Providence," Vol. 1—1800–1844

Letter of Chief Selstice of the Coeur d' Alenes to Sister Catherine, 1870.

Lucia, Ellis. *Seattle's Sisters of Providence.* Seattle: Providence Medical Center, Sisters of Providence, 1978.

McCrosson, Sister Mary. *The Bell and the River.* Seattle: Sisters of Charity of Providence, 1957 and 1986.

Tucker, Joan Pinkerton. "Beggar/Builder," videotape produced by KWSU Productions, written and narrated by Joan Pinkerton Tucker, 1993.

Special thanks to Sisters of Providence Archives, Sacred Heart Province, Seattle: Loretta Zwolak Greene, Archivist; Sister Rita Bergamini, S.P., Archivist Assistant.

LIZZIE ORDWAY

Binns, Archie. *Northwest Gateway: The Story of the Port of Seattle.* Garden City, NY: Doubleday, Doran & Company, Inc., 1941.

Evans, Walter. "The Mercer Girls." Dateline: Northwest. *Seattle Post-Intelligencer,*
    September 7, 1975.

"First U. of W. President's Installation." *The Seattle Times,* February 21, 1928.

Fish, Byron. "Retired Teachers Will Pay Tribute at Mercer Girl's Grave." *The Seattle
    Times,* May 12, 1954.

Grant, Frederic J. *History of Seattle, Washington.* New York: American Publishing &
    Engraving Company, 1891.

Kitsap County History. Silverdale, WA: Kitsap County Historical Society Book
    Committee, 1977.

"Mercer's Speech." *Puget Sound Weekly,* May 28, 1866.

Perry, Fredi. *Port Madison Washington Territory 1854–1889.* Bremerton, WA: Perry
    Publishing, 1989.

Perry Fredi, ed. *Kitsap County: The Year of the Child 1979.* Silverdale, WA: Kitsap
    County Historical Society, 1979.

"Pioneer Career Woman." *The Seattle Times,* July 6, 1947.

Warren, James. "Miss Lizzie Tamed the West's Children." *Seattle Post-Intelligencer,*
    April 6, 1980.

Special thanks to Claire Raaum, State Association of the Daughters of the Pioneers of
    Washington.

DR. MARY ARCHER LATHAM

By the Falls: Women of Determination. American Association of University Women,
    Spokane Branch, 1989.

"Dr. Latham Flees in Open Buggy." *Seattle Post-Intelligencer,* July 27, 1905.

"Dr. Latham in Hands of Jury." *The Spokesman-Review,* June 18, 1905.

"Dr. Latham Is in Serious Plight." *The Spokesman-Review,* June 14, 1905.

"Dr. Latham Is Starving." *The Spokesman-Review,* July 2, 1905.

"Dr. Mary A. Latham." Annual Illustrated Supplement to *The Spokane Spokesman,*
    January 1, 1892.

"Dr. Mary Latham Creates a Scene." *The Spokesman-Review,* June 30, 1905.

"Dr. Mary A. Latham Dead." *Spokane Chronicle,* January 20, 1917.

"Dr. Mary A. Latham Is Found Guilty." *The Spokesman-Review,* June 19, 1905.

Edwards, Rev. Jonathan. *History of Spokane County.* Spokane, WA: W.H. Lever,
    Publishers, 1900.

"Former Friend Hurts Dr. Latham." *The Spokesman-Review,* June 13, 1905.

Inmate Register and File on Dr. Mary Latham, State Penitentiary at Walla Walla,
    Washington, Washington State Archives, January 9, 1906.

"James Latham." Obituary. *The Spokesman-Review,* April 21, 1903.

Latham v. Latham. Spokane County Superior Court file, Case No. 9886, 1895.

"Mary A. Latham Faces a Jury." *The Spokesman-Review,* June 10, 1905.

"Messner Woos As Shop Burns, Bad Day for Defense." *The Spokesman-Review,* June 17, 1905.

"Own Witness Hurts Dr. Latham." *The Spokesman-Review,* June 16, 1905.

"Pioneer Woman Physician Succumbs to Pneumonia." *The Spokesman-Review,* January 21, 1917.

State of Washington vs. Mary A. Latham. Spokane County Superior Court file, Case No. 2438, filed May 17, 1905.

Special thanks to Clerks of the Spokane County Superior Court, Spokane, WA; Nancy Gale Compau, Librarian, Northwest Room Spokane Public Library; Karen De Seve, Curator of Special Collections, Cheney Cowles Museum (Eastern Washington State Historical Society Museum); David Hastings, Chief of Archival Services, Washington State Archives.

OLIVE SPORE RYTHER

Andrews, Mildred Tanner. *Seattle Women: A Legacy of Community Development.* Seattle: The Seattle YWCA, 1984.

Chase, Cora G. *Unto the Least.* Seattle: Shorey Books, 1972.

Davis, Nancy Parker. "Memory of Great Woman Lives in Ryther Center." *The Seattle Times,* June 16, 1946.

Dennis, Juanita. "Growing Up with Mother Ryther." *The Seattle Times,* October 29, 1972.

Jacobsen, Berne. "Mrs. Ryther, Mother to All Children, Dies." *Seattle Post-Intelligencer,* October 3, 1934.

"Mother Ryther, Children Home Leader, Dead." *The Seattle Times,* October 2, 1934.

Ryther Child Center. Brochures. Seattle: Ryther Child Center, 1995–1997.

Suffia, David. "Mother Ryther: 3,000 Children Kept Her Young." *The Seattle Times,* December 22, 1974.

Thomas, Leah. "Let Not Your Heart Be Troubled, Children." *The Seattle Times,* October 5, 1934.

Special thanks to Mary Anne Howard, Director of Community Relations, Ryther Child Center.

THEA CHRISTIANSEN FOSS

"Andrew Foss." Obituary. *The Seattle Times,* March 14, 1937.

"City Makes It Official: Thea Foss Waterway." *The Morning News Tribune,* October 18, 1989.

Evans, Walter. "Thea Foss: Lasting Wake on Sound." *Seattle Post-Intelligencer,* June 4, 1976.

Foss, Henry. "A Mother Molds the Character of a Boy." *Tacoma News Tribune,* May 14, 1967.

"From the Crow's Nest." *The Seattle Times,* September 12, 1935.

Green, Frank L. "Thea Foss—A Gallery of 100 Eminent Washingtonians." Tacoma, WA: Washington State Historical Society, 1989.

Johnson, Bruce, and Michael Skalley. *Foss: a Living Legend.* Printed for Foss Maritime Company, 1990.

Michener, Charles T. "A Remarkable Saga of Tugs and Towing." *Seattle Magazine,* 1966: 39–43.

Skalley, Michael. "Foss: Ninety Years of Towboating." August 23, 1982.

"'Tugboat Annie' Continues Run." *Seattle Post-Intelligencer,* August 4, 1933.

"Tugboat Annie Picture to Be Sold." *Seattle Post-Intelligencer,* June 4, 1976.

Whitney, Marci. "Thea Foss Was No 'Tugboat Annie.'" *Tacoma News Tribune,* September 19, 1976.

Special thanks to Kae Paterson, Commencement Bay Maritime Center; Tim Brewer, Vice President, and Michael Skalley, Historian, Foss Maritime Company.

DR. NETTIE J. CRAIG ASBERRY

Andrews, Mildred Tanner. *Washington Women as Path Breakers.* Tacoma, WA: Junior League of Tacoma, 1989.

Bence, Erma. "Dr. Asberry, 96, Founder of NAACP Here, to Be Honored on Tuesday." *Tacoma News Tribune,* July 23, 1961.

Bence, Erma. "Found—A Very Old Diploma." *Tacoma News Tribune,* October 2, 1975.

Federation of Colored Women's Organization, meeting minutes and notes, University of Washington—Manuscripts Collection.

Kellogg, Caroline. "Time Machine: Dr. Nettie Asberry: Music Fixed Her Vision." *Tacoma News Tribune,* December 4, 1977.

"May 11 Is Proclaimed Dr. Nettie Asberry Day." *Tacoma News Tribune,* May 1, 1961.

"Nettie Asberry of NAACP Dies at 103." *Tacoma News Tribune,* November 18, 1968.

Patterson, James H. "Tacoma NAACP Unit Is First in the West." *Tacoma News Tribune,* February 14, 1968.

7th Annual Catalogue of the Kansas Conservatory of Music, Kansas State Historical Society Collection, Topeka, 1879.

"Tacoma Woman Dies at Age 103." *The Seattle Times,* November 19, 1968.

Whitney, Marci. "Harmony Between Races Was Music Teacher's Aim." *Tacoma News Tribune,* April 18, 1976.

BERTHA KNIGHT LANDES

Arnold, William. "Exhibit on Seattle's First Woman Mayor." *Seattle Post-Intelligencer,* July 5, 1974.

"Bertha Knight Landes." Obituary. *The Seattle Times,* November 30, 1943.

Cunningham, Ross. "Seattle's First-and-Only Woman Mayor." *The Seattle Times,* December 20, 1972.

Pieroth, Doris H. "Bertha Knight Landes: The Woman Who Was Mayor." In *Women In Pacific Northwest History,* edited by Karen Blair. Seattle: University of Washington Press, 1988. First published in *Pacific Northwest Quarterly,* 75 (July 1984).

Stockley, Tom. "Seattle's Woman Mayor." *The Seattle Times,* July 14, 1974.

Stripling, Sherry. "Folk Heroines: They Helped Build Pacific Northwest." *The Seattle Times,* March 6, 1985.

Suffia, David. "When Doc Brown's Cigar Thwarted a Reform Move." Seattle Historical Vignettes. *The Seattle Times,* January 7, 1974.

"Ten Take Their Places in State's History." *The Seattle Times,* November 11, 1985.

Watson, Emmett. "Big Bertha." *The Seattle Times,* February 21, 1984.

FAY FULLER

Duncan, Don. "Climbers Commemorate Fuller's Rainier Ascent." *The Seattle Times,* August 9, 1990.

Duncan, Don. "With the First Woman atop Mount Rainier," Driftwood Diary. *The Seattle Times,* January 14, 1973.

"Fay Fuller Reaches Top of Rainier." *Tacoma News Tribune,* August 10, 1890. Reprint, July 1, 1976.

"Female Mountaineers' Clothes Streamlined." *Tacoma News Tribune,* July 11, 1943.

"First Woman to Climb Rainier Liked Annual." *Tacoma News Tribune,* March 12, 1950.

"First Woman to Conquer Mountain Dies." *Tacoma News Tribune,* May 27, 1958.

Fuller, Fay. "A Trip to the Summit." *Every Sunday,* August 23, 1890.

Hunt, Katharine. "First Woman to Climb the Mountain Visits City." *Tacoma News Tribune,* August 17, 1950.

Kellogg, Caroline. "Time Machine: Bloomer-Clad Fay Fuller's Trek Shocked Tacoma." *Tacoma News Tribune,* March 7, 1982.

Linsley, Jeann. "Women Commemorate Fuller's Historic Ascent." *The Seattle Times,* August 10, 1990.

McIntyre, Bob. Transcript of Interview with Mrs. Fritz Von Briesen, August 18, 1950, Mount Rainier National Park Service.

Molenaar, Dee. *The Challenge Of Rainier.* Seattle: The Mountaineers, 1971.

Potts, Betsey. "Fay Fuller—First Woman to the Top of Mount Rainier." *Columbia Magazine* 10 (Winter 1996-1997): 24-29.

Schullery, Paul. *Island in the Sky: Pioneering Accounts of Mount Rainier 1833-1894.* Seattle: The Mountaineers, 1987.

Smith, Ernest C. "A Trip to Mount Rainier," read April 11, 1898. Manuscript from the files of Mount Rainier National Park Service.

"Summit Salute to First Woman to Climb Rainier." *The Seattle Times,* August 12, 1990.

Whitney, Marci. "Notable Women: First Woman to Climb Rainier." *Tacoma News Tribune,* February 15, 1976.

Special thanks to Longmire Library employees, especially Kathleen Jobson; National Park Service; Mount Rainier National Park; Alex Van Steen, veteran Rainier summit guide with Rainier Mountaineering, Inc., and Alex Van Steen Expeditions, LLC.

KATHLEEN ROCKWELL

Browning, Robert. "Klondike Kate of Gold Rush Fame Dies at 77." *Seattle Post-Intelligencer,* February 22, 1957.

"Kathleen Rockwell." Obituary. *The Alaska Sportsman,* May 1957: 28–29.

Kilroy, George. "Alaskans of Other Days." *The Alaska Weekly,* August 14, 1931.

"Klondike Kate Finds North Only Memory." *Seattle Post-Intelligencer,* August 4, 1933.

"Klondike Kate Flies North to Seek Word of Husband." *The Seattle Times,* October 21, 1946.

"Klondike Kate, Here for Fete, Rolls Cigarette, Reminisces." *The Seattle Times,* November 29, 1937.

"Klondike Kate Home as Bride." *Seattle Post-Intelligencer,* July 22, 1933.

"Klondike Kate, 65 and Happy, Returning to Wilds She Loves." *The Seattle Times,* August 16, 1944.

"Klondike Kate Succumbs at Home in Oregon." *The Seattle Times,* February 21, 1957.

Mann, May. "I Was Queen of the Klondike." *The Alaska Sportsman,* August 1944: 10–11, 28–32.

"Rush Leaves Klondike Kate Cold." *Oregonian,* October 26, 1948.

Schillios, Rolv. "Dance Hall Girl." *The Alaska Sportsman,* March 1956: 8–11, 30–33.

———. "Dreams and Reality." *The Alaska Sportsman,* April 1956: 16–19, 38–41.

Rochester, Junius. "Seattle's Gift to Vaudeville, Alexander Pantages." *The Weekly,* February 29–March 7, 1984: 34–35.

Stanton, Patty. "Kate's Vivid Career in Klondike Recalled." *The Seattle Times,* July 15, 1973.

Stockley, Tom. "Klondike Kate: 'Queen of the Goldrush.'" *The Seattle Times,* June 25, 1972.

"Uses Her Money Then Jilts the Girl." *The Seattle Times,* May 2, 1905.

Welch, Doug. "1937 Girls Shock Klondike Kate." *Seattle Post-Intelligencer,* November 19 ,1937.

"Whitehorse—Letters, Photography." *Alaska Magazine,* December 1973: A3.

JUDGE REAH MARY WHITEHEAD

Bechdolt, Jack. "Judge Reah Whitehead Sums Up Her Position." *Seattle Post-Intelligencer,* October 10, 1915.

Dumett, Ray. "The Washington Alumnus—Personality Sketch." University of Washington Alumni Association, January 1925.

"First Woman Judge Here, Reah Whitehead, Dies." *The Seattle Times*, October 15, 1972.

"Justice Reah M. Whitehead Resigns." *The Seattle Times*, November 10, 1941.

"Miss Reah Whitehead Takes Position on Bench." *Seattle Post-Intelligencer*, January 12, 1915.

"Miss Whitehead Honored by U.S. Women." *The Seattle Times*, March 8, 1926.

Neighbors, Dorothy. "Successful Seattle Women." *The Seattle Times*, February 23, 1941.

Suffia, David. "Reah Whitehead, Pioneer Woman Justice of Peace." *The Seattle Times*, January 3, 1975.

Starbuck, Dr. Susan. "Yesterday's Women Judges: Role Models for Today." *Judiciary*, winter/spring 1985: 7.

Whitehead, Reah. "Women Succeed in Law—Find It Good Background." *The Seattle Times*, February 7, 1926.

"Woman to Be Named as Assistant Prosecutor." *Seattle Post-Intelligencer*, November 28, 1908.

"Women Lawyers Meet." *The Seattle Times*, August 10, 1947.

Special thanks to Robert Henderson, Public Information Officer, Office of the Administrator for the Courts.

IMOGEN CUNNINGHAM

Bensley, Lis. "Imogen Cunningham: Of Flora and Effective Seeing Exhibition of Floral Imagery." *The Santa Fe New Mexican*, December 6, 1996.

Coleman, A. D. "Cunningham—Still Going Strong." *The New York Times*, May 6, 1973.

Clemans, Gayle. "Granddaughter Recalls Public, Private Side of Photographer Imogen Cunningham." *The Seattle Times*, August 31, 2009.

DeFore, John. "A Woman's Place Is in the Darkroom." *San Antonio Current*, September 12, 2001.

"First Take: Indelible Imogen." *Columns*, December 2006: 42.

Gehman, Geoff. "Biographer Preserves Image of Pioneer Photographer." *The Morning Call*, March 27, 1994.

Grundberg, Andy. "Photography View; Revisiting a Modernist Pioneer and a Poet of Urban Life." *The New York Times*, January 5, 1986.

Hackett, Regina. "Pioneering Women Who Called the Shots." *Seattle Post-Intelligencer*, December 19, 2002.

Hagberg, Marilyn. "Using a Camera to Give Flowers and Plants Eternal Life." *The San Diego Union*, December 23, 1983.

Kramer, Hilton. "Imogen Cunningham at Ninety: A Remarkable Empathy." *The New York Times*, May 6, 1973.

Kramer, Hilton. "Remembering Cunningham and White." *The New York Times,* August 1, 1976.

Lorenz, Richard. *Imogen Cunningham Ideas without End.* San Francisco: Chronicle Books, 1993.

Muchnic, Suzanne. "Photographs Upstage the Imogen Stories." *Los Angeles Times,* October 22, 1985.

"100 Alumni of the Century." *Columns,* December 1999: 16–23.

Raynor, Vivien. "Art; Portrait of the Artist: Sass and Sensibility." *The New York Times,* June 21, 1981.

Thornton, Gene. "Cunningham: Doing Anything That Pleases Her." *The New York Times,* November 15, 1970.

Zajac, Ina. "A Fair to Remember." *Columns,* June 2009: 29–31.

Special thanks to Meg Partridge and the Imogen Cunningham Trust.

ISABEL FRIEDLANDER ARCASA

Anderson, Eva. "Silico Saska Was Entiat's Indian." *Wenatchee World,* circa 1955.

Arcasa, Isabelle [*sic*], and Robert H. Ruby. "No Wrath Like That of an Indian Chief Scorned." *Columbia Magazine,* Fall 1987.

Barham, Melvin. "Isabel Arcasa Keeps Indian Heritage Alive." *Wenatchee World,* November 23, 1980.

Brown, John A., and Robert H. Ruby. "Isabel Arcasa, a Centennial Centenarian." *Columbia Magazine,* Fall 1989.

Connolly, Tom, S.J. Manuscript prepared from interview taped with Isabel Arcasa, May 5, 1979.

———. "Stories about Isabel Arcasa." *Colville Tribal Tribune,* December 1, 1989.

Greene, Bernice. "Interview with Isabel Arcasa." October 18, 1977; October 25, 1977; Manuscripts from North Central Washington Museum collection, Wenatchee, WA.

Greene, Bernice. "The Oldest Colville Indian in the West! Isabel Arcasa Celebrates 100th Birthday." *Colville Tribal Tribune,* December 1, 1989.

Schmeltzer, Michael. "Our Pioneers Are Part of the Present." *Spokane Chronicle,* May 26, 1983.

Special thanks to Maybelle and Sheila Gendron, daughter and granddaughter of Isabel Arcasa; Father Tom Connolly, S.J., of Sacred Heart Mission, DeSmet, ID; Father Patrick Twohy, S.J., of Swinomish Spiritual Centre, La Conner, WA; Mark Behler, curator, North Central Washington Museum, Wenatchee, WA; Jessica Sylvanus, Research Assistant, Okanogan County Historical Society, Okanogan, WA.

MAUDE C. LILLIE BOLIN

Dietrich, Bill. "Washington Indians: Indian History Tells a Tale of Two Worlds— Struggle and Survival." *Seattle Times,* December 16, 1985.

"Feminine Campaigner Uses Unusual Method." *Yakima Daily Republic,* July 22, 1942.

"First Solo Air Flight." *Toppenish-Review,* November 15, 1929.

"Flying, Relay Riding, Music and Trade of Milliner are Mastered by Toppenish Woman as Life Pleasures." *The Yakima Daily Republic,* October 4, 1929.

"Four Have Close Call at Superior." *The Daily Missoulian,* July 17, 1931.

Foster, Ruth—Manuscripts from the files of The Toppenish Mural Society.

"Freak Planes, Girl Pilots Intrigue Tex." *Spokane Chronicle,* July 31, 1930.

Haugen, Borg. "Pow Wow City Takes on Color with Banners and Cowboys." *Yakima Sunday Herald,* June 20, 1948.

An Illustrated History of Klickitat, Yakima & Kittitas Counties. Chicago: Interstate Publishing Company, 1904.

"Indians Wearing Festival Regalia Present Play." *The Yakima Daily Republic,* 1936.

Mays, Theo. *100 Years—100 Women.* Yakima County: Yakima Valley Museum, 1989.

"Mrs. Bolin Undaunted by Recent Wreck in Montana." *The Yakima Daily Republic,* July 22, 1931.

Murphy, Joseph, and Gilson Ross. *Letter to Commissioner of Indian Affairs,* 21 March 1950. Yakima Valley Museum Archives.

"Pow Wow Events Slated." *Yakima Sunday Herald,* June 12, 1960.

"Relief for China Drive Will Start." *Toppenish-Review,* May 15, 1942.

"Relief Fund Drive Nears $500 Goal." *Toppenish-Review,* June 19, 1942.

Rupp, Virgil. *Let 'R Buck: History of the Pendleton Round-Up.* Pendleton, OR: A Time for Growth, 1985.

"Toppenish Focus of Agriculture." *Yakima Sunday Herald,* 1960.

"Toppenish Woman Tells of Stunt." *Yakima Republic,* November 26, 1928.

"The Yakima Indian Reservation and the City of Toppenish." Pamphlet. Toppenish, WA: Toppenish Commercial Club, 1916.

Yakima Valley Museum files, clippings from unidentified newspapers:

"Bolin Home May Be City Museum." Circa 1960s.

Haugen, Borg. "History of Yakima Valley Washington." 1919.

"Jeanette Wesley 16 Year Old as Sacajawea." June 15, 1948.

"Maude Bolin in Airplane Crash." July 18, 1931.

"Mrs. Bolin Back from Plane Tour." August 19, 1930.

"Rodeo Invitation." Circa 1960s.

"Toppenish Plane Brings Home Honors from Pasco Annual Air Jubilee." May 17, 1930.

"Woman Flies Cross Country," August 31, 1928.

Special thanks to Lowell Evans, Toppenish Mural Society; Martin Humphrey, Archivist/Librarian, Yakima Valley Museum; Colleen Veomett, Librarian, Yakama Nations Library; Virginia Tubbs, Umatilla County Historical Society, Pendleton, OR.

PANG YEE CHING

"Angel Island: Ellis Island of the West." Angel Island Immigration Station Foundation, www.a-better.com/angel.island.htm.

"Chinese Workers Played Roles." *The Spokesman-Review,* July 14, 1940.

Cowles, Cheney. "Chinese Community Concepts Changing." *Spokane Daily Chronicle,* June 24, 1972.

"Golden Legacy, A Chinese Historical and Cultural Project," Golden Legacy Web Page, www.kqed.org, KQED Instructional Television, San Francisco, Calif.

Lowe, Felicia, Daniel Quan, and Ann Williams. "Gateway to Gold Mountain: A Journey Remembered." Pamphlet. San Francisco: San Francisco Public Library, July 1–November 30, 1996.

Lee, Douglas W. (publications editor 1983–1985). "The Annals of the Chinese Historical Society of the Pacific Northwest." 1984.

Lill, Lucile Lee, and Mark, Joyce Lee. Interviews, 1997, and written records, 1996.

Powers, Dorothy. "Lee Yuen Believes in His Herbs, 7 Children, 5 Grandchildren." *The Spokesman-Review,* 1951.

"Spokane Chinese Leader Dies at 82." *The Spokesman-Review,* October 10, 1972.

"Trio of Chinese Laid Northern Pacific Ties." *The Spokesman-Review,* August 12, 1945.

White, Aubrey L. "Chinese Burials of Early Day Recalled by Dwight." *The Spokesman-Review,* December 6, 1943.

"Yee C. Lee." Obituary. *The Spokesman-Review,* January 7, 1993.

Special thanks to Lucile Lee Lill and Joyce Lee Mark, Mrs. Lee's daughters; Nancy Gale Compau, Northwest Room of the Spokane Public Library.

HAZEL WOLF

Brodine, Virginia Warner. "Environmentalist Honored on 100th Birthday." *People's Weekly World.* 1998: 9.

Broom, Jack. "Honoring Hazel Wolf—As an Energetic Seattle Environmentalist Turns 100, Friends Prepare a Big Bash and (Of Course) a Good Deed." *Seattle Times,* March 4, 1998.

Coffey, Laura T. "A Century of Tireless Activism." *The Seattle Daily Journal of Commerce,* August 22, 1996.

Cushman, John H. "Hazel Wolf, 101; Fought for the Environment." *The New York Times,* January 24, 2000.

"In Memoriam Hazel Wolf's Century 1898–2000." *Audubon,* March/April 2000: 153.

Jamieson, Robert L. Jr. "A Golden Century for Hazel Wolf/Birthday Tribute to Honor Legacy of Longtime Activist." *Seattle Post-Intelligencer,* March 21, 1998.

Mann, Carolyn. "Hazel Wolf: Ninety and Still Fighting." *Sierra* 1988: 63-67.

Ryckman, Lisa Levitt. "She's Watching Out for the World." *San Francisco Chronicle,* January 15, 1986.

Slivka, Judd. "Hazel Wolf, Fighter for Ecology and the Little Guy, Dead at 101." *Seattle Post-Intelligencer,* January 21, 2000.

Starbuck, Susan. *Hazel Wolf Fighting the Establishment.* Seattle: University of Washington Press, 2002.

Taylor, Rob. "At 99, Hazel Wolf Wins Recognition." *Seattle Post-Intelligencer,* September 12, 1997.

Terkel, Studs. *Coming of Age: The Story of Our Century By Those Who've Lived It.* New York: The New Press, 1995.

Wolf, Hazel. "Deportation Then and Now." Speech at Lifetime Learning Center. November 5, 1998.

———. "Great Women in My Life." Speech at Hazel Wolf High School. September 7, 1999.

———. "The McCarthy Period." Speech at Rainier Beach High School. May 24, 1990.

———. "Speech for the Big Bash." Scottish Rite Temple. March 21, 1998.

———. Speech to American Immigration Lawyers Association Conference. June 10, 1999.

SUSIE REVELS CAYTON

Cayton, Horace. "Good Woman's Helping Hand." *Seattle Republican,* July 23, 1909, p. 1. Accessed via Washington Digital Newspapers, November 17, 2022.

Cayton, Horace R., Jr. *Long Old Road: An Autobiography.* New York: Trident Press, 1964.

Cayton, Susie Revels. "Sallie the Egg Woman." *Seattle Post-Intelligencer,* June 3, 1900.

Cayton, Susie Revels. "The Sunday Forum." *Seattle Republican,* October 19, 1906. Accessed via Washington Digital Newspapers, November 17, 2022.

Du Bois, W. E. B. (William Edward Burghardt). "The Great Northwest." *Crisis* (National Association for the Advancement of Colored People), Vol. 6, September 1913, pp. 237–240. Accessed via the Internet Archive, Dec 1, 2022.

Goshorn, Michelle L. "Susie Revels Cayton: 'The Part She Played.'" Seattle Civil Rights and Labor History Project. Undated. Accessed via https://depts.washington.edu/civilr/susie_cayton.htm on November 28, 2022.

Hobbs, Richard S. *The Cayton Legacy: An African American Family.* Pullman, WA: Washington State University Press, 2002.

Morgan, Marilyn. *Trailblazing Black Women of Washington State.* Charleston, SC: The History Press, 2022.

Mumford, Esther Hall. *Seattle's Black Victorians, 1852–1901.* Seattle: Ananse Press, 1980.

Taylor, Quintard. *The Forging of a Black Community: Seattle's Central District from 1870 through the Civil Rights Era* (Emil and Kathleen Sick Book Series in Western History and Biography), Second Edition. Seattle: University of Washington Press, 2022.

Taylor, Quintard, and Moore, Shirley Ann Wilson, eds. *African American Women Confront the West: 1600–2000*. Norman: University of Oklahoma Press, 2003.

Wagner, Tricia Martineau. *African American Women of the Old West*. Guilford, CT: TwoDot Press, 2007.

EMMA SMITH DEVOE

Arksey, Laura. "DeVoe, Emma Smith (1848–1927)." Historylink.org, December 27, 2005. Accessed October 28, 2022.

Bjorkman, Frances M. "Women's Political Methods." *Collier's*, 20 August 1910, 22–24. https://ia902301.us.archive.org/29/items/sim_colliers-the-national-weekly_1910-08-20_45_22/sim_colliers-the-national-weekly_1910-08-20_45_22.pdf.

DeVoe, Emma Smith. "Mrs. De Voe in the Field." *The Woman's Tribune*, May 12, 1906, p. 23. Gerritsen Women's History Collection of Aletta H. Jacobs. Accessed via ProQuest Historical Newspapers, November 5, 2022.

Emma Smith DeVoe papers: boxes 1–6 accessed via Washington Women's History Consortium (https://wshs.contentdm.oclc.org/digital/collection/devoe); boxes 7–23 accessed via Primarily Washington (https://primarilywashington.org/collection-tree), November 11, 2022.

Jennings, Linda Deziah, ed. *Washington Women's Cookbook*, published by the Washington Equal Suffrage Association, 1909 (accessed via Michigan State University Libraries Digital Repository, November 30, 2022). https://d.lib.msu.edu/fa/72#page/12/mode/2up.

McConnell, Carolyn. "The Road to Women's Suffrage Began in Washington State." *Crosscut*, March 20, 2020.

Ross-Nazzal, Jennifer M. *Winning the West for Women: The Life of Suffragist Emma Smith DeVoe*. Seattle: University of Washington Press, 2011.

Stevenson, Shanna. *Women's Votes, Women's Voices: The Campaign for Equal Rights in Washington*. Tacoma, WA: Washington State Historical Society, 2009.

Uncredited article. "Mrs. Emma Smith DeVoe Has Been Doing Really Remarkable Work as an Organizer and Raiser of Equal Rights Funds in the West." *Woman's Journal and Suffrage News* (Boston), July 6, 1895, p. 209. Accessed via University of Washington Libraries, November 15, 2022.

Ware, Susan. *Why They Marched: Untold Stories of the Women Who Fought for the Right to Vote*, Chapter 13, "Mountaineering for Suffrage," pp. 181–193. Cambridge, MA: Belknap Press of Harvard University Press, 2019.

Wilhelm, Dorothy. *True Tales of Puget Sound*, Chapter 8, "Parkland: Give Us a Vote and We Will Cook." Chicago: Arcadia Publishing Inc., 2019.

"Women to Call on Wilson: Committee of Voters Will Confer on Constitutional Amendment." *The Washington Post*, April 5, 1913, p. 2. Accessed via ProQuest Historical Newspapers, November 5, 2022.

"Women Voters in Capital to Battle for Their Sisters." *The Washington Post*, August 10, 1913, p. 5. Accessed via ProQuest Historical Newspapers, November 5, 2022.

KARA MATSUSHITA KONDO

Ayer, Tammy. "75 Years after Japanese Internment: Poetry Tradition Ripped Away from Yakima Valley along with Creators." *Yakima Herald-Republic*, February 18, 2017.

Ayer, Tammy. "Uprooted and Interned." *Yakima Herald-Republic*, December 6, 2016.

Brigolin, Lauren. "Our Kate Pinkerton Tells a Story of Japanese American Injustice." Seattle Opera blog, July 20, 2017. Accessed December 5, 2022.

Burton, Jeffery F., Farrell, Mary M., Lord, Florence B., and Lord, Richard W. *Confinement and Ethnicity: An Overview of World War II Japanese American Relocation Sites*. Seattle: University of Washington Press, 2003.

Fugita, Stephen S., and Fernandez, Marilyn. *Altered Lives, Enduring Community: Japanese Americans Remember Their World War II Incarceration*. Seattle: University of Washington Press, 2004.

Gold, Eric. "Within Makeshift Walls: Portland Expo Center's Era as a Prison for Japanese Americans." *Oregon Humanities*, December 6, 2016.

Heuterman, Thomas. *The Burning Horse: The Japanese American Experience in the Yakima Valley 1920-1942*. Pittsburgh: Carnegie Mellon University Press, 1995.

Hirabayashi, Lane Ryo, Hansen, Arthur A. *Barbed Voices: Oral History, Resistance, and the World War II Japanese American Social Disaster*. Denver: University Press of Colorado, 2018.

Kara Kondo interview, Denshō Visual History Collection, Denshō Digital Repository. Accessed via https://ddr.densho.org/, December 8, 2022.

Kara Kondo papers, Yakima Valley Museum.

Kashima, Tetsuden. *Judgment Without Trial: Japanese American Imprisonment During World War II*. Seattle: University of Washington Press, 2004.

Kondo, Kara. "Camp journal" excerpts, Kara Kondo papers, Yakima Valley Museum.

Kondo, Kara, ed. *Profile: Yakima Valley Japanese Community, 1973*. Published by the Yakima Valley Japanese Community, 1974.

Kondo, Kara. *100 Years 100 Women, 1889-1989*. Yakima, WA: Print Masters of Yakima, 1989, pp. 169-170.

Lee, Bill. "Kondo Leaves Behind a Positive Legacy for Valley." *Yakima Herald-Republic*, Aug 5, 2005. Accessed via Kara Kondo papers, Yakima Valley Museum.

Provenza, Nick. "Japanese: They Survived Hard Times." *Yakima Herald-Republic*, August 21, 1978. Accessed via Yakima Valley Libraries, December 8, 2022.

Raffa, Justin, and Mattox, Sarah. "Forte: 'Heart Mountain Suite' Brings Kara Kondo to Musical Life." *Yakima Herald-Republic*, October 25, 2019.

Summary from *Personal Justice Denied: Report of the Commission on Wartime Relocation and Internment of Civilians, 1982-1983*. Washington, DC:

Commission on Wartime Relocation and Internment of Civilians. Accessed via
https://www.archives.gov/research/japanese-americans/justice-denied, November
28, 2022.

Troianello, Craig. "Government's Effort to Repay an Old Debt." *Yakima Herald-Republic*, May 9, 1980. Accessed via Yakima Valley Libraries, December 8, 2022.

Unsigned obituary. "Kara Kondo, Yakima County Community Leader, Passes." *Pacific Citizen*, August 19–September 1, 2005.

Special thanks to the Yakima Valley Museum and particularly John Baule, the
museum's archivist, for their assistance.

INDEX

ABOUT THE AUTHOR

Northwest native L. E. Bragg was born in the shadow of Mount Rainier and raised in the Greater Seattle area. A graduate of the University of Washington, Ms. Bragg spent six years living and teaching school on the Colville Indian Reservation in eastern Washington. She and her family reside on the eastern shore of Lake Washington.

L. E. Bragg's books celebrate the history, scenery, and cultural diversity of the Pacific Northwest. Her first two books, *A River Lost* and *Seattle, City By The Sound*, are picture books written at a level for young readers, as well as for adults to enjoy reading aloud. She is also the author of *Idaho's Remarkable Women* and *Washington Myths and Legends* for Globe Pequot.

ABOUT THE REVISER

Christy Karras has lived in and written about Washington for many years, covering travel, recreation, culture, and community for publications including the *Seattle Times*. A longtime Utah resident, she is also the author of *Remarkable Utah Women* and *Scenic Driving Utah*. She lives in Seattle with her very patient husband, Bill, and their spoiled pets.